John Rodda, with whom Steve Ovett has collaborated on his autobiography, is Athletics Correspondent of *The Guardian*. He has covered every Olympic Games since 1960 and is co-editor, with Lord Killanin, of *The Olympic Games 1984*.

Merry Xmas 1985
from Helen v Steve.

STEVE OVETT WITH JOHN RODDA

Ovett

An Autobiography

GRAFTON BOOKS

A Division of the Collins Publishing Group

LONDON GLASGOW
TORONTO SYDNEY AUCKLAND

Grafton Books
A Division of the Collins Publishing Group
8 Grafton Street, London W1X 3LA

Published by Grafton Books 1985

First published in Great Britain by
Willow Books, Collins 1984

ISBN 0-586-06531-8

Printed and bound in Great Britain by
Collins, Glasgow

Set in Times

Contents

Preface   7

1 Brighton Milk Race   9
2 'You'll Never Be a Champion'   23
3 Stride for Stride   41
4 Lost in Lane Eight   59
5 The 'Perfect Race'   75
6 And Then There Were Two   90
7 'I.L.Y.'   105
8 The Inevitable Goodbye   131
9 The Best of Years   144
10 A Kind of Break   168
11 In Step with Seb   185
12 Another Personal Best   201
13 Sergeant Norman's Law   221
14 Almost Spiked on Bondi   239
15 'Have a Nice Day'   253

Checklist of Races   271

Preface

If there is one thing that I know about myself it is that you can predict that I will be unpredictable. I have actually gone on record as saying that I would never have a book, let alone a biography, written about me; yet here I am putting the finishing touches to the impossible reality. So what changed my mind? Well I suppose the main reason must be to put the so-called records straight. Over the years I have sat back watching and listening to the various reports, studies and statements about my sport 'athletics', and of course in particular the many colourful if not libellous appraisals of my performances and character by the 'Ovett' experts of the media.

So now I have a chance to get my own back – to tell quite simply my side of the story, and to show that there is always another side to every Scoop or World Exclusive, and that the changing, slightly glamorous world of athletics is not always quite what it seems.

This book does not set out to glorify, project or enhance any image. On the contrary, there are more than a few related instances of which I am embarrassed and others about which I will always remain extremely sad. But they are there, they have not been cut out or conveniently omitted so that only the best is on view, for that would be unfair – not so much to those who read this book but, selfishly, to me. I felt that I had always to reflect on all of my feelings and experiences, good or bad; and all those decisions and actions that I made in my past I had to drag up and question again, so that I could satisfy myself that this book has a true feeling for my past and is not some concocted patchwork of half-forgotten memories.

I have read books in the past that have left me stunned by the magnificence of the portrayals of the individuals concerned. They came across as lofty heroes whose life styles were so perfect that it left me feeling that all attempts to emulate them were almost certainly doomed by about chapter three. This book is regretfully different: it functions on the principle that any idiot can become an Olympic champion provided that they have a lot of luck, work hard and cross the finish line first in the final.

Still, enough of what my editor would call the hard sell, it's time now for a few dedications and to thank the people who really have made it all possible. First, the most important, my parents: I love them and thank them for loving me in return. Second, to every one of my friends and family in and out of sport, thanks for the time shared together. Third, to Matt, Harry and Andy, thanks for putting me through Hell – after all it's only pain. Fourth, thanks to John and even more so his wife Yveline, who through most of her pregnancy had to transcribe my various ramblings from tape to paper. Lucy, their beautiful daughter, must have heard more about me before birth than Simon Turnbull did when he took it upon himself to write a biography about me without even meeting me. (Sorry but I just couldn't resist that.)

And lastly to my wife Rachel – I.L.Y.

STEVE OVETT
Brighton, August 1984

1

Brighton Milk Race

It is true that fear and running go together. You run faster because you do not want to be beaten, you are afraid of defeat. I think I was five when I first experienced the feeling.

We were living in Colman Street, Brighton, at the time, an area of terraced council houses where there was a big open space – a communal area would I suppose be nearer the correct definition – at the back where I used to play with the other lads. I cannot recall why, but one morning I hit another boy over the head with a milk bottle. Blood was spilled, the bottle shattered and I took off down the road running, I felt, faster than I had ever done before, without getting out of breath or feeling pain anywhere because I was too consumed with fear. I dashed into the house, upstairs, waiting for the ring on the door bell, frightened about what I had done to the boy and what was going to happen to me. Sure enough, the mother turned up . . . and then there was that long wait before my father returned from work and administered the punishment which I can still recall.

A better memory of running as a five-year-old came through the family ruse to get me to fetch the paper and the cigarettes from the shop at the end of the road. 'See how fast you can do it, Steven,' was the carrot from my father. 'I'll start counting – one, two, three . . .' Off I flew and when I burst through the door back home Father was saying, '. . . twenty-five, twenty-six, twenty-seven'. I was a little too young to realize that these were the only figures he counted. But looking back, it gave me my first taste for record breaking, a glowing feeling when I hurtled through the door hearing '. . . twenty-four, twenty-five'.

Colman Street was my first home. I was born when my mother was only sixteen, so we lived with her parents. Then an odd thing happened when I was four or five. We went for the weekend to my other grandparents, who also lived in Brighton, and when it came to going home on Sunday afternoon I said I was going to stay with Pop – that's what we called grandfather Albert. I suppose it was regarded as a childish request. Pop just said, 'Oh, leave him. He'll go when he's ready.' But that did not happen for another five years. For all that time I lived with Pop and Grandma.

Looking back it seems strange and I suppose there were a variety of reasons: it was cramped in Colman Street; I saw little of my father because as a market trader he was working so hard; and perhaps the fact that my mother was so young also had something to do with the break. Of course Mother and Father were living only half a mile away and I saw them frequently, but it was something which happened and I, and I know my mother, find difficult to understand.

The fact that I did not live at home for many of my early childhood years might seem surprising to some people, but it would be wrong to leave the impression that there were divisions within the family. Quite the contrary, we had a close-knit unity often found among market people.

Pop had a barrow, and then a stall, when he was very young in the original Brighton Market in London Road. Like most of its kind, the social need which was met cluttered the highway so the council provided a site which is now Brighton Open Market. Pop moved in there where unit 21 – 'Albert's' – sold farm produce. When I 'joined' the family business – in my early schooldays – the market was in a transitional stage. In the smart covered area, the stalls had given way to lock-up units – not quite shops – which are familiar in many market towns. Pop's three sons worked the market and I know it was tough. My early recollection is of Father going off at six in the morning to open up and put the 'flash' out – displaying the goods as attractively and as invitingly as he could. Because it involved poultry, eggs and meats it all had to be brought out each morning from the refrigerator and put back at the end of the working day – about six o'clock.

Those days were hard, when I look back now, harder than I realized, but there was a lot of fun. There is a camaraderie among market people which comes through the humour that cushions the fact that you are virtually surviving from week to week. There is no guaranteed, regular wage packet; in our case it was a matter of Pop and his sons buying the produce, most of it from local farms, and re-selling it at a profit. You develop a sharp attitude towards buying and selling no matter what it is, goods or services, something which some of the people who now deal with me in business are surprised to encounter. I question everything and in part that comes from my family tradition; the need to be sure that if you are after a bargain you are going to get one, that you are not being 'conned' or done down. I suppose that might account for my reticence, now that athletes can enjoy commercial benefits, to deal with entrepreneurs and agents.

I first began to 'work' in the market about the age of eight. I liked being with Pop and my father, of course, and enjoyed listening to the banter among the stallholders, the laughs over stories in the *Daily Mirror* etc, the gambling on horses, dogs and anything sporting. My father was a fanatical sports fan but there was not much time, or money, to go to the big events. They went to White City for an athletics meeting once when I was very young and I can recall Father telling me about going up to see one of Henry Cooper's fights with Muhammad Ali – I think it was the one at Highbury. He was in one of the cheapest seats and admitted that from his distant spot he could not see much, even though he had a pair of binoculars; but that did not matter for he had been part of the big occasion, an experience to talk over back in Brighton. Most of his other sporting contact in those early days was, I suspect, in the betting shop, just round the corner from the market. Many times I was sent off to find Father, pushing open the betting shop door into a crowded room, bits of paper strewn everywhere, the noise of the course commentary and thick blue haze of smoke just above my head. There were losses, which caused the occasional family row, but there were also some good wins, which meant there were a few extras.

I suppose that when I was living with Pop I was spoiled, but at home I never wanted for anything. Naturally, with our market connection, we were always well fed and in other ways, in my pre-running days, I was never conscious of being deprived. When it came to athletics, the support which my parents gave was remarkable. It was, like for so many parents I suppose, the first priority that the Ovett children should not face the struggle or miss out as they had done. My father worked himself to a mild early heart attack and my mother looked after the family and worked part time to ensure there was enough for us. Understandably my father was keen to ensure that his sons did not follow his experience: he won a scholarship to Varndean Grammar School, but by the time he was fourteen he had to leave in order to help his father in the market. Before and after I was at Varndean, my father worked to ensure that I would not follow those steps.

The market had a happy atmosphere. My early 'working' days usually involved weekends when I would go off to a farm and help load up with eggs or chickens. At Christmas it was more serious because the Ovett family had a reputation for supplying very good fresh turkeys. We used to buy them in, usually the day they were killed, bring them into Brighton to a cooling room which we hired for the week and then pluck them. At first, some of them – thirty-pound birds – seemed as big as me, hanging there from the rack.

The plucking is done with thumb and forefinger to prevent damaging the bird's flesh. If you do one, for the family Christmas dinner, I suppose it could be fun. But here we were plucking hundreds. My fingers used to be raw – I couldn't understand how such a delicate feather could have such an effect. Then there were the feathers flying up with all the dust in them as people moved about and that gave you a terrible cough. It was the most hectic time of the year and must have started me wondering whether, as the senior son and grandson in the business, I really wanted to take up my inheritance.

Even this arduous task had its funny side. My father used to make up the orders, but many times – in spite of everyone's vigilance – Mrs Jones would go off with a twenty-pound bird, having ordered a twelve-pound one, returning after the festivities to say how delighted everyone had been and how surprised they were that there was so much meat on a twelve-pound bird . . . not knowing the panic there was to find and prepare at the last moment a twenty-pound bird for the lady whose order had gone so gratefully astray. Could we face turkey at Christmas dinner after that? As far as I was concerned I just murdered it – you had to get your own back.

My father has now branched out into wholesaling which I suspect and hope has a little less hassle and greater reward. Unit 21, 'Albert's', in Brighton Open Market is still in the family.

My mother's industry did not stop at looking after a husband and three children. When a market café became vacant she took it over and of course had some of her supplies from Albert's stall. Later she ran the Rotunda, a cafeteria/restaurant in Preston Park, alongside the main Brighton–London road, which was only a ten-minute walk from the house in Harrington Villas to where we later moved. She now runs a delicatessen as well.

My early schooldays were spent at Balfour Primary School, just round the corner from Harrington Villas. My first competitive experience came in soccer, but it was my speed rather than ball skill which won me a place in the Brighton Primary Schools team. I could invariably push the ball past a defender and run round him. Pop and Father encouraged me in those days and Pop felt at first that I had a gift for high-jumping.

My earliest memory of running in inter-schools sports, aged ten, was of disaster and tears. In school playground races I was so good that it was obvious I was going to win the 100 yards at Withdean Stadium in the Brighton Primary Schools Championships – and when I lost I burst into tears and I was still crying when I did the high jump. There is a story that I only won that event because one of the judges was my teacher and she held the bar on after my best jump. It was apparently the only way to stop the crying; my first athletic victory needed the help of an official.

I was fortunate enough to pass my 11-plus which guaranteed my entrance to Varndean Grammar School, a massive building situated in a vast campus in the Surrenden area of Brighton. It had a high reputation among English grammar schools for its academic achievements, but following the traditional lines of such places sporting individualism was submerged by the team games of football and cricket. However the young Ovett spirit was not daunted and sprinting technique was exercised frequently on the soccer field as an 'attacking' left back; and perhaps more obviously chasing the ball on the edge of the cricket field.

The only opportunity to display my true talent came during the Open days when the lower school was paraded in front of the parents in white plimsolls, white socks, white shirts, usually ill-fitting, which all added up to a traditional English school's sports day. Ovett junior won everything.

Athletics, schooldays and family life entwined very happily. Unlike some musical prodigy I did not suddenly one day hoist myself on to the piano stool and tinkle through a few Chopin Etudes which I had just heard on the radio. My family were not suddenly struck by that awesome sort of talent demanding a change in their life style. The process towards being an Olympic champion and a world-record breaker evolved slowly; I went through the normal athletic school-age groupings, without always winning in my class, but it soon became clear that I was talented and my parents wanted to nurture the talent. One evening after a schools sports day, my father decided that he was going to take me somewhere to develop my talent along the right lines for the future – Brighton and Hove Athletic Club was the obvious choice, based at Withdean Stadium.

Withdean Stadium – now called Brighton Sports Arena – is a big plus for living in Brighton. I've had some wonderful times there and one or two sad ones. It is a natural amphitheatre, with a steep slope on the southern side, covered in beech trees; on the other there is sufficient rise to make the track nestle neatly, and be sheltered. However, one temptation for exhausted athletes in the finishing straight is a pub, the Sportsman, a mere ten yards away from the outside lane. There have been calls to put the track on the international map, build more stands and turn it into a sort of Gateshead of the south. It has had international events; probably one of the most notable was in 1956, just twelve months after I was born, when many of the Olympic team had their final competition before departing to Australia and the Games at Melbourne.

My first three visits to Withdean Stadium did none the less leave me disillusioned. No one appeared to be concerned about newcomers of my age and my father and I were left to our own devices on the back straight of the track. On the fourth occasion my father's patience snapped. Stopping several seniors in mid-training session, he asked where the coaches of Brighton and Hove AC were, only to be told that they did not always come down on training nights. Someone was pointed out across the track and Father went off to seek help. But eventually it took a letter to the club secretary to bring results. I could easily have been lost to the sport during that period if it was not for my father's persistence, which no doubt came from his own experience as a sprinter in the RAF. Not only did he want me to develop my talent but also to find the sort of fun which he enjoyed in athletics in his younger days.

After breaking the ice, club nights on Tuesdays and Thursdays became part of my training pattern when I would join in with the rest of my contemporaries. We tried everything: sprinting, hurdling and the jumps. It was during this period I achieved notoriety for my record breaking in my age group on the track – and in the field; it looks as though I am still Sussex record holder for the junior boys' long jump with 20 feet 6 inches. The whole of this period was experimental. Looking back it was the best way to be at the time instead of specializing in one particular distance. Through the training programme and the varied competition I was strengthening my whole body for later years.

My first experience of athletics in the wider world beyond Brighton and Sussex came in 1970 in the English Schools Cross Country Championships at Blackburn. I was moving into the world of my athletic heroes – not David Bedford or Brendan Foster, the stars who stirred the crowds at Crystal Palace, but runners who were virtually my contemporaries, one age group up perhaps, athletes like Andy Barnett and David Glassborrow. These were the athletes whose progress I studied in the *Athletics Weekly* column 'Spotlight on Youth', where I read about their training schedules and tried to adapt the work they were doing to my own needs. I spotted them at Blackburn, their track suits weighed down with badges. It was the fashion to have a badge for every achievement – on the fields of Blackburn you could tell who the 'Field Marshals' were.

The eight-hour coach trip from Brighton to Blackburn brought a world of new experience. The English Schools Association organize their national events in a way you would expect of schoolteachers, with discipline and order, which is only achieved through a lot of hard work and forward planning. When the Sussex coachload arrived at that northern outpost, we trooped into a school hall to be assigned a billet for the weekend. I was taken off in a mini by a man whose name I don't think I ever knew. An overall covered his clothes but I was a little puzzled because he looked too frail and pale and his finger nails were too delicately manicured for those of a mechanic. We drove off to a tiny terraced house where my host told me that he and his wife were going out for the evening and my tea was on the table . . . after that journey from Sussex, the night before the big race my meal was bread, butter, jam and a pot of tea.

The man disappeared upstairs and while I was spinning out the bread and jam, trying to think it was more, his wife appeared, also in an overall with an immaculate hairdo and eyelashes that seemed to touch the back of her neck. After a little small talk she disappeared again, leaving me to watch television and wonder what I had come to; after all, a fourteen-year-old did know all the facts of life and I was wondering about the sort of life people who lived in Blackburn led. Suddenly the living-room door was swept open and all was explained. The woman waltzed in, twirling towards the television in a sequined dress, followed by husband in white tie and tails – and gloves. 'We're off then, make yourself at home, have a cup of tea,' said the woman as, presumably, they departed to the local version of 'Come Dancing'.

Next morning I came down to breakfast and nothing was said. I did not have the courage to ask them if they had won. I was not due at the school until midday, but they took me there three hours before and I spent the time in an empty hall trying not to think about the race. They were of course well meaning and in their way kind, but it was a very unathletic beginning to my running career away from home.

The race was a disaster. It was pouring with rain all day and by the time my event started the course was churned into a quagmire and at one point looked like a river. I am a fluid runner and this was a course for sloggers. When I'm running in such conditions I still look relaxed in my style, although I am pushing it hard. It was desperately tough and when I got back to the changing rooms in the school, there was my father, Pop and my uncle, looking like characters out of *The Grapes of*

Wrath, soaking wet and bitterly disappointed. After all my success in Brighton and Sussex, I know they thought I was in with a chance of winning: I think I finished twenty-seventh. They had been standing out in the awful weather all afternoon without so much as a cup of tea – cross-country races are held in the remotest spots – and when I saw them I thought, 'What have I done to them? All that travel, the misery of the weather and I finish twenty-seventh.' Their first reaction was 'Why didn't you try harder?' which upset me, and has done many times since. I can look relaxed and easy, when in fact I've really got nothing left. It is the same today on the track: I don't have that tense, tortured Zatopek look in the last fifty yards, twisting my head in contortions, but believe me it still hurts. It did that afternoon at Blackburn.

My family went off damp and bedraggled, to travel home to Brighton. I went back to the billet – bread, butter and jam – and then out with the rest of the Sussex lads. I was desperately tired and tried to resist the idea of 'celebrating' in Blackpool, a bumpy diesel-train journey away from Blackburn. We went, only to find of course that in February most of Blackpool was closed. My legs were hurting, almost numb with tiredness, and after buying fish and chips we went into an amusement arcade, one of the few open. The warm stuffy atmosphere only made me more tired but I spotted a haven. I made a bee-line for one of those machines which simulates driving a car, and put a couple of quid into it. No, it had nothing to do with my love of motors, just that it had a seat which I had bought for fifteen minutes . . . heaven.

Five months later I had a very different experience of an English Schools Championships – my first major victory on the track. I won the 400 metres in a record 51.8 seconds, a time which was only beaten a couple of years ago, and I had something like a fifteen-yard margin over the second runner. I was the favourite because I had produced a time of 51.6 seconds in winning the Sussex title a month earlier; being favourite is something I have had to live with ever since.

This first experience of winning away from home was the climax to a marvellous weekend. The English Schools Championships was and still is the biggest festival of the sport in Britain and, for all I know, in Europe. For me it was the first time I was marshalled into a parade behind the Sussex Schools' banner with hundreds of other competitors. I was fascinated by the whole weekend, competing in several rounds before the final. It was a two-day jamboree, events like the shot and the jumps going on somewhere outside the arena. There was of course billeting again and the whole affair was a remarkable example of the British ability to organize. I was so concerned about the enormity of the organization and the way the meeting was run that I think it took my mind off racing. Anyway I treasure that memory of running at such an event for the first time, with my family watching. Going back to join them, after winning, in one of the temporary stands and seeing them so ecstatic was the first of many such moments; sadly Pop was to share only a few.

I competed in two more English Schools Championships meetings, a third place in the 400 metres with a time of 1 minute 55 seconds. They were important meetings in my development, bringing hundreds of local heroes together and putting their feet firmly on the ground; even the schools athletic world of England was a big place. I was fortunate winning in two of my championships, but the victories apart, I learned something about coping with big meetings. Unhappily, since the athletic calendar is now so crowded, the English Schools does not get the widespread publicity it deserves. It is nevertheless a valuable part of the British athletics pyramid.

Three weeks before the last of my English Schools Championships I won the 800 metres in the Sussex Schools at Withdean setting a UK record for a sixteen-year-old of 1 minute 52.5 seconds. It was a miserable occasion, cold, rainy and depressing, when the cinders stick more to your back than your spikes. A family occasion, with Mother and Father and uncles in the stand to watch me, I went over to the family for a chatter. Then I rejoined my friends and I can remember looking over and seeing that my family had moved from their seats, which seemed strange. When I prepared for the sprint relay they were missing and I think I must have been puzzled by it, because usually you knew where the Ovetts were by the noise they made cheering for me. After the race, another victory I recall, I saw a friend coming across the track towards me. 'Steve, I think you'd better come with me,' she said and I sensed that something was wrong.

As we were walking away from the track she told me that my grandfather had died. He was then living in Tongdean Court, a small block of flats close to the stadium, and as I walked in there was a policeman, my mother and father were crying and I think that there were other people around. Pop was lying on the floor, still wearing the cardigan which he always seemed to wear. My emotions seemed shut off. When I heard that Pop was dead, I was drained and cold but now, standing in his living room, emotions seemed to me out of place. I could do nothing about his death – it was obviously impossible to bring him back. My thoughts were of the good times we had had together and whether I was going to be able to remember them all, for that now was all that remained of our love. My family were distressed, and some were intent on consoling me, but I did not need that. All I wanted was time to reflect, and to touch my grandfather for the last time.

2

'You'll Never Be a Champion'

Athletics has given me an immense amount of pleasure over many years. But there was one weekend when I think I became a little frightened of it. I was about fourteen and went away for the first time to a coaching course at Crystal Palace, organized by the Southern Counties. The man in charge of my group was Frank Horwill, the moving force behind the British Milers Club whose work rate from the athletes under his control became almost as famous as his brusque attitude towards the Establishment of the sport. At fourteen I knew nothing of him or his methods. I thought at the time I was training quite hard, but under the Horwill influence I came to understand a new dimension of pain and to be introduced to the athletic adage: 'If it's not hurting then it's not doing you any good.'

We started the morning with a six-mile run, having to sprint the last quarter mile; then it was into the weight-training room for another session; then after a teabreak it was off to tackle some hill work to be followed by sprinting. At the end of the day I had done as much training as I would do in a fortnight. The following morning at eight there was Frank driving us all on into a session of 200-metre runs – about forty of them I think – and of course the whole course was grinding to a halt as Frank called 'Faster, Faster, Faster'.

I became a bit disillusioned. By lunchtime I was almost living proof that there was life after death. I rang home and told my father what this man Horwill was putting us through. 'Just stick it out for the rest of the day and I'll come up and collect you,' he said – which he did and Ovett junior stretched his aching legs along the back seat of the car and slept all the way home to the seaside. Father had to carry me up to the house, crying, I was in such a state.

Before going home all the athletes were required to go through a series of tests. During one of these Frank was urging more effort when an athlete behind me, waiting his turn for the long jump, blew a raspberry as a riposte to one of Frank's remarks. Frank thought I was the culprit and has had to live with his outburst ever since: 'I know it was you Ovett. You'll never be a champion, you haven't got what it takes . . .' There are many coaches who have the same attitude towards training as he does. Basically his method is developed from the Arthur Lydiard (Peter Snell's coach) school of coaching – hard work and a lot of it. Today Frank is less fierce about it all and has produced some fine athletes. He remains today a good friend.

In contrast to Frank's 'encouraging' words were those I heard a few years later. 'Well, boyo, you've got something on your hands here,' was the remark to Harry Wilson which I associate with the fact that someone else knew I had unusual talent. The man with the Welsh lilt was Cecil Smith, one of Britain's senior coaches.

The occasion was a Southern Counties invitation training camp for athletes at Crystal Palace in January 1973, the first I had attended; Harry Wilson was in charge of coaching the middle-distance squad to which I was transferred from the sprinting group. I have never really liked the idea of group training and having worked with the sprinters to whom I was assigned I did not like what they were doing and had been allowed to join the middle-distance men, some of whom were internationals. At the age of seventeen I found I could cope with the sort of

training session these senior athletes were undergoing. I
do not think at the time the significance of that fact struck
me. It was yet another piece of life's jigsaw slotting into
place at a timely moment.

Barry Tilbury was my first coach but when he moved
away and tried to handle the role from long distance,
with my father as intermediary, it did not work so my
father took over. By the time I met Harry, I knew that
my father's experience of training had been exhausted.
Thus Harry came on to the scene at an appropriate
moment. Like many coaches he was dogmatic, a brash
extravert, with peak cap and whistle shouting at you in a
style I gather Percy Cerutty organized for the training
of Herb Elliott, Australia's world-record breaker and
Olympic 1500-metres champion of 1960. I thought at the
time he was a little over the top, but then that was Harry.

For two years, 1973 and 1974, Harry was extremely
valuable because he took me beyond basic training
methods and showed me how to utilize certain training
techniques. Harry pulled me away in effect from the off-
the-peg style of training – taking something out of a book
– to a tailor-made training. He gave me sessions which
were helping him to find out more about my long-term
prospects. I was getting to that age when I liked to train
with other runners at the club because of its sociability,
but the training I needed for developing the talent I
possessed required that I move away from that style.
Many people drift through their athletic life doing the
wrong type of training and are quite happy about it --
Harry showed me that by experimenting one could find
out strengths and weaknesses, what I should work on and
how I should do it. Had I been regularly with a group of
six or eight runners then I might have emerged as yet
another 'Ford' off the assembly line. Harry also helped
me out of the last stages of adolescence and rounded me

off from being a brash, rather arrogant character – which was probably no more than a defensive mechanism.

I quickly realized that while I had been training hard in my earlier years, much of it was a waste. During the double-games period at school, for instance, I would leave the footballers and go off on a ten-mile run, then after school play squash and finish up with circuit training when all that was really needed at that age, thirteen and fourteen, was a four-mile run.

Perhaps a better example of Athlete Lost was a session I copied from Jim Ryun's book which my father had read. Ryun apparently included a session in which he did 40 times 400 metres: since he had been a world beater as a junior I suppose I thought I should go out and do it too. We used the cycle track at Preston Park in the middle of winter for this exercise, each with a torch, with my father flashing his as a starting signal and I using mine to warn him that I was finishing the recovery. I am not sure which wore out first, the torch or my legs. I have since learned not to imitate other famous athletes and that is why I have been reluctant to get involved in writing articles or a book about coaching. I do not want youngsters to copy me blindly. That is not the way to develop or enjoy running, it is more likely to disillusion and destroy. You cannot truly duplicate: I am sure I could not cope with Seb Coe's training and my schedules would not suit him – and neither of us would benefit from the work Steve Cram does.

In the first two years of our relationship I would see Harry perhaps once a fortnight and in between be in touch by telephone, tailoring his work to suit me. I believe many athletes have failed to achieve their natural fulfilment by reason of the attitude towards coaching and the rather selfish attitude of some coaches. Coaching after all amounts to teaching and if we followed the pattern of normal teaching then I think we would benefit: at primary school we have one type of teacher; through junior school we have another; in the comprehensive system or college we have several specialists; and at university we move to the tutorial stage. There ought to be a greater acceptance of this system than exists in athletics and a different attitude on the part of coaches and athletes. We could learn a lot from the coach – athlete relationship of some of our great athletes, discovering, I think, that David Bedford reached a point where he was coaching Bob Parker – his coach – to coach David Bedford. I suspect the same would be true of Brendan Foster and his coach Stan Long. Not many coaches know much about international racing and certainly a coach new to the top level needs to seek those with understanding and expertise in the business of international competition and all that goes with it.

There is, I think, a touch of the sadist in many coaches, not of course to the point where they would inflict permanent harm, but towards that 'if it doesn't hurt, it's not doing any good' attitude. Some athletes need a little bullying, the whip hand. That has never been my relationship with Harry although there were many times, in the early years, when he tried it. For instance, he might have suggested a session of eight 300-metres runs in 36/37 seconds (which is sub-50 seconds for 400 metres) and the recovery would be a 100-metres jog in 20 to 30 seconds. I would turn down that sort of idea flat. Harry, I felt, thought I was not working hard enough and that if I did more, then the end result would be a better athlete. I have never accepted that theory. Instead I might attempt four or five 300-metres runs, just as I might step up a suggested session because I felt I needed more volume; it goes back to my belief in tailoring training to individual needs, a subject which I discuss in the following chapter.

Certainly since 1978 I have worked out my own training, with advice from other people, one of whom was Harry. He has of course been described as 'Steve Ovett's coach', which we both knew was not truly the situation, but as far as I was concerned it was not of such significance that the world needed to be told otherwise by me. Harry Wilson and I have been good friends over those years. He has shared my ups and downs in athletics and I have been grateful for the part he has played in my life. Some people said, quite viciously, that anyone could have coached Steve Ovett to the top. This is probably true, but one thing I do know is that I would not have enjoyed it half as much with anyone else.

My first real step into the world of senior competition came on Friday the thirteenth of July 1973 – lucky for some. In my heat of the AAA Championships at Crystal Palace I faced the American runner Mark Winzenreid. The qualifying system was the first past the post in each heat and three fastest losers. Mark accordingly went off bent on getting that first place, intent on dominating a heat in which he considered no one would offer a real challenge. Surprise, surprise . . . I stayed with him until the final 10 metres and lost by only a fifth of a second in 1 minute 47.5 seconds, a UK record for seventeen-year-olds. My family were delighted and we were about to return to Brighton with an unexpected prize of the record when it was announced that I had qualified as one of the fastest losers for the following day's final – panic and elation.

The final turned out to be one of the finest 800-metres races seen in Britain, Andy Carter of Stretford producing a UK record of 1 minute 45.1 seconds with me being dragged round in the wake to record yet another UK age record, 1 minute 47.3 seconds. The race though left me depressed because of my lack of ability to deal with the athletes of this calibre. Quite simply, they just ran away from me, which on the track was a completely new experience.

Two weeks later I was invited by the British Milers Club to take part in the City Mile at Motspur Park – on the cinder track – where before the war Sydney Wooderson broke the world 800-metres and one mile records. My family took me to the meeting where I met Harry who was one of the BMC officers. His advice on the race was just to stay in the pack and to hang on as long as possible. The field included Nick Rose and other more established milers from all over the country who had been gathered with the prime intention of breaking that elusive four-minutes barrier.

The pace was quick. When Nick Rose broke with 600 yards to go I was left in the pack, trying to maintain my rhythm. I do not remember much until the final furlong when Harry shouted from the outside of the track, 'Go on, you can do it. You need twenty-seven seconds.' I took off, sprinting as hard as I could around the top bend. Turning into the home straight I was gaining on Nick and for one moment thought I might catch him. I closed and closed but Nick's strength kept me out of reach. He crossed the line in 3 minutes 58.4 seconds and I followed only three or four yards behind.

I walked slowly round the track to join Harry in the back straight and he came running to meet me with a beaming smile and stop-watch in hand: 'You've bloody done it. I've got you at 3 minutes 59 seconds, and so have a few others. Congratulations.' As I continued walking, coaches and athletes shook my hand – they had all clocked me under four minutes. Sitting on the infield, pulling on my track suit, the result, after what seemed a long delay was announced. 'First N. Rose, 3 minutes 58.4

seconds. Second S. Ovett, four minutes nought-nought point nought.'

There were groans from the crowd and disbelief from fellow athletes, to the extent that a group actually questioned the official timekeepers on their judgement. However they would not budge or accept that either I had broken four minutes relatively comfortably or Nick's time was much slower. The distance separating us at the finish did not relate to the times given. It seemed to me that the officials did not deem it proper that a seventeen-year-old should be breaking that magic barrier – it was just not on. So I was left with membership of that exclusive club of Four Minute Milers.

The disappointment was soon forgotten when I received my first international invitation for a senior Great Britain match. This is it, I thought: the big time and bright lights. My début on the world stage of senior international athletics came at Sotteville, in northern France, reached by boat and a long coach trip. The British Amateur Athletic Board did not intend to spend much money on this trip as the main team that weekend was competing in the European Cup Final in Edinburgh. So for those in Sotteville there were no GB track suits or vests – I was fortunate enough to have a team mate in Pete Browne who had been an international for a few years and had taken the precaution of carrying a spare track suit. That one went the rounds of the team and was fairly sweaty by the end of the afternoon. Team talks preceded the action, but must have been wasted on me because I finished third.

The big moment of my year was still to come, the European Junior Championships in Duisburg, West Germany, the biggest junior competition in which one can take part. There are plenty of stories about overcrowding in team villages, four and five to a room, but on this occasion it was three to a room and two to a bed. I was one of the unfortunate ones who did not draw the short straw, so I was allocated the left side of a rather small and lumpy double bed. My sleeping partner on those heavy, warm evenings shall remain anonymous.

After reaching the final through heats and semi-finals I was the favourite to win and felt that there would be very little opposition from the rest of the finalists. As I walked on to the track the junior women had just finished their event and Lesley Kiernan of Havering AC, my girlfriend at the time, had just taken the silver medal, beyond all expectations. After that, being a chauvinist, I just had to win the gold.

As he stepped up to the starting line, S. Ovett did not realize that there were a few surprises to come. My opposition included a Belgian, a West German and an East German who were going to have a dramatic impact not only on this race but also on world athletics in the future. The Belgian was Ivo Van Damme, who took two silver medals in the Montreal Olympic Games and was killed in a car accident; the West German was Willie Wulbeck, who in 1983 won the world 800-metres title in Helsinki. Little did I realize that afternoon in Duisburg that my task was going to be immeasurably more difficult than I believed.

After the gun sounded I relaxed and drifted with the pack for the first lap, thinking it was only a matter of time before I made my move and the others settled for second place. However, at the bell two individuals swept past me and seemed to be sprinting as though it were a 400-metres race. Wulbeck and Van Damme had gone and I was left 15 metres adrift chasing in despair into the back straight. The gap closed all the way round that last 300 metres and there were times when I thought the race had been lost, but I dug deep and pushed hard for the final 20 metres and closed my eyes. Those last three or four strides seemed to go on and on as though it were all in slow motion. Inch by inch I moved past one and then on to the shoulder of Wulbeck, and one desperate lunge sent us both through the tape together. Both of us were looking at one another wondering who had taken the gold – it went to a photo finish. It seemed my vest was thicker than his and I won by four hundredths of a second. I returned to my team mates in the stand only to be congratulated on my marvellous tactical ability in leaving things to the last minute and giving my rivals no room in which to counter attack!

I won that one, but lost selection for the Commonwealth Games in Christchurch, New Zealand, as the selectors believed in or preferred to take experience over youth. The end result was that I was left in England and the athlete who took my place, Colin Campbell of Polytechnic Harriers, ran 1 minute 52 seconds in his first-round heat and was eliminated.

My success at Duisburg brought a response which many young middle-distance runners, and today those in other events, receive from the United States. A seventeen-year-old being offered, without the ordeal of the examination room, an education in the States sounds tempting. I know that many have accepted such offers and if they have not actually regretted doing so they have not always enhanced their athletic careers. My Duisburg victory did not just bring one offer – in a short space I had twenty letters and four American coaches approached me directly or by telephone. One actually came up to me as I was putting my track suit on at a Southern Counties meeting and offered me a place at a college in Wisconsin. He left a little surprised when I said, 'No thank you, I am quite happy where I am' – which was true.

I was fortunate in that I had Harry Wilson, who was

fully aware of what these offers meant and could explain it all to me. We were having a coffee after a training session at Crystal Palace when I told him about all the letters. I was not, like some athletes, starry-eyed about the offers – the market trader in me sparked the response, 'If they are offering me all this, life on a college campus, all found – then what do they want of me?' Harry had the answer to that question. The system at that time – which I understand is little changed in many establishments – is that you could have two or three college matches a week, in each of which you might be required to run two or three races – a total of perhaps nine races when in England the accepted form is one or two a fortnight.

At whatever level of education in the States there is a high degree of competition and rivalry between the various establishments and many coaches survive or fall on the success of their teams. It stems of course from the national interest generated in college basketball and football. Athletics is really a minor sport there, but if a school or college can produce a winning middle-distance runner then that is a plus for the coach. Since all this racing would take place from March to June, I would be in poor shape for the British domestic and international programme when I returned home. Harry provided several examples of athletes who had gone down this particular American drain and not surfaced again.

Those offers were valuable to me in another way. My parents had always said that they would support me in my athletic career, but I knew that this had been and was going to continue to be something of a financial strain, with two other children to bring up. Here, whatever the deficiencies of the American system, was an opportunity for me to relieve them of that burden. The offers gave me a little feeling of independence and, when they reiterated their support and belief that I would be better off at home in Brighton, it strengthened the family purpose and bolstered my confidence.

There was too another interlocking factor – I had recently started training with Matt Paterson, something which Harry welcomed. Ultimately Matt was to become the most important person in my athletic life, because he was there, most days running with me, knowing what I had done, last week, last month and last year. While Harry still had a valuable role to play, more and more Matt became the person with the finger on my athletic pulse – he knows me as far as the business of running is concerned better than anyone else.

The season after my victory in the European Junior Championships was baffling – my first in the senior division and a winter in which I missed three months training through glandular fever was in effect going to be a write off, or rather a chance to build up for the Montreal Olympic Games, which was really Harry's plan. I think because of this looking ahead to the following year, I did not really come to terms with the challenges I was to face and surmount during the summer of 1974.

I won the AAA 800-metres title in a race I ran badly, drifting off the pace and then coming through to pick up seven places in the final 200 metres. It was the first time I had shown such a finishing kick at Crystal Palace, but to me the runners in front were just dying and I went through to win in 1 minute 46.9 seconds. Two weeks previously I had won an 800 metres for Britain in Poland in a tenth of a second faster and I did not really expect to find that speed again; it was uncanny. So too was my first sub-four-minute mile, four days after the championships, the Brigg Mile at Haringey in which I ran each of the first three laps outside 60 seconds and then blasted the final one to achieve that magic figure of 3 minutes 59.4 seconds, exactly the time Roger Bannister achieved in the first four-minute mile twenty years before; my little piece of history was that I became the youngest man in Britain to get under four minutes.

All this running was, I felt, illogical. I really should not have been going like this in my first year as a senior after the illness of the winter. Yet it went on and I felt there could have been more to it than the silver medal I took in the European Championships 800 metres. Even that memory has a slightly unsatisfying taste about it. Luciano Susanj of Yugoslavia was, like me, a man with a finishing kick and when he went down that back straight of the Rome Olympic Stadium he virtually had the gold medal dangling from his neck. But as he went for home I was boxed, badly positioned and although I got out and chased him into the silver-medal position I was angry. There was no way I would have caught him, but I know I could have gone under 1 minute 45 seconds instead of finishing with a time of 1 minute 45.77 seconds. I knew from the excitement of Harry that he had not expected such a run and when I sat up in the stadium and watched the 1500-metres final, in which Britain did not have a runner, I realized that these events are made for men with a finishing kick and resolved then always to think in terms of doubling up in the 800 metres and 1500 metres.

The day after the Rome 800-metres final, I was sitting on the verandah of the team hotel with some of the other athletes when Andy Norman, a very much slimmer version than the present one, sidled up to me and asked if I would like to run in the Coca Cola meeting at Crystal Palace. This is the oldest established invitation meeting in Britain and athletes are keen to compete because always there is a full house and the International Athletes Club who organize the event and the sponsors make sure that all the athletes are well looked after. I had run there the previous year finishing ninth in the mile – not exactly worth recalling.

By now, having won the silver medal, the IAC were naturally keen to have me in the meeting and Mr Norman came up with the 'Can I have a quick word with you' routine, so I moved away from my group. He asked me if I wanted to run in the Coke meeting and I simply replied, 'No, it's not possible.' This brought a puzzled look and 'Yes of course it is.' Whereupon I explained that I was not returning directly to London since I was going on holiday with my Italian girlfriend, who lived in London. We had planned to back-pack our way to places like Rome, Florence and Venice, an explanation which either went straight through him or over his head. He ignored it and suggested I could fly back, run and then fly out to Italy at the IAC's expense.

I declined because my girlfriend was just about to start her thirty-six-hour train journey from Victoria Station and would arrive on the final day of the Championships. He seemed not to be put off and adopted what I now realize is his policeman's look: by the time the conversation ended, with me not running in the Coke meeting, my girlfriend and I could have had a free holiday in Barbados, or anywhere else in the world for that matter. What he did not seem to appreciate was that I did not want to run again that season. I just wanted the holiday I had planned.

Mr Robert Harland of the Coca Cola organization who used to be involved in the meeting was with us. Many years later Andy admitted to me that, as I rejoined the athletes at another table, he said to Robert: 'Right – you wait, if that so and so wants to run next year . . . we'll see about that!' Maybe that is why some people regard him as abrasive if not slightly ruthless. Anyway I went off round Italy with Toni my girlfriend; I lived to tell the tale and the Coke meeting was very successful, I understand, without me.

My holiday was also a great success. We toured most of Italy, France and Switzerland with backpacks and inter-rail cards which allowed us unlimited rail travel. We went to Florence, Pisa, Venice, Lucerne, and then back through France taking in Paris, Bordeaux and then to Dieppe for the ferry to Newhaven. It was an exhausting sort of rest but one which satisfied the Rome silver medallist. It gave me time, instead of rushing back for another athletics meeting, to reflect on my years at Varndean and consider my future.

I enjoyed school and looking back I think it helped that Varndean did not focus upon my athletic achievements, nor in some way set me aside because of them. Academically I was not outstanding; I think I excelled as an orator more than anything else. I was in the sort of educational environment at Varndean Grammar School which, without my concentration upon athletics, would have taken me to university. As athletics became more important so my school reports contained more 'Could do better' remarks, particularly when it came to examination work which even with my distraction because of athletics often seemed a poor representation of my studies. Varndean was, like most I suppose, a team-game school, a sentiment that was reflected in my report of 1973: Games 'Fair' – that was the year I won the European Junior 800-metres title in Duisburg.

I was in the top grade and that meant the main objective was the Oxbridge entrance examinations; everything was geared to getting people in my group to one of the leading universities. I fell short of the requirements in that respect, not helped by my glandular fever when I lost several months of schooling, but I passed 'A' level art with a Grade One. I had always been interested in every form of art – drawing, oils, design – and Grade One gave me the opportunity to go to an art college or polytechnic. I chose Brighton because I wanted to be based at home for my athletics and the forthcoming Montreal Olympic Games.

I completed the first year foundation course and then applied, like everyone else, for a specialist course, graphics in my case. At my interview I was questioned about my athletics and answered, honestly, that I put preparing for the Olympic Games higher than my art studies. If I had been asked to leave on that count I suppose I could not have complained. The outcome of the interview was that I was not up to specializing in graphics but they would have taken me into the fine art section, even with my Olympic priority. Instead, they suggested I did the foundation course again, giving me the opportunity to specialize in the fine art area and to work on my Olympic preparation.

In theory it sounded an ideal method of continuing my studies, but in practical terms I could not cope with the repetition of lectures and other work which I did in the first year. Finally I talked it over with my tutor and decided to withdraw; looking back it was unfortunate that this aspect of my life should end in this fashion, but considering the home environment in which I was living, where most things revolved around the prospect which the Montreal Games held, it was not surprising that something like this occurred. Hundreds of sportsmen encounter this problem. The academic regime in Britain still remains stifling in the constraint it imposes. One or two institutions, such as Bath University, have nibbled at the problem by adding a year to an academic course for sportsmen so that they may concentrate upon their training. There are, too, opportunities for the mature student to study for a degree in later years. There is though much greater need for flexibility in the academic world so that not everyone has to be pumped through the system between the ages of eighteen and twenty-five, which for many are the most fruitful sporting years. Many sportsmen turn for their further education to colleges which specialize in teaching physical educationalists. Loughborough University provides the scope for these students, but, once qualified, teaching PE in schools, when much of your day is spent on your feet, may not necessarily be the best job for an athlete – or for that matter other sportsmen.

Despite the frustrations, first at Varndean then at art college, at least my parents were fully aware of why their elder son was slipping. They realized – unlike one of the masters at Varndean who wrote, in an end of term report 'I hope he will not let his athletic activities interfere with his academic work this summer' – that there were rewards in athletics and that the hypocrisy of the amateur rules would eventually be swept away. They also knew that my greatest gift was my running. And if I failed then there was always a vacancy in the family firm. My father and his family were never people who had gone off to work at nine and finished at five, with a wage packet at the end of the week or the month. They had lived by their wits, by their own output, in a variety of ways and it was natural for my parents to encourage me to turn my athletic talent into a 'living' if that was within the rules.

So life at home revolved around my athletics. The evening meal was scheduled early or late, depending upon whether it was a circuit training night or a session in Stanmer Park; wash day came round when the pile of track suits, shorts and socks reached a certain level. If I came in and felt hungry I had only to ask and Mother would supply steak and chips. That might sound like a child being spoilt but in fact it was to meet a need. With my parents coming to support me at meetings, and later on my mother acting as a buffer between me and the press, athletics became the prime purpose in my mother's life. As a teenager it was of immense help and comfort to me, just the aid and support which I required to hone my talent. Without it I may not have succeeded, but at twenty-four, after the Moscow Games, my attitude had naturally changed. As an adult I wanted to and was perfectly capable of standing on my own feet, of fending for myself. Yet I could see that my mother was 'hooked' on her son's athletics and could see no other way than that she should be associated with it.

3
Stride for Stride

There have been several people who have played an important part in my success and it would be difficult and invidious to set out a league table. However, I do set one person aside for his constant support and sacrifice – Matt Paterson has for ten years been companion, friend, training partner, cushion, buffer, a man whose own athletic career has suffered if not nosedived by training with me. Instead of the victories and performances he might have achieved, his satisfaction – and much of mine I should emphasize – has come from pounding the roads of Brighton, Preston and Stanmer Parks, and the Downs together. Rain or sun, hot or cold, early morning or latish nights – we have matched stride for stride in the process of preparation.

When people hear of this partnership, which has been the most crucial part of my athletic development, they often ask why Matt does not figure in any kind of medal winning. He has been Sussex champion at 1500 metres, 5000 and 10,000 metres but no longer; and he has finished once or twice in the first hundred in the national cross-country championships. The answer is that he does not have my talent. Then, you may ask, am I not being held back by training with him, ought I not to be up a division or two, working at a better quality in training? My response to that is I am uncertain, but my feeling is that I am pitched at the proper level of training and always have been, whereas Matt is probably overdoing it. The theory is supported by the time a couple of years ago when, after a tiff which started from a misunderstanding, he went off to train on his own. He concentrated on work for a marathon and ran it in 2 hours 22 minutes, no mean performance for a man around forty (one of the most closely guarded Paterson secrets, after the contents of his Tartan wallet, is his age).

On many of our training sessions Matt finishes shattered, or somewhere near it, and I am convinced that he would have achieved greater performances at his own level without me. There have though been certain occasions when I have suffered the same agony. One such instance was the Harlow Marathon in 1976–7 after the Montreal Games. Matt and I had decided to have a weekend away camping, going out to Essex to see some of the club lads run the marathon and then on to the Chilterns for a long Sunday run. We picked up directions from an official at the Harlow race who pointed out that there was a five-mile loop and a ten-mile one. We ran the short one thinking we would meet the race field coming from the opposite direction after a gentle five miles, but unfortunately we mixed the loops and the running went on and on. From the start I did not feel good after a night under canvas and my first training session since my two months end-of-season rest. I realized that I was going into a state of hypothermia and despite Matt's exhortations I just had to stop and sit down on the nearest kerb, even though it was cold and raining. When you get into that condition you become fractious and I tried to resist Matt physically pulling me along. Eventually we got back to the dressing rooms and I stood under a hot shower for half an hour feeling very very ill as marathon runners came and went thinking 'Fancy that Ovett running a marathon – he looks in a bad way.'

Our relationship began out of Matt's natural inquisitiveness. In my early days with Brighton and Hove AC people apparently were almost warned off me. I was a high flyer, it was said, a young man best left alone. It was the sort of attitude which emerges, I find, through typical misunderstanding. Tuesday night was the big training evening. Most people worked hard but I treated it as a gentle session and went down there more for the sociability. A lot of people wondered how I was able to produce my performances on training that looked so casual – overlooking the point that the hard work of preparation was done elsewhere. Matt I think was interested enough to find out and after I returned from winning the 800 metres in the European Junior Championships he asked me to give a talk at his school. That evening we went out for a training run, five miles over the Downs, and soon after that running together became a regular pattern.

It was in fact in the build up at the end of 1975 that Matt suggested I add a morning training run to my work. Harry thought it was a good idea so I learned reluctantly and painfully to get out of bed when I did not really want to. Fortunately Matt was living about four hundred yards away from me and was like an alarm clock, getting me up on the dot every morning and waking me through a three-mile run before I went off to school. In retrospect I can see that it was of tremendous value to start running twice a day at that time, when I would otherwise have not got down to it for a year or two.

The training relationship built in other directions. Running together on a stint of two hours loses its boredom when you can talk with someone. We have a laugh, swap jokes, and have received some odd looks in the past from Brightonians who see us stopped, doubled up with laughter. When you are doing a training session on your own, on the track or around a circuit it is helpful, perhaps even essential, to have someone with you watching, knowing what you are doing. There is in the intensity of the work that has to be done a touch of insanity: to have someone on hand as I have had was important. We think alike, have I suppose become almost telepathic.

I realize now that while I was heading towards the middle spot on the Olympic podium, it was taking Matt nowhere fast. Certainly he has had a lot of fun from his part, but there have been many times when his training has been exhausting, when perhaps he has not been able to give a hundred per cent to the children he has been teaching or to his family. There were often times when his batteries were on low ebb, but he kept at it believing that if he was not with me on the next session I would not train so hard. His satisfaction was seeing my rise to success. There were times when I thought he took it to an absurd degree. One Sunday he was about to go on a long training run when he had to take his wife Lynn to hospital. He returned to do the run and then went back to find that his daughter Fiona had joined the family. There were plenty of times when he would get back home feeling very frail from a training session. Whatever the description I attach to Matt, and 'training partner' is almost derogatory, it puts him as the most important person in the Ovett preparation for success and one of my closest friends.

Leaving Brighton and Hove AC in 1981 and setting up Phoenix AC with Matt was something which evolved over a period, a result of daily conversations in training. As a result of my popularity after winning an Olympic gold medal there were hundreds of youngsters joining Brighton but schoolteacher Matt, sensitive to children and particularly the way they are taught, was unhappy about what was happening. Brighton was very much a club of parts, with the juniors, seniors and women's sections separate and only working together on a few occasions a year.

Matt was concerned that lots of youngsters were not receiving proper attention on training nights because there were only a few coaches. It seemed that nothing was going to be done to change the set-up in order to make the sport more interesting for the young newcomers. Matt went on moaning about the position and eventually I told him that if he was unhappy he should leave.

'I don't want to leave the kids,' he said. The natural response from me was, 'Well, form your own club.' We mulled over the idea for a long time, working out what was needed, and finally Matt made up his mind to form a new club and asked me to join him in the venture. I had no loyalty to Brighton and Hove – in my early days they had left me alone to get on with things which, looking back, I think was wrong. Initially, few of the Brighton youngsters came with us – a good thing because it gave us time to get on our feet and set our ideas into action.

Probably the most important part of the Phoenix philosophy is to preserve the needs and aims of the individual within a club atmosphere. There are team events, cross-country races, road relays and track matches which can help team spirit in a club, but athletics is essentially an individual event and it is no good trying to pull against that fact. Phoenix was formed for the individual, not the team, and we do not pressurize members, young or old, into running week after week, to go round the country trying to win team trophies. We teach the youngsters to understand that if there is a team race and Charlie Bloggs does not want to compete then he is not the one to blame for defeat. He might be preparing for an individual event the next weekend: at Phoenix we put that first. We also try to avoid the power structure which seems to bedevil the higher echelons of the sport. We have a committee, but co-opt people on to it for all kinds of tasks. It is working well, but I am sure that in twenty or thirty years' time someone will come along and say, 'There are not enough team competitions in this club, let's go off and start another club . . .' That I suppose is inevitable, but for the present we feel we are trying to meet a need by watching hundreds of members, mostly under the age of sixteen, as best we can. The most important factor is that we all get a lot of fun out of doing it.

In the early days of training, Harry would get me to do interval sessions (repeating a set distance of running with a period of time for the body to recover between each run), working hard to produce a particular heart rate, thus ensuring that the body pump was working at a specific level. It was said that anything above 170 to 200 was efficient but beyond that it was beating faster than the blood could flow in and out, so it was therefore not having the desired effect. Once the heart dropped back to 120 then the recovery had been achieved and you could do another repetition.

That was the theory, as outlined by Harry, behind this particular approach to training. We have now learned, through accumulated research over the years, that the physiology of an international athlete does not conform to that theory. In my case, I would tell Harry that my heart beat was going over 200 and that I was still finding it quite comfortable to work; by the same token sometimes I found that even though my heart beat had dropped to 120, my legs were still hurting and I could not run quickly enough to manage another repetition.

So many athletes – and here you can understand the danger of working in groups – set out to do a training session of repetitions with predetermined recovery times. By the last few repetitions, the time of the run is not being achieved because of a slavish attitude to the recovery rate.

The work of the training session therefore becomes less valuable. If, for instance, an athlete is running a series of 400-metres laps in 58 seconds and the last three are achieved in only 61 or 62 seconds and he is struggling and not working at racing pace, then clearly some of the training is wasted. From the outset I questioned the value of this system with Harry, and we developed together tailored training sessions to benefit me. I place a great deal of importance on the fact that by knowing my body well enough I have been able to stay at the top longer than most other athletes. Many runners accept what their coaches say, in spite of their own feelings, and they either come down with problems or they have an athletic lifestyle in which one year it works and another year it unfortunately does not.

In my case I have refined the situation to the point where I know exactly what my heart rate should be throughout. For instance, in a session of ten 400-metres runs, I know that if that session is achieved in a certain pattern then it is a case of two plus two making four – which for me is being able to run 1500 metres in 3 minutes 30 seconds within a few days. I know from how my body feels after that session that I am ready for a fast run. I can do a session through the woods without the benefit of a watch and still know that I am going well. Instinct, and the knowledge that I have the greater part of the year's training behind me, tells me I am in shape for something special.

Tailoring a training session to an individual's need does not necessarily mean the end of sociability. I like to do some of my training with the club at Withdean Stadium and as part of our goal to help the individual develop rather than herd people together, we adopted a fairly simple system with hill work which enables everyone to benefit equally. Usually in doing a series of runs up a hill together, the strongest runner reaches the 300-metres point, or whatever distance has been chosen, first and then has to wait for the slowest, before everyone turns and walks down together. It means in effect that I get a much longer recovery period than the slowest man and that some runners are being pushed too hard and others not hard enough. The sum total is that very few are achieving the optimum benefit from the session. In the Phoenix Club sessions, when the leader reaches the top of the hill everyone stops and jogs back and we start the next one together. I have to do my recovery quicker than the slowest man, or boy, but it means we are all working together in a more sociable situation. When I am getting back to fitness, after my end-of-season break, then I do not get to the top of the hill – someone is ahead of me. It is a logical system for coping with everyone's fitness.

Similarly on the track, we break our training sessions into groups – not of age, but ability. If you watch the Phoenix Club sessions it looks like a hotchpotch: we don't have the ten-year-olds there, the thirteen-year-olds over there and the fifteen-year-olds somewhere else. That system is wrong, because it is not age but ability and fitness that must be the criteria. Some ten-year-olds are much fitter than thirteen-year-olds. It does not matter if you get 6ft-1in lads of fourteen working with a 5ft-3in ten-year-old, which is what the mix at Phoenix produces. If a lad is struggling at the end of a session or in the coach's view taking it easy, then he moves up or down to the next group, as the case may be. In competition, at club level, the same attitude applies – you might have a twelve-year-old up against a fifty-five-year-old in one event because their performances are roughly level.

I cannot see why this approach could not be extended to cover both sexes. There are plenty of women runners who would benefit from competition against men. In

Britain our girls are struggling to find races where they can run two minutes for the 800 metres; there is just not the competition for them to get the feel of running that fast or to discover what is needed to achieve it. As a result, when they come up against the Russians or girls from other Eastern European countries, they are hopelessly out of their depth. They have to think in terms of not racing the opposition, who are going to get to the finish in something like 1 minute 56 seconds, but running somewhere close to their own best – which means finishing 20 metres or more behind. It is an entirely false situation and causes a lot of frustration amongst our girls. A simple step in the right direction would be to have girls racing against men in domestic events before they are pitched into the real thing.

One of the values of breaking records is to know that your body can go faster, giving you a sense of confidence. It does not matter that there are pacemakers, for in the end the record breaker has gone faster, stepped across into no man's land; he has another potential advantage against future opposition. Our girls would certainly have something like that feeling if they started to know what sub-two-minute 800-metres running is like in club competitions, and that can easily be provided by races against the opposite sex. I know that this sort of thing does go on in some clubs, but it is against the rules – silly rules in my opinion – which the UKAAA will turn its attention to I hope when it comes into being.

One insight into my success must be linked to the training and racing I have done in cross-country and road events. Two of the best examples of Ovett's 'abnormality' in this direction must be my running and winning a half marathon in just over 1 hour 5 minutes in 1977, two weeks before my 1500-metres UK record in the World Cup;

and my victory in the national Junior Cross Country Championships over six miles in the same year, just over three months before setting the UK mile record. No one, and certainly not a top 800-metres runner, has had the same sort of span.

Cross country and road racing are integrated for me. Work over the country is the very basic part of the sport – it starts at school when the soccer pitch is too muddy for a game and the PE master sends you off on a cross-country run. The popular image is of a hard slog in the mud. Although that is not always the case it is hard, strengthening work and races of anything up to nine miles, the distance of the English Cross Country Championships in March, provide me with a competitive sounding board through the winter. Because of the shortening of our winter days you move on to the road during the evenings for some of this work and after the cross-country racing season ends there are short-distance road races, up to ten kilometres, and road relays, which again I have always used. Over the country I have won the Inter Counties title (1978) and finished fourth in the National race (1978). This year Steve Cram, just back from a trip abroad, ran in the English Championships at Newark in March and finished eighty-first. I hope that, with the advent of commercialism in the sport and the belief of certain athletes that they need to protect their image, our middle-distance runners will not turn away from cross-country running as part of their preparation just because on the competitive side they may not be winning.

Cross-country and road running have provided the basis of the pyramid for me throughout my running career. Even as a 100-metres and high-jump expert at school I ran over the country in the winter. Because I have speed there has been less inclination and need for me to concentrate on speed training. I work on the road and the country over long distances, sometimes longer than I should perhaps, and because of this I take longer to get to a peak of sharpness for summer track events. When I do I seem able to hold my form much longer than most, benefiting from years and years of solid winter work, building strength and stamina. I am therefore able to produce peak performances in September, and even October. By that point the European season is over and the Australian one has not begun. If the season was to spread that long, I would have to resist the temptation to go on running. Unlike many of my contemporaries I take a complete rest, which may last as long as two months, in the autumn with absolutely no running at all – not even to catch a bus.

I can do this now because of the years of training which I have built up and also because my training is strongly related to strength rather than speed. I think that other people are coming round to the belief that the 'diary obsession' – doing specific training on specific days and relating it to what you did this time last year – is now out of date. Athletes like Steve Cram who have been forced to rest because of injury have in the end found they have not lost fitness by such inaction – so long as there is plenty of work in the 'bank'.

I term athletes as being 'speed orientated' like Seb Coe or 'endurance orientated' like myself. Seb has the speed and works on that aspect of training to produce such purple patches as his three records in forty-one days in 1979, but he has, up to this year, certainly not shown the ability to make his training pattern work as far as an 800-metres championship is concerned, where endurance is needed to get you through heats and the semi-final prior to the main event. He began 1984 running in road relays, which to me looked like a change of approach. That, together with cross-country racing, has been part of my athletics from my early club and school days. I have concentrated on it because I have enjoyed it – perhaps a little too much.

As you get older the ability to move from one pace to another, to sprint, declines. This coupled with over-endurance training has led me to work upon the area of sprinting a lot more in recent years to maintain the proper balance. Although the ability to kick is one of my great assets, I think my position in this respect was further complicated after my leg injury of 1981, the result of a collision between S. Ovett and some church railings towards the end of a training run. An operation became necessary, for a time my body became unbalanced and this, as much as the ageing process, blurred my acceleration when it came to the final lap.

Ninety per cent of my winter training is on the road through necessity, because of weather and darkness, and in summer the work is equally divided between road and track. I hope all this does not destroy the romanticism which has been built up into what I call the road-running industry. The jogging fashion suddenly turned to a passionate love affair with the marathon and, while the basic outcome is that a lot of people are taking exercise that they would not otherwise have done, the commercial world has not missed a trick as far as I can see. There are volumes on how and where to run on the roads; people suddenly become experts on how to train for marathons; suddenly there is a need for special jogging suits, liqua-paks, diets, anti-gravity boots and how to cope with jogging and a normal sex life. I read about the deep mystique of road running, the soul searching and the fact that you meet yourself out on the road – I've never met myself anywhere, let alone on a stretch of road in the middle of Brighton. People of course are making a living out of it all, which doesn't worry me too much as long as they do not baffle everyone with their complexities and take away the joy it all brings.

With the fashion for running marathons there are now plenty of people about every day of the year running somewhere, on roads, pavements, parks or precincts. Obviously Matt and I train in the quietest parts possible, but everywhere we go the number-one menace – a dog – may be lurking. I am a dog owner, my parents have a dog and I understand and appreciate the animal, but my anger with some Brighton dog owners is well known. Perhaps some people would not understand my attitude but they must remember that when I encounter a dog I am often under stress, trying to concentrate on a hard piece of work. I would just as easily be ruffled if another runner was to bump me, or if Rachel was to miss timing a lap or a circuit. So if Fido wants to come and play, or bark, let alone bite me, then I become irate.

Dogs should be under the control of those in charge of them at all times. Most dog owners have their animal on a lead in the street or in a public place, but when it comes to the park they are left to have a run. Yet many dogs will not respond to a command when something unusual happens . . . and to a dog, a runner in striking colours amounts to the unusual. Immediately that dog runs after the runner there is danger. The runner is concentrating on what he is doing, he may be very tired near the end of a session, he may not be aware of the animal until the last moment. That is the time when he might react in a way which frightens the poor animal.

I use a 1000-metres circuit in Stanmer Park in training and I was doing a session of six circuits with only a short recovery period. Matt was training with me as usual and as we finished the second circuit a dog came running after me – Matt was in my wake away from the trouble. I called to the owner to control the dog but he just laughed.

I went away on the third circuit and the same thing
happened. By the fourth I was pushing the work hard
and when the dog came bounding and yapping at me
again I lost my cool, more so because when I stopped the
owner was smiling. 'He won't hurt you,' he said. He was
upset at the expletives I used in telling him to control the
animal before I kicked its, and his, teeth in.

I know one should not get to that point, but dog
owners do not seem to understand the stress which
runners suffer. There would be no such reaction from
any athlete anywhere at all if the dog owners exercised
their responsibility. On the next circuit the same thing
happened so I turned and chased the dog, and the owner,
with Matt guffawing in the background. The end product
was a ruined training session which was not as bad as two
other occasions when I have had to go off to hospital for
stitches and injections after being bitten. That of course
stops training and competition.

For some time at Phoenix we have been worried by a
Doberman that lives in a house backing on to Preston
Park. The animal just roams the park and we have had to
use club members as diversions so that the training groups
can do their work unhindered. Imagine what a fully
grown Doberman might do to one of the ten-year-olds in
our club. Can you blame us for being concerned? I think
it is time that local authorities gave consideration to the
system which operates in Sweden, where sections of parks
and open spaces are for the use of dogs and their owners
and the area is fenced off. They need a large enough
space in which to run, I accept, and that ought to be
provided. There is after all the added question of hygiene
to be considered as some parks are badly fouled by
animals.

There are other hazards which face runners: newspaper

boys who come out of gateways without looking, motor-
ists who drive alongside you and then accelerate to turn
across your path when you come to a side road, or drivers
who accelerate when you are running across a road.
There are I am afraid a lot of idiot drivers. Pedestrians,
too, sometimes seem transfixed as you run towards them.
I suppose some are trying to make up their minds whether
it is that runner they see on the telly – Seb Coe or
someone – when they see this figure approaching, but I
am amazed at the way they just stand, sometimes two or
three across the path. If another pedestrian was walking
towards them they would not block the way; as a matter
of courtesy they would step to one side. Why not the
same attitude to runners? We do not want to bump into
anyone but in many instances it is far too hazardous to
run in the road. Even in the quiet roads I often approach
someone from behind, with a warning cough or a call,
but the fright I sometimes cause as I pass someone is a
reminder that we live in the era of the mugger.

I say elsewhere that I believe part of my talent is an
instinctive feeling about when I am ready to race. I have
never been an athlete whose training regime is based on
last year's work. I can be in a period of hard training
when most athletes would not want to race, but I know
from experience and a certain feeling that I am capable
of running really well. When that happens I phone up
Andy Norman and say 'I'm in shape to run a good time'
and within forty-eight hours or so I'm off to a race in a
helpful climate and hopefully good competition.

Andy I know has been described as my racing manager
– which demeans our relationship. As far as that side
of the sport is concerned it has always been a loose
arrangement. He shows me the European calendar at the
beginning of the year and I go through the events, picking

those I want to run in and noting others. If I want to run somewhere then I ask Andy. We talk about the structure of athletics, we discuss its future and, as I write elsewhere, I was very much involved, through Andy, in helping to construct the AAA registration scheme. In many instances I make my own arrangements, but there is certainly no one else in the sport whom I trust to do the job – he has known me for virtually all my athletic life and I know that he can be relied upon to make the arrangements which are best for me. He does exactly the same sort of thing for a growing number of athletes and a lot of other people benefit. I know that if the promoter in Oslo or Koblenz or other meetings wants me to run then Andy will ask that other British athletes who need the experience be invited. That is the sort of 'market' bargaining I understand and encourage.

Like every athlete my training is geared in the long term to major events, like the European Championships, the World Championships and of course the Olympic Games, but for many of my races I make what really is a last minute decision. The programme may be pencilled in but the final decision comes nearer the event. It may seem haphazard and I suspect that the press used to think that it was part of my Garbo act to turn up for races without too many people knowing. All it is really is to utilize a race as I would utilize a training session. I do not plan a month in advance: it is almost day to day with me.

I have been out on a training run, felt good and got back home to ring round and search for a race. Matt will be out with me, struggling to keep up when I'm floating along and he'll turn and say, 'My God, boy, you need a race – to slow you down.'

We have adopted this approach in training the youngsters at the club. While the main goal may be the Sussex Schools or the English Schools, if someone is going well in training, perhaps because they have had a week of good sleep or less school work, we will try to find them a race, almost as a natural outlet for them. After all, you can build your training programme towards a particular race or races, but the body mechanism cannot read an athletic calendar. You need to watch for the signs and if the training is producing a need for a race, then that need should be met. You cannot simulate racing in training; time trials may be of some help but there is no substitute for a race and training runs can be misleading to the unwary or the inexperienced.

It takes me three or four races early in the season to get myself into the right physiological shape for competition. I can be going faster in training early on in the year than I am at the peak of the season, but the first few races never reproduce that speed. Physiologically you are not in shape for a race, or as Andy has often put it to me 'the tissues need breaking down', phraseology which I cannot recall reading in any coaching manual.

There are times when the body seems to deceive you. I have learnt over the years that easing down for a race can have an adverse effect. I can have a bad run in a race I have prepared for, even though I have run hard, and yet a day or two later have another race and run exceptionally well. I do not necessarily rest before a major race; in fact I have had some of my best runs after a hard morning training session. The body does not always respond to rest. I have come to understand more of my body mechanism and the way it functions and thus become more sensitive in my response.

I think a classic example was in 1983 after the World Championships, when many athletes were jaded and tired towards the end of the season. During a race in Oslo I instinctively knew after the first lap that there was something special coming up. It was not a spectacular time,

3 minutes 50 seconds, but I knew that while I was running it there was a lot more there; it was coming so easily that it was ridiculous. I realized immediately that somewhere in the next fortnight there was a world record to be taken and I astonished the reporters at Oslo by going straight up to the press box and telling them that I would break the world 1500 metres days later in Koblenz. Such post-race words from the Ovett lips had them jamming their fingers in the typewriters. Well, yes I was wrong, the pacemaking at Koblenz went awry, but a few days after that I achieved the target in Rieti. I knew that night in Oslo that I could have taken the world record; yet here I was after the disappointment of the World Championships at a time when I might have been tapering off at the end of a season broken by injury. Instead my body was ready to run faster than ever before.

4

Lost in Lane Eight

An incident at the European Cup semi-final in July 1975 at Crystal Palace proved the final straw in my relationship with the media. It was at that point I, together with my family, decided that my progress as an athlete would be hindered and upset were we seen to be part of an operation which only added up to a distortion, a mis-representation of what Steve Ovett was doing in the sport.

By then I was a fairly experienced international runner, having taken the silver medal at the European Champion-ships in Rome at the end of the previous season. I had always been reluctant to be part of the ritual of trotting up to press conferences after a victory. Most of the questions – though not all – were a banal repetition. 'How old are you?' 'Where do you live?' 'What is your best time?' were some that used to annoy me because all it needed was a simple piece of homework to find that out. I did not feel any responsibility to promote my sport in talking to the press – I did that out there on the track, by winning. That is what happened at this European Cup semi-final.

In beating the Pole and the Russian in this race I achieved my most important victory to date, and my second-fastest 800 metres, 1 minute 46.7 seconds. I was taken up to the press box and answered the usual ques-tions, but a row blew up when the subject moved on to the European Cup final later in the summer.

In answer to a question about that race I replied, 'I do not intend to run.' When I added, 'I'm sorry, but it doesn't come into my plans' I sensed that they thought I was being arrogant. Some of the reporters felt it was an outrage that this young athlete had decided that he would not run in the final in Nice. What I could not quite comprehend was why I should be questioned about something which was going to take place in a few weeks' time, when here I was part of a British triumph still going on out there on the track and about which the crowd were going berserk. This little scene in the press room seemed unrelated to the events of the moment. Added to this was the fact that all along it was my intention to have a quiet season in the year prior to the Montreal Olympic Games.

When I added that I did not want to run because I was going to Athens that weekend to watch my girlfriend, Lesley Kiernan, compete in the European Junior Championships, all hell broke loose. Instead of questions, I found I was being told how to behave; that I was being unpatriotic. I thought 'That's it' and got up from my chair, moved it forward and said that I wanted no further part in the interview. The gesture with the chair was taken to mean, 'You can ask it questions and make up your own answers.' I think the reaction of one reporter who said 'You will run for your country' incensed me. This was amazing. Here was a newspaperman, supposed to be asking questions and getting the facts, instructing me where I was to run next. That, as I understood, was the role of a selector. I left them to it to join my parents who were out there in the packed arena, waving the union jack at every British victory. The Ovett family is not unpatriotic.

If I was being in any way selfish it was due to the fact that I wanted to win an Olympic medal the following year. I hadn't been running well and I did not want to end up in the pre-Olympic season losing to international competitors whom I knew I ought to beat – that would have been psychologically damaging. So the plan had been to wind down the season after the AAA Championships, in August take an early break from training and then get into Olympic preparation. I suppose I could not expect my questioners from the media to weigh up all that I drove home from Crystal Palace with Matt to hear on the radio the beginning of the tirade about 'unpatriotic Ovett'.

I shut the matter out of my mind by not bothering to read all the advice the newspapers were offering. I simply immersed myself back in training again. Later, in fact, I did accept the British Board's invitation to take part in the final in Nice, but because I was fit, wanted a race and believed I could win – three good reasons for changing my mind. No doubt those reporters in the Crystal Palace press box preened themselves on the good job they had done in putting Ovett to rights. But the manner of my victory in Nice probably showed some of the men who were to be my rivals in Montreal the following year a little more of my talent than I wanted to reveal.

After this incident, though not entirely due to it, the family decided we could do without the media. It was a conscious decision taken because of the intrusion and interruption it would cause. The Ovett household was deeply into the quest for an Olympic gold medal and I think my family were influenced by previous British hopes, such as David Bedford, who had come under pressure from the media, had been a willing part in this form of promotion and had failed to win. Any action to get S. J. Ovett to the top place on the podium was under consideration and we therefore decided to keep our distance.

Unlike people in show business, we did not have PR people who could set things up and feed out information when and how we wanted. People in the pop or film world can take the rough and tumble which the media provides, for that is part and parcel of their world. They are earning thousands, maybe millions, and it doesn't matter at the end of the day if your image is tarnished or you have been misrepresented so long as your financial future is secure. I personally did not feel responsible to the media. I promoted athletics by running well. Sport as a whole is littered with people who are very personable, who love promoting their sport and themselves and the end result is that they often lose.

For over five years then I had little to say to press, radio and TV; the telephone at Harrington Villas was virtually always answered by my mother, who fended off the questions – she became quite expert at it. I looked upon the press as a superficial side of the sport, something which was on the periphery, not related to the heart and soul of athletics and therefore something which one could do without. And the fact that I would not conform to their rituals meant that I was bound to be presented as the bad guy. I was peeved that there were certain journalists who, because of my silence, were not getting the facts. I could see that because I was not giving my view it was helping the distortion. But our decision was made and we stuck by it and I've never really regretted it.

After the success of 1975 I turned to the long, hard winter's preparation for the Montreal Olympic Games, with the 800 metres and 1500 metres as my goals. But ambition soon became clouded by an injury that put me out of training for three months.

I started to get a niggling pain in my right knee, which became gradually worse to the point where I could not run for more than a quarter mile before it became inflamed and swollen. My ambivalent attitude towards injury and illness was developing. I did not immediately seek treatment, preferring to think that it might go away; it did not. Then I went to Bert Parker, my physiotherapist, who decided that rest was the best approach. I took a month off and it seemed to have disappeared but on the first day back I ran half a mile and there was the pain again. That was soul destroying. I took another two weeks off and came back and it was still the same.

In the end I went to see Dr Peter Sperryn, who was one of the British Board's medical officers. Having examined the knee he advised me to go and see Hugh Burry, a New Zealander and a consultant at Guy's Hospital who was I believe a former rugby player and a coach – a man who knew and understood sportsmen. I was lucky for he was about to return to New Zealand. He discovered that I was in fact suffering from a condition in which the knee cap had shifted slightly as a result of a particular exercise I was doing and it was rubbing against a ligament. He put me on a special course of exercises to maintain muscle fitness in the problem area and gave me large doses of a special type of aspirin. The pain eventually disappeared.

Looking back I suppose I was extremely fortunate to be directed towards a man who spotted the problem immediately and to catch him just before he was leaving the country. Even though I have always been reluctant to seek medical care, I would react differently if we had some form of instant hot line for athletes above a certain standard. In 1975–6 there was little, apart from a scheme run by the International Athletes Club in conjunction with physiotherapists, to give athletes medical support. We are still a long way off a satisfactory scheme but there have been improvements and moves towards linking with organizations like BUPA. Sportsmen cannot expect to have the specialist attention they require always through the National Health Service; that in my opinion is unjustified. With the increased amount of training, the greater stress put upon athletes – and many other sportsmen too – a stronger medical backup has to be provided, for which the sport must pay. Such a service is essential and today, with the vast income the sport is receiving from the performances of a few athletes, it is only fair that a percentage of this money be set aside for what is no more than an insurance policy for the sport.

Having lost virtually four months' winter work I was in a fairly desperate state in the spring of Olympic year. It was then that Harry Wilson made one of his good decisions – getting me to a place for altitude training. Ever since the 1968 Games which were held at Mexico City over 7000 feet above sea level, there has been a greater understanding of the difficulties of trying to race at that level without proper acclimatization. We drew experience from the Kenyans and Ethiopians who live all their lives at altitude: when they came down to sea level they were producing some super results. Many lowlanders were finding that by training at altitude they produced better performances on returning to their natural environment. Harry decided that if I underwent such training it might compensate in part for the time lost through injury.

It was a good idea which went wrong. Harry picked Lake Tahoe in Nevada for the venue and I went off with Tony Simmons and Ian Stewart. When we arrived there was a foot of snow and blizzard conditions. For Tony and Ian it was a desperate situation to be in because this was going to be their last Olympic Games; for me I was just hoping to salvage something from a winter gone wrong. We tried training for a couple of days but it was ridiculous. On long runs, which proceeded in indian file, one man was assigned the task of leading and protecting the other two from the elements and finished up looking like a mobile snowman. Added to that, we shared a room and had no proper facility to dry out our daily supply of wet training clothes.

By the time Harry was due to arrive we had made up our minds that Mexico would be a far better place to get in some proper training. We had even got round to looking up airline timetables in order to hustle Harry round to our way of thinking. The atmosphere was pretty desperate when we went off to the airport to meet him. As we peered through the frosted-up glass of the airport's only waiting room across the arctic panorama, his plane pierced the clouds and was followed by a shaft of sunlight, the first we had seen for two weeks. Uncannily, as the aircraft taxied to a stop the clouds dispersed, leaving Harry to walk down the gangway beneath a sky of imperishable blue. Against this backdrop he was understandably taken aback by our simmering attitude. We gave him a roasting. Someone had to be a scapegoat for our frustrating fortnight, although we could not really blame the weather on Harry as we should have known that the elements at this time of year in this area were impossible for running. The locals were upset with the warmth which Harry brought in because it disturbed their prime ski-ing time; as far as we were concerned the trip showed a need for more research and pre-planning.

After two weeks with Harry at the altitude training we returned to England for some very low level competition. After the break in my winter training and the frustrating period at altitude it was very much a period of trial and error. I progressed towards the Olympic Trials in June, with mediocre times but satisfactory competitive performances. The 800 metres followed a predictable pattern with me winning comfortably in 1 minute 46.7 seconds. The following weekend the 1500 metres provided the crowd with a novelty and me with a breakthrough.

The distance was relatively new to me and for most of the race I was boxed in, bumped, pushed, shoved and back in the pack. I seemed to have time to think in all this bustle, which in my case was probably not good for me. With 50 metres to go from a boxed third position a gap appeared, courtesy of David Moorcroft who suddenly veered towards lane three. For once I could use my 800-metres speed. I went up a gear and moved to the front with 20 metres remaining. In my elation I inadvertently set a precedent – by giving a victory salute before actually winning the race. Three strides from the line I turned and waved with both arms aloft towards the block of seats in the main stand where I knew my parents were sitting. Another instance of arrogance from this young upstart from Brighton – or even more sinister, a link with a deodorant company?

Having qualified for both events I sat down to discuss my future racing plans with Andy, who by this time was getting me into the sort of races I needed. He tried to pitch me into the situation of a travelling racer, conditioning me for the time when I would need three hard races in different parts of Europe within a few days. He wanted me to get used to the normal everyday hassle of airports, queuing for baggage, waiting for transport, losing sleep and to be able to absorb all that without my racing being affected. I can recall after the Olympic Trials a journey to the middle of the nowhere to a race in Saarijarvi, in Finland.

I arrived in Helsinki on midsummer holiday, which as far as I could see was the one day in the year when Finland closes. The airport was deserted, no one to meet me, no taxis or buses. I began to panic so I phoned home on a transfer-charge call. My parents got hold of Andy as

I waited by the phone. He called me back and asked what my hotel was like, whereupon I explained about deserted Finland. Then he became angry when I told him I had only ten pounds on me. 'Have you got an American Express card,' he said. 'Andy,' I replied, 'I'm an unemployed nineteen-year-old – and as far as American Express is concerned that does not do nicely.' I then hitch-hiked into Helsinki, went into a hotel and persuaded them to ring Mr Norman who promised to meet the hotel charges.

The following day I journeyed – one train and two buses – to Saarijarvi which is in the middle of an unending forest, and Finland has plenty of that. All the towns and villages seemed deserted but when I reached my destination panic set in again. It was not difficult to realize that people were flocking to the stadium and the meeting had already begun. I thought, 'No, after all this I am going to miss the race.' I couldn't find the competitors' entrance so I went up to a gate and tried to explain I was Steve Ovett. Today they might understand but not in 1976, so I ended up paying eleven Finnmarks to get into the stadium. I was directed to the meeting organizer and rushed up saying I was Steve Ovett of Britain for the 800 metres. He gave me a polite, calm look and said 'Yes . . .' so I said, 'Well, what do I do?' 'You run tomorrow' was the reply.

I had a twenty-four hour recovery before I won the 800 metres, defeating John Walker who was at the time the world mile record holder. It was a slow race, which they always were in those days, and I surprised John who thought he could out-kick anyone over the last 200 metres. It was, one month before the Olympic Games in Montreal, valuable experience. It also helped me to realize that you need to find out as much as you can *before* you go to a meeting abroad: take more than ten pounds, don't panic, find out what day your race is run and, whatever else you do, don't go to Finland on their midsummer holiday.

My first Olympic Games was in fact daunting. After my arrival in Montreal I quickly became disorientated from the reality of sport as I understood it. Once you arrive in the Olympic city, you become just a number – the event is so vast it is overwhelming. In some instances this can be a good thing. You become submerged and in my case I found that part refreshing. I could go away and do my own thing without being troubled. But in Montreal the security was almost claustrophobic, which was understandable after the massacre of the Israelis four years previously in the Munich Olympic Village.

Britain, as usual, took a very large team and we were living five and six to a small apartment which was very different to the way most of us lived at home. Those who had had experience of living in colleges or university could be expected to acclimatize quickly, but, for the many who had come from a home environment, living together in such cramped conditions as part of the biggest sporting achievement of their lives added to the problems.

I was sitting on my bunk one afternoon when Denis Watts, one of the national coaches and somebody who was to prove so helpful a year later, came dashing in full of excitement about a giant of a Cuban whom he had seen producing some fantastic times in training. 'What event is he in, Denis,' I asked, to which came the response, 'The 800 metres.' Denis realized that for once he had slipped from his always diplomatic attitude. I was about to start my Olympic competition at this distance and this news item was the last thing to help preserve my morale. Denis was no bad judge for the Cuban, Alberto

Juantorena, not only won the 800 metres in a world-record time but the 400 metres as well.

My 800-metres heat was without difficulty but Juantorena surprised me. The power was undoubtedly there but tactically he looked raw, pushing and jostling in his heat and being unable to chop his enormous stride to fit when the pace was slow. In fact he came very close to being eliminated through his tactical inexperience. There was no such problem for Juantorena in my semi-final for the pace was fast and the Cuban loped along in the clear without athletes around him. When it came to the back straight he just shifted up a gear and was away. I realized then that he was capable of getting under 1 minute 44 seconds and thus breaking the world record. I had gone to the Games after the winter setback with a realistic target of going a shade under 1.45 and in doing so taking a medal, but Juantorena's large frame and a stupid rule about running in lanes finally blotted out my hope.

For a short period the IAFF (the international governing body) ruled that, for the first 300 metres, the 800 metres should be run in lanes. The most naïve of the eight finalists, Ovett, was drawn in the eighth lane which means that I was running almost half the race 'blind', without the normal pace-judging aids. The rule was introduced to cut down on the bumping and boring in slow races, but it cut across the concept of the event completely and was definitely unfair to the runners in the outside lanes. In the 800 metres pace judgement is crucial. A second too fast on the first lap and you are dying in the finishing straight; a second too slow and you are out of the hunt for a prize. So how do you gauge your speed – the answer is simple, by other runners and by markings which are on the inside lane of the track, the same as road signs on motorways. However, I was isolated in the outside lane, with none of these familiar aids to assist me. I did not know what was happening until I turned into the home straight on the first lap: Juantorena, on the inside, went by about seven yards up. They had not been running very fast and yet they had an enormous advantage over me as I was back in seventh position. I had never been so far down at that stage of a race before. I should have been with them to give myself a chance but I realized I had made a mistake and misjudged the pace. Against top-class runners you cannot afford that, let alone anyone of Juantorena's ability. I picked off a couple of people but I didn't have it in me to claw back that amount. I finished in front of Luciano Susanj, an experienced sprinter-type 800-metres runner who had won the European title two years previously ahead of me; he was in lane seven and that only helped to prove the point that the rule was bad. It was changed the following year.

The moment I heard the lane draw I was resigned to the fact that my first Olympic final was going to provide a major problem for me. Fate had dealt me a duff card and, although I went out determined to make something of the situation and in fact ran my best time I did not expect any rewards. There was no way I could have beaten Juantorena and looking realistically at the way the race was run I could have achieved no better than fifth place.

As I had suffered the knee injury back in the winter and then the farce of that training spell in snowy Lake Tahoe a fifth place ought to have brought some sort of satisfaction, but it left me feeling pretty depressed. Harry had to return home in the middle of the Games because of his work and I really needed someone to talk to about the race and the coming 1500 metres, so I rang my father. He quickly realized that one long-distance phone call was not going to be much help so he offered to come out to Montreal. I was taken aback because the idea had never

been discussed nor mooted during the year; frankly, with
the support my parents had given me, there was not really
the kind of money left for buying instant transatlantic air
tickets. He told me not to worry and within forty-eight
hours I had a call to my room from the British Olympic
office to say that my father was waiting to see me.

He did not try to galvanize me into action or psyche
me up; that is not his way. But in being there and through
general conversation he put the events into their proper
perspective. I needed someone who was very close to tell
me that I was only twenty and that I had run in a world-
record race. The fact that I failed to reach the final of the
1500 metres in no way indicates his mission was a failure;
rather the contrary because he was on hand for the
second disaster.

With only the heat winner assured of a place in the
semi-final I was determined to qualify in that position. As
it turned out, that meant a fast run because Thomas
Wessinghage broke with 600 metres to go and I followed.
It was all stops out to get first place, which I managed in
a personal best of 3 minutes 37.9 seconds. After running
that time my spirits were lifted. I felt now I was in good
shape and went into my semi-final with a new attitude.
All was going well coming round the final bends into the
last 150 metres: I was just behind John Walker with Dave
Hill of Canada leading and Dave Moorcroft just behind
me. Suddenly Hill tripped and went down. I fell over the
top of him, lost my rhythm and balance and actually
touched the track with my outstretched hand before
getting back into my running, only to find that Walker
and Moorcroft and others had gone and I trailed in fifth
and failed to qualify.

The nightmare of it all was only completed when I sat
in the stand and watched the final; it was a gentle three
laps, then a big 300-metres kick by Walker with four or

five scrambling for the other medals. As I watched I thought, 'There they are playing my tune' – it was just the sort of race I win. The Montreal experience though was not a total loss. My father was obviously downhearted but pointed out that two personal bests from my first Olympic Games was by no means a failure.

'You cannot account for someone falling over,' he said. This made me think about how much store people put on winning an Olympic medal, the opportunity of which only comes every four years, yet luck can play such a crucial part. Watching films of past Games I realized the number of people who were missing through injury or illness; or like Jim Ryun in 1972 who fell; or who peaked, physically, in between Olympic Games. Were these people failures? I therefore resolved that for the next Olympic Games I would be better prepared, having something extra so that if this sort of incident or something like it occurred I would be in a better position to cope. I would not be pushed around.

Of course history records that John Walker won the Olympic 1500-metres title in 3 minutes 39.17 seconds and for me it was fitting that this man above all others in this era should take the crown. The favourite did win and rightly so. John Walker is the greatest miler I have ever seen. I use that accolade not only because of the speed he was producing in the early seventies. He had the awesome capability of being able to run under 3 minutes 50 seconds in the mile on one day; then get on a plane to somewhere else in Europe and a couple of nights later turn in 3 minutes 34 seconds in the 1500 metres. Living out of a suitcase, he could trail around Europe for six weeks producing a series of marvellously consistent performances.

I was reading about John Walker long before I was part of the international racing scene. I now realize that he was not only ahead of his time on the track but also (together with Rod Dixon) made the European athletic circuit economically viable. We owe a lot to John Walker, for his record-breaking exploits generated so much new interest in athletics that it became possible to start building an entirely new structure for the sport. Crowds turned out to watch him and television came on to the scene to provide more finance, thereby making it possible to meet the expense of bringing athletes from around the world. Thus Oslo, Stockholm, Helsinki, Koblenz, Zurich, Nice, Berlin, Lausanne, Milan and many other places were strung together as staging points for athletes from all parts. It was Walker who laid out the carpet for today's athletes; in my estimation he triggered off the new developments which have so reshaped the sport.

There were of course others before him in a similar mould and they came from Australasia: Herb Elliott, the Olympic champion of Rome in 1960, provided a magnet; and after the Tokyo Games Ron Clarke and Peter Snell played a similar role. But, at that time, there was neither the ease of air travel nor the sophisticated television coverage to produce the economic viability which Walker created. I liken John to Muhammad Ali whose fighting skill and charisma did so much to awaken people to the possibilities of satellite television. His fights in the seventies were generating two and three million dollars; today lesser boxers are benefiting to the tune of eight to ten million dollars. In athletics we now have the Permit Meetings in which promoters may offer participation money. That has come a little late for Walker, but I am glad to see that he is still running with us and turning in performances close to his 1975 world records. Few men get the sort of applause that John receives when the runners are introduced just before the start of a big event; it is richly deserved.

Andy Norman once said of the marauding Kiwi, that if you parachuted John Walker into the Sahara he would find a race, win it and then make sure the promoter paid his airfare home. I think his resilience to the constant air travel has shaken a few of his fellow competitors. I know that tennis players are on the same trek, but they are much better cared for and when they go out and beat someone else 6–4, 6–0 they are probably nowhere near a hundred per cent; Walker and the rest of us cannot hide behind a score – it is the stop watch which ultimately strips you to naked athleticism.

Walker has not given up pioneering. He has moved on from 'have spikes will travel' to 'have spikes, wife and daughter will travel'. Meeting promoters are now having to find second air tickets for spouses and we have to thank John for that. How he manages to cope with his baby daughter as well is something which I may one day discover. Elizabeth Walker at three knew more about airline timetables than nursery rhymes. I can recall walking down Prince's Street, Edinburgh, in 1982 with my wife Rachel, John's wife and Elizabeth.

'Where's Daddy, Elizabeth?' I asked.

'He's back at the hotel.'

'Is he alright?'

'No, Daddy is tired and sick.' This was perhaps Miss Walker's misreporting of Daddy saying, 'Elizabeth, I'm sick and tired of you' – which on race day I can understand.

The only man to upstage Walker in this side of the athletics business in Dwight Stones, former holder of the world high-jump record, who took his wife, baby daughter and au pair girl round the circuit. The next raise in these stakes should be interesting.

5

The 'Perfect Race'

My first British record was preceded and followed by a row. The Debenham Games of 1977, held at the end of June, was going to be one of the more spectacular of the invitation meetings: I was to race John Walker, the Olympic 1500-metres champion, over the mile; and Mike Boit of Kenya, who missed the Olympic Games because of the African boycott, was due to face Alberto Juantorena of Cuba, the world-record holder over 800 metres and the Montreal gold medallist, over two laps. I was in good shape, looking forward to proving to myself that I could do better than I had managed to achieve in Montreal.

The day before the race I rang Andy just to tell him I was OK for the race and check details about travel and tickets. Andy sounded depressed and talked about the political manoeuvrings behind the scenes. Just as I was about to put the phone down he said, 'Boit's maybe in the mile, but I'll talk about that to you tomorrow.' That last point worried me because I wanted the opportunity to see if I could beat Walker, not Walker and another of the world's leading 1500-metres men which would have complicated the matter. It seemed strange to me and I did not think it was fair that people who had bought tickets for Boit versus Juantorena now might see the Kenyan in another race. If he was injured and had to withdraw, that would just have been bad luck for the ticket holders; but to publicize a race and then drop it in this way was unfair, just as it was unfair to me to put someone into my event at the last minute when it had

been a longstanding arrangement which was eagerly
awaited by the British public as well as myself.

When I reached Crystal Palace I met Mike. While he
never says very much, he was clearly unhappy about
being moved out of the 800 metres and told me the story
behind it – the Cubans did not want him to run against
Juantorena at this invitation meeting. It was obvious they
treated Juantorena as a political tool, which would be
blunted if he were defeated by the man he did not face in
Montreal. I saw Andy, who was organizing the meeting,
and pointed out that if the Cubans had agreed to these
races they should be made to honour their agreement.
They were, he said, threatening to withdraw the whole
party of athletes. That was becoming my mood too and I
told Andy I was considering going home. I talked to
Harry who did not come down really on either side of the
argument as I believe he knew I was in good shape and
needed to race. Less than an hour before the race was
due to start I told Andy that I did not want Boit in my
race and that he should go back to the 800 metres. If the
Cubans pulled out . . . well let them. I was getting fairly
steamed up which is something to be avoided before such
an important contest.

Half an hour later a compromise was reached which
was unsatisfactory in many ways but left me facing Walker
as expected. However, we had the ridiculous situation of
two 800-metres races with Boit in one and Juantorena in
the other. The mile, after all this, turned out to be one of
the most exciting events since it lived up to expectations
which had been anticipated. The pace was never really
hot until, with 300 metres to go, Walker turned on the
speed. I chased him, held on until the straight, with Ari
Paunonen of Finland after me. I think the Finn was eager
for my scalp since he had beaten Seb Coe in the European
Junior Championships earlier, but I moved clear with 60

metres to go and took the UK mile record with a time of 3 minutes 54.7 seconds. The crowd were on their feet going berserk because I was the first Briton to beat Walker over his favourite distance so it was a good day for Britain. It would have been a very good day for athletics had Boit and Juantorena met as well. Unhappily though there had to be a nasty taste at the end of the day to go with the euphoria.

I joined the queue at the table where runners collect their expenses, with athletes congratulating me on my victory and record. It came to my turn and I filled in the necessary form – seven pence a mile, a hundred miles from Brighton and back, seven pounds – and pushed the piece of paper across the table. The official looked at it, nodded his head and said, 'No, we can't pay seven pounds.'

'Why,' I replied.

'It's more than the second-class rail fare and that's our limit.'

'How much is the fare?' I enquired.

'Six pounds forty-eight.'

'You're joking – we're not arguing over fifty-two pence.'

'I'm not, you are – take it or leave,' was the offer.

'I have just helped fill the stadium, broken the British record, beaten the Olympic champion,' I pointed out. 'And if that's your attitude you can keep your six pounds forty-eight . . .'

Most of the following day's papers buried the victory over Walker and the record in favour of 'Ovett Coward', 'Boit Boycott', 'Ovett shies away from Boit' – I had apparently made him run a farce of an 800-metres race, kicked him out of the race he wanted to run. No one, as far as I could see, mentioned that he was moved because of the wishes of the Cubans – or the fact that I was the only British winner that day.

After my first British record in June I became involved in some, for me, unusual races in 1977 – one of which was a 5000 metres at Gateshead in mid-July. I cannot remember now why I should be running that distance at a time of year when I needed to be sharpening up for 800-metres and 1500-metres events. I think I might have been yet again persuaded by a certain Andy Norman. I was to face Miruts Yifter, a short, balding Ethiopian of indeterminate age who was a bit of a mystery quite apart from the question of his years. He missed the Montreal Games because of the African boycott, but in the pre-Games warm up meetings he had produced some sensational looking 5000-metres running.

I flew up to Gateshead on the day of the race, in order to reduce the break from home routine, and found that Tyneside had a very hot afternoon. Dave Black and Bernie Ford, two of our best 5000-metres men, were in the field and I can remember my apprehensiveness as I finished my warm-up, feeling very hot indeed and looking down at Yifter (he's very short) and thinking he probably feels cold. We set off and coming along the straight the lap board said 12, which for an 800-metres runner like myself was like the Chinese drip torture – eleven, ten, nine . . . With the pain increasing I thought, 'What am I doing here. I could be at home watching this on television.'

As we got deep into the race I was getting hotter and hotter while Ron Pickering, the BBC television commentator, was apparently saying, 'He's looking so relaxed.' With about four laps to go I was feeling very rough, but around me there was plenty of heavy breathing so I kept at it with Dave, Bernie and Yifter. All I could do was hang on over the last three laps while the world looked on waiting for the big kick. Dave was leading and I was just at his shoulder, with Yifter trapped on the inside; that was all I could do, but it was no hindrance to the Ethiopian. With 250 metres to go he just reversed, as it were, and went round the outside – a flash of dark brown skin disappearing into the Gateshead horizon was the last I saw of him until the prize-giving. The coup de grâce was swift and merciful. He finished 30 metres clear of me at the tape. When I turned into the final straight I realized I had absolutely nothing left; I was wobbling from lane to lane with the feeling that I was not going to finish. In fact Dave and Bernie, who do not have a finishing sprint to save their lives, were gaining on me. I could never have faced the lads at the club had I been outsprinted by these two, so I tried to raise a gallop. Reaching the line I collapsed with my face burning.

As I walked back across the field to the start some minutes later to pick up my track suit, I resolved to have a long recovery period before I tried that athletic torture again – like several years. When people ask why I do not run more 5000 metres races, the burning memory of this day is etched in my mind as a deterrent. The statisticians and the analysts lifted my morale somewhat by pointing out that my time of 13 minutes 25 seconds put me in the UK top ten and my last lap was 59 seconds. But the Ethiopian's final circuit took only 54.6 seconds and it did not surprise me when he went on to two World Cup double victories and a double in the Olympic Games at Moscow, in the 5000 and 10,000 metres.

By winning the European Cup Final 1500 metres in Helsinki in mid-August, I thought I would naturally be selected for that event in the World Cup of 1977. Selectors I have come to learn do not always act in a logical manner and I later discovered that my appearance in the race at Dusseldorf only came after some fairly heavy arguing and an ultimatum from Denis Watts, a man who was to play a crucial part in the performance I achieved. Denis guided Ann Packer to an 800-metres gold medal and world record at the Tokyo Games of 1964 and also helped in the development of Lillian Board who died so tragically after taking a silver medal at Mexico in 1968.

It was only after the euphoria of the Dusseldorf victory had died away that I learned that Denis had put his professional reputation on the line over my selection. This was the inaugural World Cup competition, with a mixture of countries and geographical areas like Europe and Oceania taking part. It was a prestigious event and, as so often happens in these circumstances, politics crept under the door of the selection room. There was a strong case from the Eastern Europeans for selecting Josef Plachy of Czechoslovakia for my distance though the evidence seemed slim. The British took a different view and were backed by the West Germans for whom Ilsa Bechtold said in the selection meeting, 'Ovett is a winner.' It still did not look as though I would be selected until Denis pointed out that it would reflect upon his integrity as the middle-distance coach to the European team if Ovett did not run the 1500 metres. He would therefore stand down. It was not a threat, just a man of integrity putting his view, but Denis knew the furore that would be caused and the selectors then looked just at the athletic facts and I was picked.

Having batted so strongly for me, Denis naturally wanted the best possible performance from me. There are occasions when some athletes, and I am one of them, need to have someone around upon whom they can rely implicitly for the little ordinary everyday items and arrangements. You need someone who is there, but is unobtrusive; someone who appears at the right moment and says the right thing at the right time. Denis Watts was that man. We have the same sense of humour – there was a lot of laughing to punctuate my mental build-up to this contest – but there was also the reassuring tap on my shoulder to wake me to go off to the stadium for the race. Numbers, pins, warm-up area arrangements – all seemed to appear without my having to think about them.

While I was thinking in terms of winning this race, which included John Walker the Olympic champion, I had the feeling that Denis knew I could win as well. He never raised the topic of tactics, never actually said what I might do or how I might win, but I knew that he was convinced I had the ability to win. He had the capacity to convey all this over the few days we were together, stoking my sense of well being without any drama or patronizing attitude.

After all the tiny last-minute preparations, runners sometimes go to the starting line with a feeling of being in the best possible shape. I did that night in Dusseldorf and there can be no doubt that the presence and the professionalism of Denis Watts over the previous days had much to do with it. If there was one factor which did not fit into this 'on a cloud' progress, it was my decision at the last moment to wear a new pair of spikes. They were lighter, much better I felt than any other pair I possessed, so I decided to use them; it was a gamble – the first time I wore new spikes in a crucial race.

The evening was still, calm and warm and the stadium not as overpowering as you might expect of a two-tiered soccer stadium. There was a crowd of 50,000. What I did not know about was the plot to beat Ovett. John Walker, who was obviously keen to avenge his defeat of earlier in the year over a mile, and Thomas Wessinghage had worked on a strategy to stretch me out. Thomas needed a fast pace anyway and was prepared to take the race out. Also running was Dave Hill, the man whom I almost fell over in the Montreal Olympic final. His presence was a reminder to me to keep out of trouble in the early stages of the race.

Thomas took it out fast for the first 400 metres, then Walker to 1000 metres, where Hill made his bid. However he dropped the momentum slightly. It was a fast pace, yet I did not really appreciate it as my mind was preoccupied with thoughts about positions: not getting boxed in; not tripping over Dave Hill again. My mind was too busy to absorb the speed at which we were running.

As we went past the bell, Hill was still in front and I eased on to the shoulder of John Walker who was then in second place, with Thomas still in touch a close fourth. It was the perfect position for me and down the back straight with the speed increasing I sensed that Walker was preparing for a sprint, but was still trapped. So at 200 metres I thought 'Go, now' which acted like a trigger and I was away. I kept repeating 'Keep going, keep going' but I could not resist taking a look back – I was stunned at what I saw for they were 20 metres down on me and I only had 80 metres to go. I could not believe that I had gone that far away from them and my thoughts were, 'I've won, they can't make up that.' What I did not realize at that point was that Walker had dropped out just as I broke, which was so out of character. He had no real explanation for it, and to this day I cannot understand why he did it.

I discovered that the first 100 metres of the last 200 metres took me only 11.9 seconds; and that the overall time, 3 minutes 34.5 seconds, was a UK record, the seventh fastest of all time in the world. I was within tenths of the European record – something I missed, according to the following day's reports, because I waved in the finishing straight. In fact I realized at the end I could have run a lot faster, but to me during the race winning was all important and the elation I felt down the straight is something I would not have swapped for another record – or better press reports.

I regarded the event as a breakthrough; 3 minutes 34.5 seconds seemed so easy. The world record stood at 3 minutes 32.2 seconds – yet my body was not tired and when Thomas Wessinghage came over to me at the end and just said 'Unbelievable . . . unbelievable. I have never seen acceleration like it' it came home to me that here was a significant moment in my career. I had realized the victory I so much wanted and achieved it with such a time, yet my body was not tired – it was in fact so easy.

Geoff Dyson, who was formerly Britain's chief national coach, said after seeing a film of the race that it should be shown as the definitive example of middle-distance running, which coming from someone so acknowledged and respected throughout the sport internationally was a marvellous accolade. But before that came the welcome and congratulations of Denis as we went off the track. He was in tears and the joy and enthusiasm of this man, almost at the end of his career as a professional coach, was another memory of the night. Denis and I went off for a quiet pint, or maybe it was two, and ever since then, whenever there has been the opportunity, I have travelled to the tiny Cumbrian village of Wray, where Denis now lives, to resume the celebrations.

During the winter months of 1977–8 I enjoyed what must be my best cross-country season to date. Training and competition flowed easily, with victory in the Inter Counties Championships and fourth place in the National race, an event over nine miles. I arrived therefore at the beginning of the summer season of 1978 in probably the best shape I had been. However, a problem loomed through strange circumstances – the Commonwealth

Games in Edmonton and the European Championships in Prague fell within a month of one another. It would therefore have been a daunting task for any athlete to compete successfully in both and in my case the problem was compounded by my ambition to take part in any championship at both 800 metres and 1500 metres. The decision was fairly simple since I believed that the European event held a greater priority, so all my preparation was geared towards racing in Prague in August.

I was not alone in this thinking. One Sebastian Coe thought very much along the same lines and consolidated his bid for a European title at 800 metres with an outstanding run in the Yorkshire Championships in May with one of the fastest times in the world of 1 minute 45.6 seconds – it was the beginning of the Coe–Ovett saga which has now stretched on through two Olympic Games. Our first clash came behind the Iron Curtain on a rather bleak, damp evening in the European event. The race had all the characteristics of a classic battle – Coe the front runner with blistering pace and slight frame, while I was supposedly the one with the kick finish. The contrast between us was fascinating not only to a waiting world, but also to this participant.

I expected the pace to be fast, but a first lap of under 50 seconds was devastating to say the least. Seb meant business. I was second, focusing my mind on maintaining contact and in a semi-tranced state into which runners often withdraw to maintain concentration. Entering the back straight I suddenly became aware that Seb was slowing and my mind pondered on the possibility in those few metres when I was closing on him. I flicked through the alternatives – was this a tactical move in order to force me wide round the top bend or was he simply tiring? Indecision and the time it took me to make up my mind cost me the race. I stayed behind Seb around the top bend in the first belief that it was tactical and he was ready to kick again. But I was wrong: that first lap had taken too much out of Seb and he was dying. I went past him easily to the roar of the crowd and pushed towards the line.

I never believe that any race is won until you hit the tape, but on this occasion, with my only conceivable rival defeated, I thought I had done all that was required to take the gold medal. Twenty metres before the line a tall figure in a blue vest changed all that. Olaf Beyer from East Germany stunned the sporting world and one Steve Ovett by winning the European 800-metres title in 1 minute 43.8 seconds, one of the fastest times ever recorded. As I pulled on my track suit I mused on the irony of the event: having beaten the man most people considered unbeatable at this distance I was defeated by an unknown, leaving me with my second silver medal at this distance in European Championships.

I decided that was enough. A change of colour was definitely necessary, so I entered the 1500 metres – not, as some people assumed, dejected by my defeat but more determined to bring back Britain's only gold from the Championships. Speculation over the outcome of the final was high. After one defeat people saw dangers and possible threats from all quarters. 'The Finn looked good in the semi-final' would be whispered to me at lunch by one of the coaches; or 'Watch out for Eamonn, he's got a kick like Beyer.' If the East Germans could spring one surprise, why not two?

With 250 metres to go all doubts, rumours and cynics were silenced. I had hit the front in the final and knew this time no one was going to catch me. My winning time was 3 minutes 35.6 seconds. I was asked if I had anything to say to the reporters and breaking my silence I sent a message to the press box wishing them all a Merry Christmas.

I returned from Prague and the European Championships feeling exhausted. It was probably more a reaction to all the froth surrounding the Coe–Ovett clashes and coming back with a UK record for 800 metres and the gold for the 1500 metres. I just flopped. Andy asked me what I wanted to run in the Coca Cola/IAC meeting, which was the final promotion of the year at Crystal Palace. My honest answer would have been nothing, but I knew I ought to run as the only gold-medal winner from the Championships. Coe I knew was going for the 800-metres UK record – which he achieved. I did not feel like running another 1500 metres so quickly after the European Championships and the only other alternative was the two miles. I decided to run in this event, but with the way I was feeling it was surely only going to be a token appearance.

With Henry Rono of Kenya in the field there was a very good chance that he would take off and I would finish up inconspicuously somewhere down the field. That is the way I approached the race and I did no serious training, just gentle jogging on most days. So the outcome, a world two-miles best of 8 minutes 13.5 seconds for me and victory over Rono, was a delightful surprise. I suppose there may still be plenty of cynics who will say it was all planned but I can only say that it was not. It has taken me a long time to acquire an incentive for world-record breaking; championship victories are far more satisfying in my estimation. So breaking a record as I did that night was all the more satisfying for the fact that the whole affair was not set up with pacemakers and pressure from the media.

I warmed up on the back straight of the track while other events were in progress and said to Harry Wilson,

'This is not the way I want to end the season, but I feel obliged to turn up.' The race got under way at a firm pace and I felt good, probably because I was not very interested, not really concentrating. It was not a burning pace and when we reached the halfway point the time was several seconds outside Brendan Foster's world mark. Rono challenged Bronislaw Malinowski, the Polish Olympic steeplechase champion who subsequently was tragically killed in a car crash, in the fifth lap and the pace was slowing down. Then Henry, as he so often did, took hold of the race by the scruff of its neck and I tucked in behind him. He was really zipping along although it didn't hurt me, and with the rest of the field falling adrift I suddenly felt a taste for the race. By the final lap I knew I was in with a chance of a victory over Rono, who had rewritten the world records that season from 3000 metres to 10,000 metres. He tried manfully to drop me down the back straight, failed and I knew that coming off the bend I would take him. I did – with a wave to the crowd and to what I thought was the end of the best season of my life.

Logically there was no way that I should have run so fast that night because I had come down from such a high pitch at the European Championships. But I was to learn that there are occasions, and for me they tend to come at the end of the season when the pressure is off, when – it can be in training or in competition – the body takes over and you just fly. It was like that for me that night, as it was I feel sure the night that Dave Moorcroft broke the world 5000-metres record in Oslo in 1981, when he sliced seconds off Henry Rono's time. Dave did not know what he was doing that night nor did anyone else – and watching him and hearing about it I remembered my run in 1978.

I saw a lot of Henry Rono in 1978 . . . and the Kenyan

has paid me one of the greatest compliments an athlete can receive. Whenever he comes to race in this country and an event is suggested he asks, 'Is Ovett in that race.' He is not concerned about anyone else, but me. We have raced one another many times and I have the greater number of victories, but of course we race more over my distances than his, which are the 5000 and 10,000 metres. He has a marvellously languid approach to his sport; I think sometimes he is a little bemused by the way the British and other Europeans put so much bustle and administration into the simple exercise of running. Although we come from vastly different cultures we touch on the same sense of humour. I remember being in Oslo for a race and Henry seeking me out:

'Ah Ovett [a mark of respect to address a person by their surname in Kenya]. You know a lot about cars.'

'Well I know something, Henry,' I said.

'I want a Range Rover – for my farm in Kenya,' he replied.

'OK Henry, you want a new one?'

'Oh no, no – I want a second-hand one, it's cheaper. But I don't want one that has been . . .' and here to get his point across Henry drew his hand in the air in a sharp up-and-down motion in the shape of several hump-back bridges. 'I want one that has been . . .' whereupon the hand movement switched to a smooth horizontal sweep.

'You want, Henry,' I said, 'one that is in fairly good condition.'

'Yes,' he said. 'Yes, one that has been straight.'

I was just about to embark on Henry's more detailed requirements, turning over in my mind the sort of contacts I had who might be into Range Rovers, when my Brighton market upbringing suddenly jerked me out of a dangerous assumption.

'Henry, have you got the money?' I asked.

'Oh, no – you buy the car for me, I pay you later.'

'Henry,' I said. 'End of deal.'

There was one occasion when I came close to knowing more about the extent of Henry's worldly belongings. Wherever he goes he carries with him a very smart Italian briefcase and I am one of the few people entrusted with it. In 1978 we were flying to Tokyo for the Golden Mile, my last race of the season, and during that very long journey Henry wanted to sleep. He curled himself up on the seat next to me, under a blanket, clutching his briefcase. But that was uncomfortable so he asked me to hold it. As the hours dragged on the devil in me began to set me wondering about the combination lock.

What sort of number would Henry pick, I thought . . . then I mulled over the question as to whether Henry would know how a combination lock would work – that you can choose your own number. Whereupon my fingers rolled the lock to zero, zero, zero and I touched the catch and the case sprang open. As the locks sprung up so did the blanket beside me and two arms reached out and grabbed the case. Henry was not so much cross as puzzled. 'How did you know the combination?' – so I explained another complicated piece of western civilization and pointed out that he could have changed it when he bought it. 'I thought they were all different,' he said.

Henry's talent on the running track is awesome. At his peak he could train for a week and break a world record and be totally unaffected by it. Like many of his countrymen he has had the benefit of going to an educational establishment in the United States and developing his running there. He and his colleagues are very gentle people and I hope that they can integrate with our sport, preserve their marvellous talent without taking on the harsh attitudes that western civilization so often produces.

6

And Then There Were Two

The year of 1978 had taken me to the top of the athletics world. Of more lasting significance, however, was the fact that it was the year in which Rachel entered my life.

It may be difficult to believe, but I am a shy person at times a little naïve in affairs of the heart. Rachel knows as it took me about three years, after first seeing her train at Crystal Palace, to get round to asking her out – and then I needed one of the athletic coaches to 'mediate' and set the romance under way. Before that happened we would merely say 'Hallo', pass the time of day whenever we were at Crystal Palace together and I would kick myself for not taking the opportunity to invite her to have a drink, a meal or something. Those closely involved with us realized that we both wanted to get to know one another, which may sound ridiculous, and finally one of the coaches came up and asked me if I really did want to take her out.

The idea had been passing through my mind for a very long time, but putting it as bluntly as that quite overwhelmed me – after three years of dithering it was rather a big leap forward. Whether in fact my fumbling, blushing reaction was passed back to Rachel I have never discovered, but soon after that I was in the bar at Crystal Palace and almost bumped into her when I was buying a round. It seemed the opening for a 'Can I buy you a drink and give you a lift home' line: to anyone with my feelings Maidstone, where Rachel lived, was on the route from Crystal Palace to Brighton even if it meant going via Cairo.

Ron Murray, Britain's leading women's high-jump coach who was in charge of Rachel's group, heard about the Ovett plan and seemed either to doubt my honourable intentions or was carrying his responsibility towards Rachel's parents a little far. It took some time to persuade him that Miss Waller would be perfectly safe in my green Citroen 2CV. After the stilted conversation through Kent, I asked Rachel if she knew a place for a light late-night snack. She suggested an American-type diner restaurant and recommended I had a club sandwich.

Naturally you want these occasions to go smoothly – after all, I had waited a long time. So after thwarting Ron Murray's intervention I was a bit anxious when ten, fifteen and almost twenty minutes went by before two coffees and one club sandwich arrived. When the food did appear my first thought was 'This must be a joke, she's having me on', for there before me was a ten-decker sandwich – half a loaf in fact.

'It's a little bigger than I thought,' I said, trying to fathom what was going on. I was beginning to think that Rachel was taking the mickey, that she was not interested in me at all and this was her way of having a joke. She slowly sipped her coffee as I plunged into layers of bread, pastrami, turkey, chicken, lettuce, tomatoes and some of the chips which were a sort of bedding for this Maidstone delicacy. Happily I soon discovered that this was not Rachel's way of having fun. It turned out that the waiter was an Ovett fan who, knowing something about the energy athletes burn up, thought he would quietly replenish my weekly needs in one go, all for the price of 95p+VAT.

I delivered Rachel to her home and we both concealed our determination to meet again at Crystal Palace the following Sunday in a casual repartee along the lines of: 'Perhaps I'll see you there' – 'Yes, maybe'. Rendezvous number two was almost missed, though this time it was not due to the protectiveness of a high-jump coach. My father announced on this particular Sunday that he too wanted to go to Crystal Palace and would drive up with me, which was the first complication. Then the car broke down on the motorway and we were delayed for a couple of hours while Matt brought another car for us.

It must seem strange that a twenty-two-year-old did not want to tell his father about a girlfriend, but that was the situation. It was July, just a couple of months before the European Championships, and I knew that a woman coming into my life at that moment would raise tensions at the Ovett house at 8 Harrington Villas. I had taken girlfriends home before and they had suffered from the fact that my mother does not find it easy to mix with women. Added to that, my parents were so intensely involved in making their son successful that women became an intrusion. I did not want this particular relationship fragmented early on. I knew that Rachel was going to be someone quite special and I wanted our relationship to develop and strengthen before she encountered my family. Thus, when the car broke down on the way to Crystal Palace, there was a long rigmarole from me about getting Matt to come up in another car and my father going back home from the breakdown – which was rejected – and then finally him going home from Crystal Palace with one of my friends because 'I want to stay on a bit'.

Ovett senior is no fool and I am sure he filed the incident in the back of his mind for future reference. We arrived at Crystal Palace at six, by which time the athletics meeting was almost over. I found Rachel all smiles, not knowing that fifteen minutes earlier she was fuming at being stood up and about to stride out of my life. Anyway, we went off for the evening and had a meal somewhere in Bromley.

In Prague then, later in the summer, there were other matters on my mind apart from medal winning. I 'won' the first Coe–Ovett clash but of course finished second in the 800 metres to Olaf Beyer of East Germany. I was not needed for a dope test and did not take part in the ritual post-race press conference, so instead of going to find my parents, who were watching the rest of the meeting in the stand, I walked back to the athletes' village for a shower and some food and telephoned Rachel from a small coin box just inside the British team headquarters. I heard someone say that you could dial London from this phone, which seemed strange to me since we were behind the Iron Curtain, but I pushed in about a pound's worth of coins and dialled the Maidstone number.

I heard the ringing tone, but had no idea whether I was getting through to Maidstone or Moscow because this was the first occasion on which I had telephoned her. Eventually the phone was answered – by Rachel. I said, 'Hallo – it's Steve' – only to have the ego-shattering response, 'Steve . . . Steve who?' After just losing the European 800-metres title they were not the words I expected from the love of my life. How many Steves were there in Rachel Waller's life? There was though no need for alarm. Rachel was merely confused at watching a re-run of the race on television and then finding she was talking to one of the participants as it was taking place.

The day after my 1500-metres victory I flew back to Gatwick, dashed home to Brighton to leave my gear and drove over to Bromley to meet Rachel after her day's work as a waitress in a hamburger bar in Maidstone. We really wanted, I think, to get away from those environments where we might be known, but that I soon realized was to be impossible. We drove out on the Hastings Road to a steak bar and most eyes were on us. There was the 'You were only on the telly last night' sort of remark and people asked for my autograph. That had happened before, but I think I felt self-conscious about it because all I wanted to do was to get to know Rachel better – and for her to know more about Steve Ovett the man, not the runner.

It may be difficult for people who have watched me running and seen my aggressive, extravert side to appreciate that there is a shy, sensitive, perhaps almost cowardly man within. Rachel was obviously very important to me and that was why I kept her, or even knowledge of her, from my family for a very long time. Eventually the late nights, and the sporadic very late nights, brought questions which I could no longer fend off; or perhaps I just let slip that I had 'taken my girlfriend home'. Anyway they eventually found out about Rachel and there were lots of questions about who, when, where and why, which I suppose is probably natural in any family. In our household though girlfriends were the target of ridicule and humour.

Setting up this defensive framework led me into a different tangle with Rachel's parents. After we had known each other a few weeks they were anxious to meet me. They knew Steve Ovett the runner, for they were athletics fans who went to Crystal Palace meetings regularly. They were also aware of the media version of Steve Ovett. What they wanted to know now was more about the man paying so much attention to their daughter. Understandable. Yet I started by treating them warily, as I did so many people about that time.

I had this consuming feeling that when I met people they already knew of me and about me – yes, through the press I suppose – and had therefore formed some sort of

view. I worried that I would not live up to their image of
me or I would rub against the grain. The best way
therefore to avoid such situations was to avoid people.
That was the negative way in which I tackled this particular problem in my life. In addition my relationship with
my parents was delicate. I had to choose the right moment
to approach them about certain things and I presumed it
was the same with all parents. That muddled thinking
compounded the confusion.

I began to think as the months slipped by, with farewells
to Rachel at the gate of the Waller home in Maidstone,
that her parents would think I was deliberately avoiding
them. They were hurt, thinking that it was Rachel who
would be embarrassed by me meeting them. And Rachel
could not understand my attitude because she had
watched me cope with all kinds of situations in the short
time we had known one another. The whole affair slipped
out of hand until there was embarrassment all round. It
seems silly when we look back on it now but at the time
it was a tangled complication, based upon my fear of
the unexpected and my inclination for the easy option,
something that I have now, thankfully, shed. The barrier
was finally surmounted one winter Sunday afternoon,
when Rachel insisted I come inside. I shook hands with
her father and my future mother-in-law kissed me and in
a few moments those agonizing months evaporated as I
finally tasted one of the cakes which had been baked
regularly for Steve Ovett's first appearance.

Rachel's first visit to my home was deliberately delayed
as long as possible – by me. I knew it was going to be
difficult and I wanted to be sure that she would be upset
as little as possible. We waited until almost Christmas;
then Rachel came over for a weekend. I met her at
Preston Park station – she was in her usual winter garb of
woolly sweater, jeans and open-toed sandals. I think it

was her 'second-hand student' fashion, but only later was I to discover that she had taken £5.00 out of her building society account to make the trip, leaving just £1.25 to her name. As we walked to the front door I wagged my finger in her face and said, 'Whatever happens in there, remember I still love you.'

Ours was a busy, noisy house. There was always a lot going on, people coming and going, and I could see Rachel was out of her environment. It was the beginning of a testing, intimidating time for her. To me it did not matter what they thought or how they acted, but I was worried about Rachel's reaction. It was, I suppose, understandable that there would be a certain amount of jealousy on my parent's part, after they had put so much work and effort into building the framework for my success, to find that someone else was coming in at the last minute to join the close-knit Ovett team. But what they would not appreciate was that Rachel had no intention of muscling in on the athletic strategy of the Ovett family in regard to their son. Her interest was usually confined in the athletic world to the high-jump area at one end of Crystal Palace; it took her a long time to get round to coming to terms with the so-called niceties of middle-distance running.

Take, for instance, the occasion on which Sebastian Coe took one of my British records. With a touch of Ovett whimsy I said to Rachel, 'Do you still love me now that Seb's taken my record?' Back came the reply, 'Oh, I didn't know you held it in the first place. That's very good . . . well done.' That sort of attitude to record breaking has brought me down to earth on many occasions.

My courting days were a lot of fun, not as cold as I am relating it here though it does reflect that throughout the period, from 1978 until after the 1980 Olympics, I had to be sensitive to things which might upset the family pattern. I always seemed to be analysing situations which involved Rachel, me and my family, trying to avoid friction or at least lessen it. I had to be very cautious, otherwise the break-up with my parents would have come much earlier and that would probably have affected my running in the Games. It was a time of anxious tension for us all.

My attitude towards the media obviously went a bit further than not talking to the press and television; I was not involved with what I would describe as the sporting social world. I did not accept invitations to association dinners, receptions and the like because I felt this would cause embarrassment on both sides with people with whom I had not had contact during the season suddenly being pitched into close proximity. Some of them would not have minded I am sure but at the price of missing these events, which frankly I did not think was very high, I kept away. 'Mr Ovett regrets . . .' would be the standard answer – until December 1978 when it became apparent that I was among the front runners for the BBC Sports Personality of the Year.

It must have been a thin year for British sport. I had won the European 1500-metres title in Prague; set a UK record of 1 minute 44.1 seconds in the 800 metres, taking the silver ahead of Seb Coe; and set a world best for two miles in the Coca Cola meeting. I would have thought that someone who had taken a world title in another sport would have topped that – perhaps that did not happen in 1978, I cannot really recall.

My mother was getting calls from the BBC asking if I was going to be at the programme, which goes out live. She said that I would not be attending because I did not take part in this type of event. But then there were strong hints that I might win the award. That put me in a predicament. Declining to be part of the crowd did not worry me because that is going to upset no one; but to win and not be there to receive the trophy would have been like accepting an invitation to a race and not turning up. Eventually we said I would go if I was the winner, which seemed to upset the BBC because traditionally no one is told until the night, something I find hard to believe.

'Yes Steve has won it,' came the whispered words. Panic set in at Harrington Villas since it meant I had to go out and buy a suit – at that time I did not own one because I was not in the sort of business where one was required. Father and Rachel also bought new clothes so it was a big family occasion. My mother did not go because she felt, rightly I believe, that it would have been hypocritical to have been pally with people whom she was constantly rebuffing over the phone; my family have never stood for double standards.

The BBC whisked us up to the TV Centre from Brighton in a Daimler and we were entertained in the executive suite before the programme. I found it a difficult occasion because I hate small talk and that was all there seemed to be; even the food seemed dangerous because it was things on sticks and I did not want to risk a stain on my suit being seen by millions. I still cannot bear those stand-up receptions where you have a glass in one hand, a plate in another and you need a third to consume anything. One man who made life easier that night was Cliff Morgan, Head of Sport at the time and a marvellous Welsh fly-half in his day. My father took his autograph book and Cliff's name was one of the first to go into it. We then went into the studio.

I found the programme thoroughly entertaining. There were plenty of amusing and dramatic incidents from the year and I enjoyed the way David Coleman, Harry Carpenter and Frank Bough operated. Their professionalism and the way they always seem to enjoy their work is something which I admire. I was so absorbed that when Coleman homed in on me with questions about what I might be doing next I could only say something banal about worrying where I could get a drink. What with all those lights and a suit and a tie I was feeling a little hot.

Normally the programme would run past midnight, but on this occasion there was an overtime ban by technicians and midnight was the witching hour. I was unaware of this as I mulled over what I would say in reply to Prince Charles who was to present the trophy. When my name was announced I walked up to the dais, Prince Charles spoke about my performances and I had just begun to express my thanks and launch forth, when one of the floor managers said, 'Right, roll the titles, that's it.' The programme was over and Ovett's first speech to the nation was never heard.

The created image of Ovett by then did cause plenty of problems. I was presented as either awkward or uncooperative, brash, aggressive, impolite and a nasty young man, or a combination of them all, depending upon which newspaper you happened to read. There was no doubt that plenty of people were put off me and did not bother to deal with me when in fact it was their responsibility to do so. One of them was David Shaw, the British Amateur Athletic Board's first professional secretary who was heralded as a man coming into the sport with a new broom to sweep out old ideas and methods.

I am sure that he did some good but I regret that he caused me several problems and brought me unnecessary hassle. When he took on the job he announced that he would have closer contact with athletes. That did not happen as far as I was concerned. He seemed to settle for using Andy Norman as a form of go-between. The most serious disagreement came in 1979 when I was threatened by Shaw with being banned from competition – in the year before the Olympic Games. It became known as the Nijmegen incident and nearly led me to taking what must be an unusual course for an athlete, legal action against the administration.

Britain had an international match against West Germany, Poland and Switzerland in June. It took place at Bremen, the day before an invitation meeting in Nijmegen, Holland, which was organized by Jos Hermans, a Dutch runner and an old friend. Two races so close together (and not far apart geographically) simulated the sort of conditions I would expect in Moscow the following year. I discussed the plan to run with both Harry and Andy and they agreed that it was a good idea. I told Jos that he would have to invite me through the British Board because athletes require permission from their governing body to run abroad. Jos, an experienced runner, knew this and contacted Shaw who, according to Jos, gave permission. But Shaw did not contact me and later denied that permission had been granted.

I competed in Bremen for my country in the 1500 metres and won a slow race, beating Thomas Wessinghage. The following morning I went off to Holland with my mother (who had travelled to Bremen to watch me run) for the second race. I won that in the much more encouraging time of 3 minutes 37.9 seconds. I thought the races had been a sound work-out as part of my long-term Olympic planning. It was a pleasant weekend until I touched down at Gatwick Airport and read the newspapers. Accusations about deserting the British team and questions about the authority by which I had run in Nijmegen were raised.

I waited to hear officially from Shaw or someone on the Board but did not. Only when I read that there was to be a committee of enquiry about my action which had the power to suspend me did I realize that my Olympic ambitions could be in danger. I spoke to my solicitor about the matter and then rang Jos Hermans in Holland who assured me that verbal permission had been given by Shaw. My solicitor then spoke to Shaw, while Jos stood by ready to sign an affidavit. I waited for the committee of enquiry to report: had there been any period of suspension I would have taken the British Board to court. However, their findings were, according to what I read in the papers, that 'a series of misunderstandings led to a confused situation'. That I felt left me a party to the confusion which I felt most certainly I was not. It left the impression as always that Steve Ovett was being an awkward boy.

The episode was damaging and upsetting. It brought a lot of unnecessary stress to me and my family, particularly my mother who again had the task of handling all the newspapers' telephone calls. I think Shaw's attitude had in part been influenced by the press in Bremen. They were incensed that I had gone off to Holland, without telling them, to run a faster 1500 metres than the one they had watched. I can see now that they might have looked a bit silly, reporting on the second day of the match in Germany when just up the road in Holland S. Ovett was turning out the fastest 1500 metres of the year. But as I have explained before, I do not run for the press and I did not feel any obligation to tell them what I was doing.

In looking back on this episode and the fact that with a bit of struggle I managed to run where I wanted as part of my Olympic preparation, I realize how damaging it is to have governing bodies of the sport who squabble in public, a matter I look at more closely elsewhere. My experience also convinced me that the restrictions imposed on the freedom of athletes in the fifties and sixties were probably damaging to the sport in Britain. In those days it was difficult to obtain permission to run abroad. I am told that athletes were always having requests to run in other countries turned down; in some cases those invitations were not even passed on by the Board to the individuals concerned. There was the over-riding belief that British athletics was best served by pursuing the archaic instrument of the two-country inter-national match as the best method of athletic expression.

Athletics is and always has been an individual sport and that individualism must always be encouraged. I know that in the fifties and sixties there were fewer meetings, without television or sponsors, but I am sure that had there been greater freedom of choice then people like Derek Ibbotson, Alan Simpson, Bruce Tulloh and Gordon Pirie would have been even more successful in championships. They, and many others, showed they had ability but they were denied the essential part of preparation – high-level competition – which I and my contemporaries now enjoy.

For most of the summer of 1979 I was a back-seat driver in the furore that followed Seb's record breaking. I was constantly bombarded by people telling me, 'Seb's running sensational times – he's in a world of his own'. It was all slightly frustrating because I knew from my training that I had the equipment to match these perform-ances, yet my attitude at the time towards running – that racing is all important, record breaking secondary – inhibited retaliation. I did not want to be drawn into the hurly-burly of a Coe–Ovett clash in which the stopwatch was to be the sole judge, particularly in pre-Olympic year. However, as in all these situations, my feelings and attitudes changed as I came to realize, as on previous occasions, that I was becoming fitter and fitter as the season drew to its close. In the final fifteen days of my season, when all the opposition was fading away, or preparing for the Olympic Games, I was left with races where the clock became my only opponent and it seemed a waste of fitness if I took it easy and won by just sprinting from the final bend.

So record attempts were on and more pleasingly the first was to be at my home track, Crystal Palace, which is notoriously slow as far as middle-distance races are concerned, and also a gamble with the English weather. However, the night of 31 August was an exception to the rule – a beautifully mild, calm evening, something akin to the climate and atmosphere which I have found in Oslo and Koblenz. I travelled up with Matt and we warmed up together behind the main sports complex and swimming pool.

Thomas Wessinghage of Germany was in the race and he too had been left out of this fashion for fast times. Between the two of us, we decided to concoct our own record-breaking formula for the mile. After the pacemaker dropped out, Thomas took up the third lap and pushed it relatively hard, although in my own mind I believe he was worried about the speed of the race and his ability to finish. I don't think he quite put his heart into that lap and push it as he might, so the pace dropped slightly. Next it was my turn and with 350 metres to go I moved past Thomas and stretched out down the back straight. I opened a gap of ten yards and that was my winning margin. My time was 3 minutes 49.6 seconds and I am, at the time of writing, the only person to get under

3 minutes 50 seconds on this particular track. It was a strange race, with only two runners in it really – it seemed to us both more like a job of work than a competitive and exciting affair.

Four days later it was time to change the world rankings at 1500 metres and the occasion was the Ivo Van Damme Memorial meeting in Brussels. Ivo had been a great friend – we met as juniors in Duisburg in 1973 and remained competitors and colleagues until his untimely death in 1976. It was therefore fitting that I should attempt to break a world record in this particular meeting before a crowd of 40,000. The result was that I went closest to a world-record mark than anyone since the invention of electronic timing – I was eight-hundredths of a second off Seb's record. If at the finishing line I had breathed in, expanding my chest, rather than breathing out, then I would probably have become a world-record holder. It was, however, a good morale booster for the year ahead.

7

'I.L.Y.'

The entry of Soviet forces into Afghanistan which brought
about the call for a boycott of the Moscow Games from
President Carter, backed by Mrs Thatcher and Australian
Prime Minister Malcolm Fraser, posed a difficulty during
the summer of 1980 but hardly, for me, the dilemma
which has been suggested. The crucial factor in all the
debate was that in Britain we did at least have freedom
of choice; as far as I was concerned there was no meddling
in that freedom. If pressure or persuasion had been
exerted on Coe and Ovett not to go then that would have
damaged the Moscow Games more seriously than the
withdrawal of many countries. Yet no one approached
me or my family directly in support of either side of the
argument. All I received was a letter from the Prime
Minister's office setting out the position. But the choice
was mine and that was largely in the hands of the
British Olympic Association. As far as the Games were
concerned I was part of that organization and the decision
to take part rested with them. Personally, I took the view
from the start that a boycott of a sporting event has no
effect other than a distortion of the result and a reiteration
of the political cause of the boycott.

Ironically, for much of the summer I could be seen
wearing a Soviet vest which was part of my running gear.
It had no political connotation whatsoever, just comfort
and nostalgia; the vest was given to me by Valeiry
Abramov, a Russian 1500-metres runner, several years
previously at, I think, a European Cup race in a typical
shirt-swapping episode. In fact I found it extremely

comfortable and wore it on many occasions, so many in fact that it led to a slightly embarrassing situation in Brussels one year when the leader of the Soviet athletes competing there asked to see me in my hotel. There was a touching little ceremony, quite formal in its way, where they presented me with a replacement. Presumably they thought that mine was getting a little tatty; the new one never fitted properly.

The proper athletic clothing, as most runners and joggers know, is vital to success of all kinds. Ill-fitting kit can end in disaster, halfway round a marathon or halfway through a mile. I have always been meticulous about this part of my preparation and have so far been very successful as you can see by looking at the record of races at the end of this book. It might give the impression that my athletic life was nothing but a string of victories, with a lap of honour and a wave to the crowd before popping up on to the top of the podium for another medal or prize. Believe me, it was not all like that. I am sure I am not the only successful sportsperson to be confronted with those problems which turn into dilemmas and then become nightmares. Cwmbran, near Newport, that outpost of Welsh athletics, holds for a me a memory I would prefer to erase. I opened my 1980 running programme at home there in May, appearing for England against Wales, Hungary and Holland. I ran 800 metres in 1 minute 49.17 seconds and a rather indifferent leg of the 4 by 400 metres; I definitely got the thumbs down from the critics. Here's why.

I had returned from an American trip having won a 3000 metres in Houston and a 1500 metres in Kingston, Jamaica. Arriving back, I had only a few days in which to see Rachel before she went off on a trip abroad. She was anxious to see as much of the world as possible during this period of her life. At the time she was at college with very little money, so she was an avid reader of those columns in *The Times* and *The Guardian* advertising cheap trips abroad. The one she picked was a 'magic bus' to Morocco, costing all of twenty-five pounds, or some such price.

The day before the Cwmbran meeting I set out early from Brighton to collect her and several rucksacks, bedouin tent etc from Maidstone; then on to Croydon to collect her friend Ruth, and finally up to a London hotel whose driveway was used as the boarding point for the bus. We arrived and parked nearby. At that time neither of us wanted our connection to become widely known and Rachel wanted to remain an anonymous tripper amongst the holidaymakers. If we had been seen together in the hotel and then waving goodbye there would soon have been questions from other bus trippers, calls back to England and the media would have moved in; that we wanted to avoid. So I sat round the corner in a café and waited for Rachel to tell me that it was time to depart.

I waited and waited and finally a worried-looking Rachel came in to say there was no bus. We walked round to the hotel and joined some other people outside who were obviously waiting for it too. Rachel kept trying to ring the bus company's number only to find it continuously engaged. Then up pops a woman, who turns out to be a rep from the tour operator, to tell us that the bus had left half an hour before and we should have been in the hotel foyer not outside. Harsh words were spoken because clearly she was washing her hands of any responsibility. I then asked her where the bus was leaving the country.

'Ramsgate Hoverport,' was the reply. Here we were at 11.30 A.M., yet I had been in Maidstone at four in the morning, half an hour's drive from Ramsgate. Frantically we piled all of Rachel's and Ruth's luggage into my two-seater Volvo and were about to zoom off in hot pursuit of the elusive if not magical bus when a forlorn-looking couple asked if we could possibly manage to give them a lift because they could not afford a taxi to Ramsgate and would miss the coach. So we squeezed in more rucksacks and, with five people on each other's laps and luggage everywhere, set off for the motorway and the coast – and I thought too a place in *The Guinness Book of Records*. We arrived and within a few minutes the bus pulled up right alongside my car and some of the Morocco-bound holidaymakers recognized me and began nudging one another – Rachel's plan to travel incognito disappeared. Anyway I saw Rachel and Ruth safely aboard, and was left to ponder what might befall them in the desert, or wherever they were heading, after such a farcical start.

Instead of a gentle drive from London to Wales at eleven in the morning, there I was in Ramsgate at three o'clock with a couple of races to run the next day. I headed back to Andy's house in Orpington, after a phone call, went for a gentle jog and then drove us both down to Wales arriving at ten at night. Within an hour or so I was off to bed, later than I would have wanted but at least believing the day's traumas were ended. Not so. I was woken at one by a hell of a party going on next door . . . singing and dancing, music, the lot. I left it a while, thinking that it might end, but by 2.30 A.M. – still unable to get to sleep – the noise was the same. I phoned reception, but the night porter clearly had dealt with other complaints and I suspect had been rebuked by the revellers for his interference.

I gave it another hour of wall-pounding, then went down to reception in my pyjamas and demanded another room. 'We are full sir,' the night porter told me. 'Look, you must have one room,' I said and he admitted that there was a spare and he handed over the key. Up I went again, found the room, took two strides in to hear 'Oh . . . Ah . . .' followed by groans and more heavy breathing which indicated to me that the room was occupied. Back to reception, a brief argument about whether the room was occupied, a visit by the porter to said room, who returned with apologies: 'Yes, some members of the staff have taken an advantage there. But would you like my room.'

By now it was nearly four in the morning and I went into a fitful sleep, waking at mid-day and getting down to find that everyone had gone to the meeting. They had obviously checked my original room and thought I had departed. I suddenly realized that I did not know what time the meeting was to start, or when my race was due. During the performance of the previous day it was one of the normal checks which was not made. I drove to the track and had just an hour to prepare for the 800 metres. Feeling shattered, I ran it in 1 minute 49.17 seconds; nine weeks before the Olympic Games that might have been a good way to fool my rivals but that was not the intention.

I was lying flat on the high-jump bed wondering how Rachel was getting on, feeling thankful that the race was over and that I could rest for the remainder of the day, when Andy came over to me and said, 'Hurry and get warmed up, you're in the relay.' My protestations about being shattered just bounced off. 'Come on, you can't let the other lads down, they're ready.' I went off on the second leg, round the bend and into the back straight, feeling as though I was going at the speed of light, when all these Hungarians, Welshmen and Dutchmen came rushing by; the England 'A' team finished fourth out of five behind the 'B' squad. I never did bother to explain to my three colleagues what had happened to me in the previous thirty-six hours – it would have taken too long and I was just too tired.

Not all my races during my build-up to the Olympic Games followed a similar pattern. I do not always have trans-European dashes followed by nocturnal meanderings in search of hotel beds and thank heavens 1 July in Oslo was not one of those. In fact, quite the opposite. I was looking for a chance to put a marker on the season with a fast run. It was just that and brought me my first world record.

The lasting memory of the occasion is that it was a long time coming, and that when it did come it confirmed my long-held feeling that my emotions do not go up and down very easily. After looking up at the clock and seeing the world-record time a few seconds after I had crossed the finishing line I was naturally delighted and extremely satisfied. However I found myself more concerned about the plight of Graham Williamson than my own achievement. Obviously the world took it as a significant performance, but running a world record was, for me, no different from many other races – after all I had been within fractions of a second twice the previous year.

That night in Oslo was a golden one for British athletics – a foretaste of the impact Coe and I were to make at Moscow in the Games where we were to start our competitions twenty-three days later. Things started to click in training coming up to the Talbot Games at Crystal Palace where I ran 1500 metres in 3 minutes 35.3 seconds, the fastest of the year in the world at that time. It was not the figures which influenced me – just the feeling that I was in good shape. As I turned into the straight at Crystal Palace with the race all but won there was a murmur in the crowd and I could hear someone (it was Steve Cram) coming up behind me. I just touched the accelerator to keep clear and the response was smooth and easy. I thought, 'Right, this is the time to go for a record.'

Two days later, having discussed my feelings with Matt, I spoke to Andy and the plans were laid. He asked David Warren to do the pacemaking. Dave was to become Britain's third man in the 800 metres for the Games and was looking for a fast race so Andy arranged for him to run at a meeting in Porsgrunn, a town just north of Oslo, on the Sunday before my meeting; he achieved a personal best of 1 minute 46.2 seconds. Meanwhile I had arrived in Oslo the day before and met my father and Alan Martin, a friend of the family. They had been holidaying in Norway. When I arrived at Oslo airport my immediate thoughts about world-record breaking were quickly set aside for the plight of another athlete, Graham Williamson.

The young Scottish miler and Steve Cram had been pitched into my race to decide who should have the third 1500-metres place in the Games, in my opinion the most absurd way of choosing an athlete and an indictment of the selectors who could have had little understanding about the preparation and planning which goes into an athlete's life. It showed to my mind a complete lack of feeling for the sport; if those selectors had been runners then they had completely forgotten what their sport was all about. To ask two young athletes to race in these circumstances a month before their Olympic event was like committing them to a duel at dawn; one of them was going to have a shattering experience.

As we all waited at the airport it became clear that Graham's kit was missing. I felt for the man, as did all the other athletes in the party. The prospect of having to run in different spikes, shorts and vest in such a crucial race was a cruel blow. A runner's spikes are like a comfortable old pair of shoes – you will keep them until they are falling apart. I wanted to say something to Graham but I stopped short, realizing I would only make matters worse. In the event, Graham's gear did not appear and Cram finished ahead of him and won the ticket to Moscow.

Within a few seconds of finishing the race I went over to Graham and tried to offer the right kind of words to comfort the guy. He had been running well; he thought he had done enough to win his Olympic place and then the selectors turned round and said they wanted more. Now Graham's Olympic hopes were dashed and he was quite distraught. I said, 'Don't worry, you're only young and there's a long time to go.' It was not meant to be patronizing. I had just achieved what I wanted to do while in the same event it was disaster for someone else; disaster which may have come about because someone stupidly did not do their job properly – putting the baggage in the right place.

But to get back to my part in the race. As I was warming up for the mile at the back of the stand I heard the sustained roar of the crowd and that familiar sound in the Bislett Stadium when something big is happening, the spectators banging on the metal advertising panels which surround the arena. It was Coe setting the 1000 metres world record. That meant that he had – for about forty-five minutes – four to his name.

My race was fairly straightforward. Dave Warren did a very good job going through 400 metres in 55 seconds and 800 metres in 1 minute 52.8 seconds with me at his shoulder. That was inside the schedule of Coe's world record at Bislett the year before and I was left to do just over one and a half laps on my own in front with Cram following me. When I turned into the finishing straight with 500 metres remaining I began to work hard, getting into a firm rhythm for the final lap. This is where concentration counts, where you shed all thoughts about turning it in when it hurts; you ingrain your mind to carry the body through the tiredness and the feeling that you just want to pack it in and walk off the track.

As I passed the bell someone shouted 'It's OK – you're on' and I remember thinking, 'Just keep this pace going. Relax . . . Relax, don't tie up.' That is the sort of thought that goes through the mind and on this occasion I remember it specifically. Your body is functioning in the correct manner so therefore you have to concentrate on your mind. In a way, instead of talking to yourself you are thinking to yourself, trying to tell your mind to keep things going as they are. There is pandemonium from the crowd, but deep into the last lap sound has become a blur, you cannot really distinguish one sound from the other.

In the final straight vision starts to tunnel, hearing begins to fade and so does your strength. All this happens as you close towards the finishing line. Probably unconsciously you know you are there, but you try to keep control because in those last few strides can come the unwanted hundredths of a second which deprive you of your goal. The feeling of pain – you have felt that before, at least you should have done because pushing your body and conditioning your mind to this sort of situation is part of training.

Two strides across the line and you explode back into reality. Everything starts falling into place: you look at the clock, you hear the crowd going berserk but it takes a couple of seconds for all this to sink into your consciousness. It does not suddenly happen – it expands around you, like coming out of an unconscious state. It is, I suppose, rather like the finish of a jigsaw: as you're running the final metres the gaps are closing and then the picture, in deliberate stages, becomes a whole. Just as the placing of the last jigsaw piece brings the feeling 'Now what?' – so too does the reality of a world record.

My second world record was more significant because of when I achieved it rather than the figures I produced. The second meeting of the year in Oslo's Bislett Stadium was on 15 July. I had always had that date in my schedule because I felt there would be a need to test my form, in good conditions, ten days before my first run in the Olympic Games. I was not looking for a record, more a race in which I would defeat significant rivals. With Wessinghage and Scott in the field, that was accomplished; equalling Seb's record of 3 minutes 32.1 seconds was a bonus, a lift to my morale.

Some of my friends were a little irritated because as I went to the front in the final 200 metres I glanced back to see how Scott and Wessinghage were responding; then in the straight I waved to the crowd, an action which slowed my momentum and thus my performance equalled rather than bettered Coe's time. To me, at that time, the record was secondary to the knowledge that I was in good shape for the Olympic task just ahead and had just beaten two outstanding runners who, because of the boycott, were to miss the Games. Wessinghage and Scott could be expected to treat any race outside the Games, before or after, as a chance to vent their frustration. Certainly Scott, who had accused me of dodging him, went to Oslo determined to bring me down. He tried by attempting to blunt my finish, misjudged his resources and finished up seventh.

Chris Sly set the early pace, but a first lap of 57.8 seconds was no good for Scott who then took up the front position and pumped more speed into the affair. I just tucked in behind him knowing that Wessinghage,

Walker and Steve Lacy, another American, were breathing down my neck. I was aware we were going fast but it was not hurting. Only after the race did I realize that we passed the 1200-metres mark just a second outside Coe's world-record schedule, but the figure which pleased me and Harry was my final lap of 56.1 seconds. This far into the race the wet track was beginning to have its effect. On all-weather tracks the rain tends to lie on the surface, or just below, and running shoes which become wet swell. I can recall wobbling a little as I accelerated round the final bend when I moved away from the rest. But it did not seem to affect the result – it just ruined my spikes.

And so to Moscow. I decided to avoid fanning the media flames of the Coe–Ovett confrontation by staying at home until the last possible moment. The British Olympic Association and the British Board agreed that I should fly out two days before my first race in the 800 metres. On the other hand, although I did not know it at the time, Coe went out earlier and, apart from off-the-cuff quotes and chats to TV and others, gave a press conference which apparently drew 600 journalists. In contrast to that sort of behaviour, the bad-guy image went with me from London to Moscow. Things began to go wrong at Heathrow where I was asked by the press why I was not wearing my Olympic blazer; a snub, someone thought. I did not give the proper explanation because it would have been too long for the instant answers reporters want at airports, but I will now explain the situation in the constructive hope that the BOA, marvellous in many things, will now reconsider their role as outfitters.

The system of getting everyone into those blazers and flannels begins with a form, which you receive even before you are selected and on which you are required to fill in all your measurements. Once selected, another

form arrives and you are requested to jog off to the
nearest appointed outfitters for another session with the
tape measure, to make sure you were telling the truth in
the first place. Some weeks later you get a call to say
your kit is ready and will you come and collect it – why
can't they send it through the post? Since I am not a new
boy, do not live near the BOA headquarters and am lazy
anyway, I do not respond like some of my fellow team
members. They immediately go along and see their kit in
boxes and the blazers on racks. Everything is labelled,
but if it does not fit exactly a quick switch when the girls
are not watching is not difficult to operate; if the track-
suit bottom is the wrong size, swap with Ovett's, or
someone's who happens to be their shape. Once this has
happened you are into a domino effect and I can imagine
there must be some point where the BOA headquarters
resembles a jumble sale at opening time. Thus when
Harry collected my gear I found that the blazer seemed
to be intended for one of our weightlifters in the heavy-
weight class.

Should I have turned up at Heathrow with my hands
completely lost up my sleeves? Would not that have been
regarded as Ovett taking the mickey? You can't win. But
I do seriously suggest that the BOA develop a simpler,
more effective and less wasteful system of distributing the
kit.

On arrival at Moscow Airport there was an opportunity
to start my 'Games' immediately and I could not resist.
After going through immigration you wait in line to have
your baggage checked and anyone who is meeting you
can see what is going on from the other side of a large
glass panel. I looked up and saw a crowd of media
men, television cameras, reporters and photographers and
somewhere at the back my mother and Matt. I joined
one queue and a phalanx of media men moved to the exit

opposite. Lights were set up, tripods adjusted, elbows flexed; my mother had disappeared behind the ruck. With everyone settled I moved to the far left to what appeared to be a shorter queue. I could hardly contain my laughter over the little piece of power I was wielding. On the other side of the glass panel everything was dismantled and everyone moved over opposite my new position. They had just settled down when . . . I spotted a shorter queue. I suppose after that I deserved all the pushing and shoving I suffered when I finally went through the glass doors. I could see a frail, bewildered young lady, obviously from the Soviet organizing committee, being buried beneath the bodies, the bunch of flowers she was intending to give me sinking with her. Eventually I got to her, took the bunch and listened to her words of welcome to Moscow. Meanwhile I was being bombarded by the media with questions like 'Are you going for double gold?' and other such banalities.

I saw my mother and Matt on the fringe of the crowd, then Nick Whitehead, the British athletics team manager, got through the scrum and pulled me towards a waiting coach. 'What about my mother,' I said. 'I must say hallo.' But Nick, understandably, was worried about having a member of his team injured in the crush and persuaded me to jump aboard without speaking to them. It worried me. After the tensions which had been building up at Harrington Villas before my parents departed for Moscow ahead of me, I wondered whether she might think I had used the crush of reporters to snub them. I was thinking about that as I settled in a seat and the coach sped us down a motorway towards Moscow. I glanced down and there, racing alongside us in the next lane, was a car with a cameraman, head and shoulders out of the window, filming me. I moved to another seat. They were there again when I got off the coach; they were there when I came out of the accreditation office; and they were even on the landing of my living quarters, where I was sharing accommodation with Harry Wilson and Ron Holman, another coach. Allowing the media in the living quarters was, I felt, an intrusion into privacy, even though they were excluded most of the time.

There were plenty of fun and games to be had with the media most days, particularly when going from the British quarters to the restaurant which was on the other side of the international zone, where all Village visitors, including the press, congregated. It became rather like a zoo at feeding time and going to lunch, in spite of dark glasses and other forms of camouflage, became like crossing a minefield. The restaurant, like all those at Olympic Games and major championships, was a danger zone – it is so easy, particularly when you are not doing much else, to go in with a salad in mind and end up clearing four courses. I resisted temptation. My heat and semi-final of the 800 metres were just the formality they should be to anyone with a chance of winning a medal.

The day of the final began well. My first thoughts as I blinked into consciousness were of realizing that I had had a very good night's sleep. I can recall reading about David Hemery, Alan Pascoe and other internationals lying restless and sweating through the night before a big race. Thankfully I have never had that trouble; I put my head on a pillow and I am away. It was a grey nondescript sort of morning, hazy with a little wind. I went with Harry for a run round the periphery of the Village, about three miles. When your body has been subjected to a training regime of two runs a day for a long period it is essential to keep to that routine. With races every evening over a sustained period you need that morning session to maintain the balance, to keep the body functions, like opening the bowels, operating in a familiar pattern.

After breakfast Matt arrived and we took a car into Moscow to the Ukraine Hotel where my parents were staying. It's a gaunt, old hotel with the foyer almost as lofty and as impersonal as a railway station. Much of the decor appeared to be 1920s with dark-stained wood-block floors partially covered by some splendid carpets. It was fairly depressing: someone with an eye to design and colour could have made it so much warmer, so much less impersonal, but maybe it was deliberate since it was built in the Stalin era. I went up to the floor where my parents had their room and we met in one of the open lounges by the lifts, an area where you could sit and talk, usually watched over from a distance by the concierge – the formidable lady who had the keys to all the rooms on her floor and 'ruled' that part of the hotel. My parents were there with Alan and Val Martin and some other friends. There was little more than small talk. Here we were on the day of one of the biggest occasions in our lives, certainly for my parents, and there was not much to be said other than 'Good luck son'. Everything that could have been done, had been done. My parents' part in my preparation had been measured in years of sacrifice; now I knew, and I am sure they knew, the parting of the ways was not far off. We kissed and touched, which was more important than small talk, and then I returned to the Village.

Running the gauntlet of the media minefield, I went off for lunch. The food was good. I was particularly fond of the Bortsch – a Russian soup – and I followed that with a small steak and chips. With an early evening final that was sufficient. I then met Harry and we sat down for a coffee together. He tried to convince me of certain tactics and I listened to him more through habit than anything else. He told me that I had never been fitter, something which I had heard from him at least twenty times before. He pointed out that there were no problems, talked about the other people in the race and what they would do. The value of talking to Harry was that if he had not said all those things I would probably have gone back to my room and started worrying; it was a release valve for us both.

There was really nothing Harry could tell me that I didn't know for, although this was the Olympic Games, the build-up and the race and the people in it were no different to many other races. In fact Harry was not involved with the tactics of the race. By this time in my running career Matt saw far more of me, knew more about the way I ticked and therefore knew my reactions to the other people in my event. Andy Norman fitted into a similar vein and between them they would be the people with whom I would discuss the tactical aspects of the race.

I spent a couple of hours sleeping, then put on my GB vest and shorts but my own track suit. The team issue – which did not fit properly and felt like serge – I packed away for wearing in the medal ceremony, alongside the spare pair of spikes, laces, pins and plasters, all of which are the tools of racing which an athlete builds up over the years to meet any contingency. Ready to race, I travelled to the stadium in an athletes' bus with Dave Warren who had, surprisingly I think, also reached the final. When we reached the warm-up track we parted.

I like to do my warming up, which is a mixture of exercises and short runs and lasts about forty minutes, on my own, something I find is becoming increasingly difficult because of the presence in the warm-up areas of television crews. I was there early for the 800 metres and they were all around me, panning in on the way I tied my shoelaces and going through my every run. It is annoying to have them in such close proximity in what is the last preparatory step before competition. I am not suggesting that this part of athletics should go unrecorded, but I think there needs to be far more control and monitoring than at present.

From the warm-up area the athletes are taken into the arena across a bridge. The Bridge of Sighs I termed it – when you walk across it you sigh to yourself, 'This is it then.' Each competitor has one of his team officials to accompany him over the bridge and then down into the bowels of the stadium to the call-up area. Nick Whitehead was with me. He knows how to handle athletes during this tense time and as we were walking across the bridge he produced a four-leaf clover which his daughter Rachel had picked. It was a nice touch – a timely diversion, though not a distraction, from the task immediately ahead.

The call-up area is where the athlete is on his own, with another twenty minutes or so to go before the race. At the door, officials check your identity tag around your neck and then you are escorted to a room with the other seven finalists. Here everything is meticulously checked – numbers (back, front and on the side of the shorts), all your clothing for any advertising and your spikes to see they conform to number and length. The Russians were extremely efficient in this process, giving the athletes confidence, but they did insist unfortunately that we all sit down. It was an extremely small room for eight people who really wanted to be up and limbering. There was nothing for it but to sit and try to keep the muscles supple with little leg and arm movements.

I tried to talk to the other people, not because I was nervous but because, twenty minutes away from one of the biggest events of my life, I did not want to waste nervous energy on thinking about it. The time to concentrate my mind was when I was out on the track. Did I speak to Coe? I think we wished each other good luck but no more. Had he wanted to speak I would have done so and I suppose the same applied in reverse – which added up to silence. But this after all was his event, he was the world-record holder, it was more his race than mine. I occupied my mind, as I always do before races, by checking that my spikes were in the bag, my pins on the numbers were OK and my clothing comfortable.

In this way the minutes pass until finally an official asks you to 'follow that man' and out you file – they are very keen to keep you in single file. You try to jog and get back the suppleness, which you think you have lost by sitting down, as you walk through the tunnel. Occasionally you hear a muffled roar from the crowd, then there is an opening in the building on to the track and you glance, for no more than a second, into a blaze of colour and sunlight. You recognize something, like the javelin run-up area, and you re-orientate yourself to the layout of the arena, something you had lost when you came off that bridge and went into the stadium interior. But still you remain in single file.

Every few yards you pass athletes coming back from the arena. Some have their heads slumped forward and are in tears, others seem to be wandering aimlessly. You never see the winners who have inevitably been removed from the debris of their event. Your mind keeps thinking, 'Concentrate, don't let this happen to me.' Eventually the single file is wheeled out into the sunlight, maybe only five minutes before the race is due to start. You have these last minutes before the starter's gun to make the final preparations. As I tied my shoelaces I kept thinking, 'Isn't it funny, you still have to remember the small things, like tying a double knot – exactly the same as I would have done in the Sussex County 800 metres.' I glanced up to the scoreboard and slowly, one by one, the eight finalists' names were being displayed in lane order. I checked the scoreboard clock and there were three minutes to go. I walked out into the arena and for the first time we were allowed to break ranks and stride for 100 metres before being called back. Track suits off and we were ushered to the start line.

I went off fairly fast and was suddenly whacked, entering the back straight, by one of the big East Germans. I thought, 'This is the Olympic final. I am not going to take that sort of tactic.' When he did it again I was ready and he bounced off me. As the running unfolded I was thinking, 'Don't make mistakes.' I was boxed in a little towards the end of the first lap, when Coe was running wide, but it was Dave Warren on my outside and I knew he would fade. I suspected that Kirov would somewhere early in the second lap go to the front so that he was clearly seen on television and do what I would call a 'Hallo Mum' sketch, even though he knew he could not last. When Kirov did this I covered the break, following him easily from about 250 metres out.

I could feel that he was dying as we went into the final bends. I kept thinking 'Where's Coe. Where's Coe' and then realized that I ought to be going flat out and I wasn't. Suddenly I remembered Prague, the European Championships of 1978, where I waited for one man and lost, so I kicked again and went into the lead with 110 metres remaining. It wasn't hurting and all I could think was that it was so quiet. I could hear or feel no one near me. 'What has happened? This was supposed to be the clash of the century with two men neck and neck down the finishing straight.' It was almost like being in a dream and when I reached the line I thought, 'You're Olympic champion. What's all the fuss been about?' It was in fact, in the moments after winning, a bit of a disappointment to me – an anti-climax.

Two strides through the line I turned and looked up at the press box and saw so many familiar British faces with looks as though they had lost money on a horse or just knocked over their drink; they were stunned and that upset me. Having achieved my goal I was now, I thought, prepared to go to them in the ritual press conference; then, as I searched for a smile, a cheer or a wave, I thought, 'No, not today.' The Italian press were jumping up and down and some Norwegians had dashed down to the front row of the seats and were shouting across to me. But the Brits maintained the stiff upper lip of, what they would like to call, impartiality.

I put out a hand to Seb and said, 'How did it go?' What else is there to say in such a situation? Of course it was later that I learned he was all over the place running probably the worst tactical race of his life. I then realized that I had been right to ignore him, otherwise I might have been following him at the back. Elation gradually filtered through, but it took a time. I had been playing out the scene with the supporting cast, not the other leading actor. I did not expect to win the 800 metres so easily and I think the race lost some of its intrigue by the simplicity of my victory. I believe that that sense of anti-climax, together with other events, affected my approach to the 1500 metres, the race I had always been gearing myself towards. If I had lost the 800 metres to Coe in a close contest it would not have done much damage – he was after all the world's fastest man at the distance and a good bit faster than me. My reaction would have been, 'Now it's all on the 1500 metres. I've got to win that.'

We both went in for a dope test; Seb was shattered and I could see that he had been crying. I felt for him. It was an event after which one of us was due to be in that state and in that moment I felt genuine empathy for him. He gave a sample quickly and was off. Suddenly, for no reason at all, I began to superheat. I went red all over and became so hot that I had to sit down. By this time everyone else had gone and I was the only one left to give a sample. The doctors came in, looked at me and were clearly concerned. I became hotter and I was stretched out, naked apart from a pair of pants, and wet, cold towels were draped over my body and constantly changed. I began to worry as none of the British team managers are allowed in the doping control area and the Soviet doctors either did not speak English or did not want to.

My temperature climbed higher and higher and at one stage I was almost into unconsciousness. I think I reassured myself with the knowledge that I had won, that it was all over and that after all the build-up to the race, the tensions and the training, the worries at home, the victory was a release from all these and I believe, in achieving my ambition, something triggered off inside me and my temperature just shot up. I was lying there on the couch for about twenty minutes when normality began to return and after taking some drinks I was able to provide the dope-testing department with what they wanted. With my lack of concern for medical matters, I never bothered to find out afterwards exactly what happened and why. In fact I dismissed the whole incident, but now I believe it may have played a part in my inability to win the second title.

By the time I had completed the dope test it was late and I left the stadium with the remaining British officials, who were strangely quiet in the car. I realized that the wrong man had won, or that was how it seemed to me. Harry had gone off for a meal with Ron Holman so I just left a note for him on the bed: 'I hope you're as proud of me tiger as I am proud of you.' I then went off into town to join my parents at the Ukraine Hotel for dinner. But the rules there are strict – I arrived after 'last orders'. We managed to get into the restaurant but there was no food. Dinner had finished and there was a firm 'Niet' for an Olympic champion. I suppose there were plenty of them that week in Moscow, so I didn't matter, but it did amuse me wondering which restaurant back home would say no to a gold-medal winner at about ten in the evening. We did manage to have a couple of drinks, and someone on another table sent across a bottle of champagne.

I had two days' rest before the start of the 1500 metres by which time the weather had turned very warm. I had forty-two consecutive victories in 1500-metres and mile races and I did not want to lose, an attitude which led me to making a mistake in the first round. I found myself racing Jurgen Straub, the strong East German, and was forced to record 3 minutes 36.8 seconds in finishing first, far faster and harder than I had hoped. I started to heat up again and on the bus back to the Village I did not feel very well. I was overcome with the feeling that I should not be there, that I had done my job and that was that. It took a fight with my inner conscience to drive home the fact that you only get this chance once every four years and the event in which I had greater consistency was still to come. The semi-final, 3 minutes 43.1 seconds, was less demanding but I was feeling tired and realized that Straub had deliberately stretched me in the heat into a tactical error.

A simple loving message from an athlete in Moscow apparently took Britain by storm – and indirectly led to the row which I had with my mother on the eve of the 1500-metres final. 'I L Y' – which, with a finger, I drew in the air in front of a television camera in the Lenin Stadium, mouthing the word 'Rachel' – was meant for a lonely, anxious, unwell lady in Maidstone. I knew that

Rachel was worried about me, about the pressure of racing in the Olympic Games, more perhaps about the building tension within my family; and she knew I was worrying about the kidney complaint which had kept her at home in bed. So 'I L Y' was an impulsive reaction to a camera probing down on me as I finished a heat of the 800 metres. It was a simple gesture, like so many which bind millions of lovers. Unfortunately, between Moscow and Maidstone there was Fleet Street, and within a few hours the media machine was in full gear.

If I had been a publicity seeker at the time, I suppose that gesture to the camera would have been the simplest way of getting on the front pages ahead of every Olympic winner, but as you know by now I was not in the business of seeking publicity. Rachel, in fact, did not cotton on to the gesture immediately. Fortunately Martin, her brother, was watching and said 'That's a message for you', but it needed a couple of replays on the video before my signal was received and understood. Rachel though was not the only one slow on the uptake. One television commentator suggested that it was 'One down, six to go'. Someone else interpreted it as a Russian symbol. One old lady actually phoned the BBC and said 'It is I Love You', which David Coleman passed on to the viewers, with a laugh, as 'one of the cranky suggestions we've received'.

The immediate reaction of Fleet Street newspapers was to call their men in Moscow to find out who was the woman in Ovett's life. As far as I am aware very few journalists knew, but it did not take much questioning amongst athletes and coaches to find out that Rachel Waller lived in Maidstone. Several reporters were on their way to the town from London, while others went through the Wallers in the telephone book. Newsmen, photographers and television crews were soon ringing the door bell and calling at local shops to find out what they could. While Rachel knew my attitude towards the press, her parents are not the sort of people who would brush off 'polite callers'. Understandably they did not like their daughter backing away from these nice ladies and gentlemen asking how she was, and whether they could take a picture of her. Finally Rachel gave in.

On the day before the 1500-metres final I visited my parents at their hotel and could see from my mother's face that something was wrong. We were in the lounge area on her floor when she threw down a British newspaper with a picture of Rachel on the front page. The tense, rather false atmosphere which had existed between us since I arrived in Moscow blew up. My parents knew that I had been telephoning Rachel in Maidstone and here, in my mother's view, was just the evidence she wanted to show Rachel was up to no good. 'We've gone to all this trouble to keep the press out' – which was absolutely true and extremely valuable – 'and here she is getting herself on the front page. All she's trying to do is jump on the bandwagon. How can you get yourself involved with someone who doesn't know you as well as I do.' Of course I had been as much responsible for that picture appearing in the paper as Rachel, who had been under intense pressure from the media and did not know how to cope with it. The picture though was the excuse my mother needed to bring the differences which had been building up between us out in the open. She had done her job in getting me to a gold medal and now she wanted to have her say. My response was that I did not want to argue about it: I still had a job to do, the final of the 1500 metres, so let's talk about it later.

My mother took my defeat in the 1500-metres final very personally. She saw what could have been a marvellous success (for which, let me be frankly honest, she had played an important part) disappear. And it was made no easier for her that Seb won and was heralded as the bigger hero, having come back from defeat and triumphed. It was a case of the nice guy wins – in the end. She took all that very personally.

I wiped my family problems out of my mind when I went out there into the Lenin Stadium for the final. I ran the best race I could but I was beaten by two better guys. In analysing that final, I do not believe that Seb would have won without Straub in the field. He was the man who grabbed that race by the scruff of the neck and pulled us round, while Seb had so much fear of defeat in him that he got past Straub and I could not. Straub hauled that race through from beginning to the last few strides. He began his run for home 700 metres out and turned in a withering third lap of 54.2 seconds. Seb managed to hang on and got him in the straight. For me though it was the East German who was the hero of the day; he threw everything into beating the last semblance of running out of two tired men, and he almost pulled it off. Deflation after the 800-metres gold; the overheating following that victory; worrying about Rachel's problems; the row with my mother – sweep all those excuses out of the window. A runner of my calibre ought to have pulled it off at his number-one distance. The one feeling I have no doubt about is that had Straub not been in the race I would have beaten Seb.

I mentioned earlier that in victory I found it difficult to say anything to Seb for fear of being patronising or misunderstood. His words to me as we shared that dope-testing room rankled. I passed him a drink and he said, 'So you got silver then?'

'No, I got bronze,' I replied.

'Oh good.'

Those two words told me more about the man than the

race did. I know they had a double meaning but I have the memory of the way he said it.

8

The Inevitable Goodbye

You have some strange thoughts during and at the end of races, usually associated with deflation, but I remember thinking, as I raised my hands to the crowd and set off on a lap of honour round the tiny Oberwirth Stadium in Koblenz, 'This can't be right. I should not be running this fast now.' I had just broken the world 1500-metres record with a time of 3 minutes 31.36 seconds, a month after winning the Olympic 800-metres title. I had already set two world records in the summer and here I was setting a third in what was virtually my last race of the season when I ought to be tailing off. The same thing was to happen in 1983 when in Rieti I lowered the time to 3 minutes 30.77 seconds on 4 September. In 1980 I came out of winter training knowing that I was supremely fit, feeling that I could go very fast, yet aware that the idea of record breaking had to be submerged in facing the challenge of championship racing in the Olympic Games – six races in the space of nine days. I had broken the 'rule' by setting records in the mile and 1500 metres just prior to the Games and this performance in Koblenz showed that even the best athletes are mystified by what goes into a supreme performance.

Back in Brighton Matt was doubting the very feat. My father, having heard about the world record from someone in Fleet Street who had phoned him as soon as the news came through, immediately phoned Matt. His response was, 'No, it's not possible Mick. You've got the figures messed up. You probably switched the seven with the one. Steve's much too tired – on a couple of days I really had to drag him round his training session. There's no way he could have broken that record.'

One of those sessions on which Matt dragged me round was on the morning of the Golden Mile at Crystal Palace, which I won, holding off Steve Scott in a harder race than I had anticipated. At Crystal Palace you expect to get away with a win in 3.54 or 3.55, but on this occasion Scott pushed me more than I expected and I recorded 3 minutes 52.84 seconds. I remember saying to Matt afterwards, 'I feel exhausted. My season should really come to an end now.' Matt pulled me out for a run the following day, when I still felt exhausted and believed I would be doing myself far more good staying in bed. Matt has done this many times, made me train when I would have preferred to play truant.

It was against that immediate background, plus the deflation that came after the Games (and all the attendant personal troubles) that I went off to Koblenz. Hardly a record-breaking scenario, yet I spell this out to emphasize that racing, in spite of all the finely tuned training methods and the increased scientific knowledge which coaches and athletes now possess, is still full of mystique. Why did I manage to run so fast? I don't know. There were however certain aspects of the meeting which gave me a psychological boost, even if I was feeling physically tired. One of these was the fact that Rachel travelled to a competition abroad with me for the first time; another was that I like running in Koblenz because of the people who organize the meeting and what they have created. It is an intimate affair in which all those involved in the organization are ex-athletes and being their one meeting of the year they put enormous effort into it. The headquarters is a restaurant owned by a committee member and most athletes stay in hotels away from the noisy part of the town. The promoter Fredy Schäfer and his team understand athletes; they handle them like people instead of shoving them around like cattle. That is the sort of meeting I enjoy. They appreciate the living and the eating habits of athletes and this creates a rapport between competitors and eases the niggling problems which tense sportsmen seem to encounter and often magnify.

There is also a feeling of humour about the meeting. The arena is small and you can just about cram in 22,000 people coming almost down to the track edge. The backdrop is a 500-ft cliff on which a couple of hundred people perch for a view of all those human ants rushing around below. I've often wondered how much they can actually see up there. But there seems plenty to laugh about and anyone who can do things for a laugh gets it – like Willie Banks, the American triple-jumper who boogies to music from his 'Walkman' and gets the crowd swinging along too; and the meeting announcer, another ex-athlete who is always getting frantic about something, and sometimes nothing. It is my type of meeting – never imposing – and of course you can almost guarantee at the end of August good weather; still, warm evenings when the Gods lean down and kiss the athletes.

With all these factors in your favour you will understand my anger at missing a third world record there in 1983 when the conditions were perfect. I felt strong yet the pacemaking went wrong. On the night of 27 August 1980, however, the situation was very different; there was in fact no plan for a world record, though one emerged on the day of the race.

Rachel and I arrived the evening before and joined Fredy, his colleagues and some other athletes for dinner. I went to bed knowing that the race might turn out fast because Thomas Wessinghage, West Germany's leading 1500-metres and 5000-metres runner, and Willi Wulbeck, the man who beat Sebastian Coe in the European Cup

Final 800 metres three years before, were both in the field. I knew that Thomas – we had been good friends for several years – was in good shape and that Wulbeck rarely runs above his normal distance unless he knows a good performance is likely. That showed me a fast race was on the cards since Thomas would have to go hard to burn off Wulbeck's finish.

I was extremely tired, as my training indicated, and Rachel and I slept late – perhaps too late, for we were woken by Andy banging on the door saying, 'You've missed breakfast and if you don't hurry you'll miss lunch as well.' At lunch Fredy came over and asked me what sort of pace I would like. I laughed: 'Really Fredy, is it my decision or has something been organized? Are you talking about it to the others?' He admitted that Thomas wanted a fast run and would take the pace through the third lap.

I knew then that we were in for a proper race, and a fast one at that. Thomas obviously did not want to be beaten by another German, particularly Wulbeck who would be quick over the final 800 metres if the first half of the race was slow. He thought too that I was tired, and as far as I was concerned he was right. It was rare to find in such a racing situation, not a paced record attempt, a man of Thomas's calibre prepared to go out on the third lap, just to win and not for anyone else's benefit. I told Fredy that I wanted to go through 800 metres in 1 minute 52/53 seconds (a world-record schedule): to have Thomas take up the front running from there was ideal. What though if Thomas did not move through? I did not want to be left out in front on my own and get beaten; the season was almost over and I wanted to finish on a high note. Nobody wants to lose in one of their last races. Who was going to handle the first two laps? When Fredy said 'Garry Cook' I suddenly realized that this race was building up into something *very* special. Garry had gone to Koblenz intending to run an 800 metres but also had that end-of-season feeling. He was glad to take over the role of running the first 800 of the 1500 metres rather than competing in what promised to be a very good two-lap event.

Garry, being an international 800-metres runner, had ample experience and pace judgement. Not only did he judge it perfectly to 800 metres, which he passed in 1 minute 52 seconds, but he also carried on to 1000 metres which was more than what was required. He hit the marks dead on and played a vital part in the record performance. When he dropped out I was left five yards in front of Thomas who should have been in front at this point. I slowed down at the front to let him pass and I remember thinking, 'Oh I'm slowing down . . . this is ridiculous . . . Thomas should be up . . . I can't really slow down . . . if I slow down, I'll lose my cadence and then Thomas will come past me too fast . . . it's all been messed up.' Wild thoughts flicking through my mind, I was sure the whole affair had died and that Thomas had left it too late. In fact he was so far back that when Cook dropped out it took him time to gather speed and go past me. When he did he was moving like a train with only 450 metres to go. He hit the front not as a pacemaker, to drag those behind him along, but with a positive bid to drain off the challenge of his rivals. He was racing with a chance of winning, so the momentum of the pace was maintained. I back-pedalled in surprise, as it were, for about 50 metres and realized that the reason why Thomas had all the stops out was because the other two Germans, Wulbeck and Harald Hudak, together with Omar Khalifi of the Sudan, were still with us. This confirmed my feeling that the race was going to be slow, outside a world record, and we had a competition on our hands.

I shifted up a gear and closed in on Thomas and with 380 metres to go I glanced back to see that the other three were still there. I began to worry. World-record thoughts poured out of my mind as fast as the Rhine flowing alongside the stadium as I concentrated on how to beat four competitors who should not have been there. I moved out slightly to overtake Thomas and that effort took me the rest of the back straight and into the bend. All of us were going flat out at that point and as we turned into the home straight I saw Thomas just behind followed by Wulbeck and Hudak. I thought that we must be slowing down because they couldn't all be that close in a world-record run. I had a kick left, not much, but I decided to use it then just in case Wulbeck had something and luckily that's the last I saw of them as I went down the straight, literally hanging on. When I reached the line my first thought was 'Thank God I've won.'

I turned to see Thomas three or four yards down and the others right on him and as I walked back along the track the crowd began to go berserk – as did that frenetic announcer. I couldn't understand him but I looked up and saw the digital clock just beyond the finishing line and thought, 'That's not bad, 3 minutes 37-point-something. Thank heavens it's over, that was tough.' But the crowd were still going berserk and I could not understand why. I looked again at the clock and realized that the way the Europeans slant the figure one – even on digital clocks – had led me to add six seconds to my time. I was stunned. It was a world record. I had gone into a race which was all set up to be very fast and was on schedule for a new world time, yet I had become so wrapped up by the necessity of winning such a competitive race that I was completely oblivious to the time. I suppose that is as it should be because winning races, not breaking records in set-up situations, must be the prime objective. Thomas and Hudak were also inside the old record, which I clipped by seven-tenths of a second; Wulbeck was just outside it; and Khalifi ran seconds faster than he had ever done before.

I know the news was greeted initially with disbelief, even from the man with whom I do most of my training. There were stupid suggestions about the track being short. In fact it was just a marvellous jigsaw in which everything fell into place – the ambience of the Koblenz track with its tremendous crowd, the perfect weather, Garry's part and then the competitiveness between Wessinghage, Wulbeck and Hudak into which I was drawn and others were dragged. Andy, who I suspect is a bit of a chauvinist, conceded that Rachel also played a part. 'We must bring her to these events more often,' he said as I walked down the back straight. Thomas was overwhelmed by the race; he just could not believe that a record could come from such a competitive event. It was a rare occasion and I am only glad that it helped to justify the special place that Koblenz has in the athletic calendar. I would dearly love to set a world mark at Crystal Palace, but the weather, to begin with, is so much of a gamble in this country. You have to be very lucky to get the conditions right; but in places like Koblenz, Oslo and Zurich there are certain times in the year when you can almost guarantee the conditions required by middle-distance runners to produce excellent performances. I was lucky having one of those that night in Koblenz. The 1500 metres in Rieti in 1983 may have been more important, more satisfying in many respects, but Koblenz 1980 was a stunning event. Yet the race taught me something: if I could run 3 minutes 31.36 seconds easing down on the third lap, there was still more to come out of that 1500-metres world record.

No sooner had I completed a lap of honour in response

to an ecstatic crowd than I dashed up to Rachel. It was the first occasion on which she had been abroad with me to a race, and when I found her she had tears in her eyes. It was the first time she had seen anyone break a world record, which is another reason why we treasure the memories of that night so vividly. Ironically, since there were no tickets left anywhere in the stadium she was given a press badge and squeezed on the end of a row of seats occupied by the British press contingent.

The joy of sharing the Koblenz experience with Rachel was heightened by the fact that it came at the end of a season that had become something of a trial for me and a burden for those close to me. I had trained very hard in my preparation for Moscow, indeed sometimes over the weekend sessions at Crystal Palace with Bob Benn I would return to his Croydon flat so exhausted that I did not want to go out for the evening with Rachel, Bob and his girlfriend; I simply fell asleep in front of the television. That caused minor upsets, understandably, with Rachel who had given up coming to see me at Brighton because of the atmosphere and my mother's attitude towards her. On top of this, Harry, Bob, and Matt were constantly being questioned by my mother about whether I was training and how hard I was training. They could see all these relationships under intense strain; they knew like me that something was going to break and no one wanted it to happen until after Moscow.

All of us, my mother, father and Rachel, had been suffering from the tensions which had built up over a long period, but I had talked it over with my family earlier in the year and agreed to make things work until after the Games were over, when I would go off and make a life of my own. I had come to realize long before the Games that I could not go on living at home much longer. I had reached the point where I wanted to live my own life and make my own decisions, but above all the point had been reached long before where my parents were living their life through me. They expected me to respond and act as I had done when I was fifteen, sixteen or seventeen; they wanted to exercise the same influence and control over my life. Of course this attitude was, I feel, a product of their involvement with my career in athletics and heightened by the impending Olympic Games, and I cannot but stress the enormous part they played in my success.

Apart from the euphoria, winning in Moscow brought me relief. I had in principle fulfilled my part of an obligation in the family relationship. The break with my family later in September came after a row over a relatively small affair; it was just the straw which broke the camel's back. I had been expecting it for months. Perhaps, so soon after the Games, it would appear wrong to some that I turned my back, an ungrateful, selfish son on my family environment. That though was merely the timing; I had, for a long time, been living a new life within the constraints which Harrington Villas imposed and when the break came it was welcome, a freedom which manifested itself in little things – like having a friend round without having to announce him or her first or explain who and what they were.

On my return from Moscow there was much talk in Brighton about honouring their Olympic champion. I was approached and said that I did not want a Mayoral reception with a lot of money being spent and no one benefiting; instead the Steve Ovett Fund for Young Athletes was launched. For ten pence anyone could run a lap of the Withdean track with Steve Ovett and receive a certificate to that effect. I signed over six thousand of these the week before the event and spent the morning of

Saturday 20 September lapping the track with up to fifty people at a time – youngsters, joggers, anyone. The fund made a lot of money. It was a rewarding, if tiring morning which started soon after eight o'clock and went on until midday. Then in the afternoon there was a ceremony at which I unveiled a plaque marking the fact that I opened the new all-weather track which replaced the cinders. (Not many people realized that the resurfacing work, which took place during the winter of 1979 and the early part of 1980, took nearly a year to complete and deprived me of a local track on which to train during my build-up to the Games.) Once the unveiling ceremony was performed, the VIPs, the Mayor, councillors, members of Brighton & Hove Athletic Club were entertained to a meal in a marquee.

My mother had been involved in these arrangements with the town hall officials and told them who would be attending from our family group so that places on the top table could be provided. Rachel stayed the weekend with us, a visit which had been planned, and spent the morning with me at the track. Yet there was no place for her. One was quickly found for her on another table. Clearly those people at the function who were focusing on me could see that something was wrong and the atmosphere was only made worse when, after a speech about me and my family, one of the officials said, 'We all know what a great team you and your mother are Steve. Don't you agree Steve?' As he said this he raised his glass in my direction. I did not agree. But he could not have been aware of the embarrassment he was causing. When I later found that my Olympic medals were being passed round, I came very close to losing my temper. I did not know where they had come from or who had brought them. I do not mind people seeing my medals, and most of all I love showing them to children. Yet here they were appearing out of the blue at an official function. My mother had apparently taken them from my drawer without asking, or even mentioning to me that she had done so. I was very annoyed and must have shown my feelings because my parents' reaction was that I had let them down in front of other people. I felt that the whole situation had reached a ridiculous pantomime performance. What a contrast to that marvellous morning, jogging round the new track with all those youngsters, knowing that every lap covered was more money for the fund.

After an afternoon of anger and bitterness, I knew that the break was not far away. Perhaps I should have returned home and settled things immediately. However, it was my sister's birthday and on returning to Harrington Villas we found that the rest of my family were about to depart for a celebration dinner, to which it appeared Rachel and I were not invited. Instead we went out for dinner with Andy who had arrived amidst the to-ing and fro-ing. Not for the first time, nor the last was Andy Norman to hear the problems of Steve Ovett. He, with perhaps the exception of Harry and Matt, knew most about how much my parents had done for me, the sacrifices they had made to help me win an Olympic title. I am sure that when he first heard about my association with Rachel he too had been apprehensive, but he did come to accept that it was a natural stage in my life. He could see both sides of the problem and, when we returned home that evening, he talked alone until three in the morning with my mother and father about the conflicting relationships. I know and respect the man's judgement and there could not have been at that time a better independent view of the situation. I think what he said made them realize that a parting had to come; that it was natural for a grown-up man eventually to leave home with, or without, another woman.

The following morning the atmosphere was very cool. My mother clearly was still upset by the events of the previous afternoon and when I asked 'How did my medals turn up yesterday?' the balloon went up. My father, decorating in the hall, joined in the event and a row ensued. Finally he gave me a choice: 'It's your mother, or her,' referring to Rachel. 'If you don't like it there's the door, you can leave' – which I had been told many times before. But this time I said, calmly I think, 'Thank you very much, I will.' I went upstairs and packed a few things, then kissed my thirteen-year-old brother Nicholas goodbye. He said, 'See you later' and I replied, 'No, not this time, I'm afraid.' Rachel went and gathered up her things and we left.

We stayed with Rachel's parents for a couple of days before taking up the opportunity to go to the United States as the guests of Nike, the shoe manufacturers whose spikes I wear. It was mostly holiday though and Disneyland and similar Californian fun outlets enabled us both to put aside the unhappy events of the immediate past.

To me the break from my parents was not a traumatic affair, only the manner in which it came about. This could not be avoided. It would have been impossible to sit down with my mother and father and talk reasonably about me moving out and going to live with Rachel. My family and I are not like that. I could not sit down and say, 'Thanks for all you have done. I truly appreciate the help and support you have provided, but the time has now come for me to move out and live my own life and therefore we won't see so much of each other.' That would have been impossible. The emotional situation was far too deep to switch off gradually. What had happened of course was that they had been living their lives through me, particularly my mother. They had concentrated their resources, their attention, most of their waking hours on Steve Ovett the athlete.

When the break came it was almost a relief and frankly Rachel was far more upset about it at the time, and is still now. Although she had seen the tension rising at Harrington Villas, been part of it, she did not expect the parting to be so brutal or so lasting. Her parents were kind and understanding, neither pushing us one way nor pulling another. They provided us with a roof over our heads, sharing their home at Maidstone until we found in October a flat to rent about a mile from the Withdean track. Rachel concentrated on her modelling course and making a home for us. It was for me a relaxing period, not having to worry about the home environment or the emotional traumas of having to think and plan for each encounter with my family.

Certain aspects of my experience are not unusual I am sure; indeed, there must surely be a parallel in some respects with the relationship between Seb and his father, who is also his coach. If someone starts living through another person, putting more importance on that person's life than their own, then things may well take a twist for the worse. My attentions towards Rachel suddenly deprived my family of something which they believed they deserved more than anybody else – I had unwittingly taken away one of the most important aspects of their life. Perhaps encapsulated in these words my attitude sounds cold and unthinking, but I had known for a long time that there was no other course. I wish there could have been. I thought that the break was as important to them as it was to me; that they had to find again their own identity and live their own lives. It was by no means an ungrateful son who closed behind him that door which, almost four years on, has not been opened again.

9.

The Best of Years

Olympic gold medals, world records and European titles have their own special place in a career, but if medals were struck for a string of performances then I think that my best hope would have been for the racing I did in 1981. To me it was the most rewarding year in spite of its frustrations; I missed world records on four occasions by mere fractions of seconds and strung together two or three of these performances within a few days of each other, which at times still amazes me. I knew that I was as physically fit as I had ever been and, without the mental stress of living at home, I was my own man moving out into an area where I made all my own decisions. I did snatch the world mile time from Seb but it was the season over all, rather than that particular run, which makes me smile.

Trackwise 1981 began in controversy – yet another misunderstanding which ended with the Ovett reputation being given the tarnish treatment by some people. The British Board followed their policy of taking the UK Championships round its constituent members by staging the 1981 event in Antrim, near Belfast. It is never a very popular meeting. Coming at the end of May, few athletes want to pitch their racing programme for a peak at that time of the year, yet an event carrying that title deserves good performances. I had planned not to compete in this meeting because, whether it had been at Cwmbran, Crystal Palace or Edinburgh, it did not fit in with my plans. I do not give a long-term commitment to such a meeting because there is always the chance that I may

Indulging in a little crowd control at Crystal Palace. (*George Herringshaw*)

On my way to winning the 400 metres in the 1970 Sussex
Schools Championships in record time.
(*Reg Hook/Sportsview*)

Winning the AAA 800-metres title from Andy Carter (1) at
Crystal Palace in 1974, my first year in the senior division. I
picked up seven places in the last 200 metres, the first time I
had shown such a finishing kick in front of my home crowd.
(*Sporting Pictures*)

The semi-final of the 800 metres in the Montreal Games of 1976. Alberto Juantorena (217), a giant of a Cuban, went on to win the gold medal in world-record time; Ivo Van Damme (103) won the silver; and I was left to wait another four years after trailing fifth. (*George Herringshaw*)

Breaking the UK mile record at the Debenhams Games at Crystal Palace in 1977, thereby becoming the first Briton to beat John Walker (1), the Olympic gold medallist in the 1500 metres at Montreal, over his favourite distance. (*Sport & General; Syndication International*)

```
1500 M MAENNER
ERGEBNIS                    PROGR. S. 76
1   405  OVETT S.     EUR    3:34.50
2   905  WESSINGHA    GER    3:36.00
3   505  STRAUB J.    GDR    3:37.50
4   105  MORCELI A    AFR    3:37.80
5   305  ISHII T.     ASI    3:38.20
6   205  HILL D.      AME    3:39.20
7   805  SCOTT S.     USA    3:44.00
8   605  WALKER J.    OCE    AUFGEG.
00:00.00
```

My second UK record in 1977, this time in the 1500 metres of
the World Cup in Dusseldorf – most significant for the fact that
it came late in the season yet felt remarkably easy. I knew then
that Filbert Bayi's world record was there for the taking.
(*George Herringshaw*)

The 1978 European
Championships in
Prague where the Coe-
Ovett saga all began.
After seeing off front-
runner Seb, I thought I
had done all that was
needed to win the 800
metres – until Olaf
Beyer stunned me, and
the world, by pipping
me to the post.
(*Keystone Press*)

An extraordinary photograph of me winning the 1500 metres.
The extra pair of arms belong to silver-medallist Eamon
Coghlan; Dave Moorcroft (734) won the bronze. (*Popperfoto*)

Above: A typical scene during the build-up to Moscow. (*Syndication International*)

Below left: Running the gauntlet of the media minefield in the Olympic Village, with 'minder' Harry Wilson in the background. (*Popperfoto*)

Below right: 'I.L.Y.' – a simple message which took the media by storm and eventually led to the row with my mother prior to the 1500-metres final. (*Tony Duffy/All Sport*)

Achieving my long-term aim of an Olympic gold medal – but in the wrong event, the 800 metres, when Seb failed against all expectations to make an impression on the event. The simplicity of my victory and the subsequent feeling of anti-climax, the overheating afterwards and my family problems meant that I entered the 1500-metres final in the wrong frame of mind. (*Keystone Press*)

All credit to Seb for having come back from defeat and triumphed, but I believe the real hero of the day was Jurgen Straub (338) who threw everything into beating the last semblance of running out of two tired athletes. (*Tommy Hindley*)

Number 13 – unlucky for S Ovett, but not so for John Treacy as he dips his way to victory in the 5000 metres at Crystal Palace a week after the Moscow Games. Four years later he won the silver medal in his first marathon at the Los Angeles Games. (*Tommy Hindley*)

Koblenz, West Germany, 27 August 1980. Good friend Thomas Wessinghage and I share a word after one of the most competitive races I can recall: in fighting off his challenge, I was completely oblivious to the time and I was stunned when I discovered that I had clipped seven-tenths of a second off the world 1500-metres record. (*Popperfoto*)

Having missed world records by mere fractions of seconds four times during the year, breaking the mile record in Koblenz on 26 August 1981 was a more fitting way to round off my most rewarding season of all. (*Associated Press*)

Another reason why 1981 was a special year for me: the manager of Shelley's hotel, Lewes, welcomes Rachel and me to our wedding reception. (*Evening Argus, Brighton*)

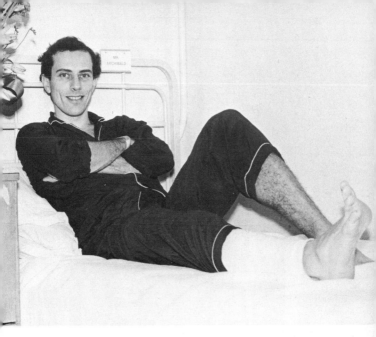

Hospitalised for the first time in my life after my encounter with a church railing in December 1981. (*London Weekend Television*)

Outside Buckingham Palace after receiving the MBE in March 1982 – a day which combined solemnity with hilarity, the latter courtesy of a certain television documentary producer. (*Sporting Pictures*)

Sharing a laugh with Seb during the press conference to announce our three-race 'showdown' in 1982, which failed to materialize due to injury and illness to both of us. (*Syndication International*)

Three men who have played vital roles in my success. *Above left:* Andy Norman, close friend and enlightened AAA administrator, a man who has done more for athletics than any other single individual. (*Tommy Hindley*)

Above right: Matt Paterson, my 'training partner' for the last ten years, whose constant support and sacrifice has been the most important aspect in my preparation for success. (*All Sport*)

Right: Not my 'coach' as such, Harry Wilson has nonetheless shared my athletic ups and downs since 1973. Spiked, and then suffering a recurrence of a leg-muscle pull, Harry was as always the man at hand when I had to drop out of the 800-metres final of the 1983 AAA Championships. (*Tommy Hindley*)

Steve Cram just wins the mile during the Coca Cola meeting at Crystal Palace – it was a tremendous race from start to finish, the sort on which our sport flourishes. (*Sport and General*)

The picturesque Paris Mile at the end of April 1984, a road race that confirmed in my own mind that I was as fit as I possibly could be for the start of the Olympic season. (*Popperfoto*)

Three potential Olympic gold medallists discuss their prospects with Ron Pickering a month before the exodus to Los Angeles. (*George Herringshaw*)

Eager attendants exhorting me to 'Stay down buddy' after my dive for the line in the 800-metres semi final – one of many dramatic Ovett pictures to emerge from Los Angeles. (*Associated Press*)

Above left: Unlocking my seized thumb and forefingers after a race in Los Angeles – just one aspect of the bizarre illness which dogged me during the Games. (*Associated Sports Photography*)

Above right: Seb offers me a helping hand at the end of the 800-metres final ... an hour later I found myself in hospital. (*Tommy Hindley*)

Entering the last lap of one of the greatest Olympic 1500-metres finals ever run. The stage was set for Britain to take all three medals, but the pains returned and I dropped out 50 metres later. (*Steve Powell/All Sport*)

then have to withdraw at the last moment and cause disappointment.

In the week before the Championships, many of the leading entrants, prompted by the decision of the England soccer team not to play in Belfast, withdrew. After watching the nightly news on television of shootings and bombings in Northern Ireland, it was understandable that some people did not want to go and I can imagine that worried relatives had a part to play in their decisions. Mary Peters, who won the Olympic pentathlon at Munich in the 1972 Olympic Games, went on television to appeal to the athletes who had turned down the invitations to change their minds. Anyone could go and pick up a ticket at London airport and fly in, she told her audience.

I knew the other Belfast, the one where you can live and run normally, because I had competed there many times before. At the time of Mary Peters' appeal Matt told me, as he had often done, 'You're going well, you need a race.' We talked about it on the Saturday morning, the first day of the meeting, and I rang Les Jones, the man organising the event in Belfast, to say that I wanted to come over and run. That caused panic because it meant delaying the 1500-metres heats until my arrival. Because of the security problems at Heathrow and my last-minute decision to take part in the event I just missed my plane. I arrived at Antrim with little time for warming up, but won my heat and the final on the following day. My time really was too slow to be of much value, but the reception I and many of the other competitors received showed that we were appreciated. Unfortunately David Shaw, the British Board secretary, chose the occasion to attack me. Apparently he thought that my last-minute dash to Belfast and having my name added to the entry was all premeditated and that, because he had known nothing about it, this was an Ovett snub. A day later he apologized for his outburst.

There are occasions when Andy Norman's planning does not quite carry the certainty which you would expect from a London police sergeant; take for instance Venice in June 1981. After three winning races to open the season I needed something fast on a good track. 'A fast thousand metres on a good track in Venice,' says Andy. 'That's what you need.' I had been to Venice before – not to run – and the idea of revisiting this beautiful city once again was attractive. The meeting promoter was delighted to hear that I wanted to run; perhaps less enthusiastic when Andy said that places would have to be found for a group of British runners who needed the competition – but he agreed. Andy has always used me and other leading athletes as a bargaining stick in this way, and I fully support the idea. One year at an Oslo meeting in which Seb and I were competing, forty other British athletes were on the programme, all getting useful international experience.

To Venice then, with Bob Benn to help out with the pace, for a quick 1000 metres. We arrived on race day in weather that was hot and humid. We stayed on the Lido, tried unsuccessfully to get some sleep in the afternoon and went in the early evening to the track which was on one of the small islands. It was a beautiful evening, still and warm, but the track was black and rubbery, like squashed tyres, and in some places it looked like the hub caps were still on. I turned and looked at Andy and said, 'This isn't a fast track'. He could see my disbelief, looked at the running surface and swung round: 'Who told me that this was fast? Where's Carlo? Carlo told me it was fast.' But Carlo, like someone out of a spaghetti western came up, shrugged the shoulders and said, 'No, it's not fast, Andy. I didn't say it was fast' with all the innocence

he could summon up. Anyway we took it in good humour
and Bob and I went off to warm up together on the side
of the track that was open to a marvellous panoramic
vista of Venice. 'This is better than working,' said Bob,
'and look at that firework display,' he added, pointing to
the flashes in the sky across the lagoon. 'Magnificent.'
We continued with our exercises, trying to psyche one
another up to make sure it was something near fast, but
to be honest we were not being very serious after seeing
the state of the track. Not as serious as Andy, however,
who sidled up and barked out, 'Bob, you've got to go
through in fifty-three.'

'Yes. All right Andy, don't worry,' replied Bob.

'And then' said Andy, oblivious to that roly-poly surface on which we were about to perform, 'you've got to
keep it going hard – hard all the way.'

Bob and I looked at one another with raised eyebrows,
while Andy went off to look after the needs of other
athletes. At that point Bob looked up and said, 'What's
happening? Everyone's leaving.' I turned and saw that
everyone was moving from the terraces – everyone, that
is, except Rachel who was sitting opposite the crown of
the bend. I thought that perhaps there was some sort of
television facility in the main stand and they were all
going off to watch that. I was confused by such a sight
just as we were about to race.

The announcer introduced the runners to the crowd
and then, suddenly, low black clouds came rushing across
the sky and the wind howled in across the water. It
was uncanny, like some biblical scene. I have never
experienced anything like it. I turned my head into the
wind, leaning my body against the force and lowering my
eyes to avoid the dust. And as we waited for the starter
to call us up Andy said, 'You're going to have to push it
hard Bob' – whereupon Bob and I almost broke down

laughing. There was no way anyone was going to push anything in these conditions, it was ridiculous. But more was to come, for hardly had we completed the first lap when those black clouds unleashed their contents; it poured as Bob 'pushed' on, unbelievably trying to respond to the words of Sgt Norman and keeping a sound pace going until the last 200 metres, when I kicked past him and only just managed to hold him off. Astonishingly he managed a personal best, albeit for a distance he did not often run competitively.

Soaking wet, we put on our sopping track suits which were waiting for us on the grass verge and hustled over to the cover of the stand. All I wanted was to get back to the hotel for a shower and a meal, but because of the wild weather the ferries had stopped. We had to wait, cold and shivering, until about one in the morning before the elements calmed and the boats resumed their ferrying. By the time we reached the hotel, the restaurant had understandably closed for the night and Andy found himself with a fairly belligerent group of hungry athletes on the one hand and an unco-operative night porter at the hotel on the other. He then found a small café about to close for the night and by brandishing a large amount of lire managed to persuade the owner to produce sandwiches filled with a variety of meats and cheeses and fifteen cups of coffee.

Next morning we made the long taxi-boat trip to the airport, only to find our flight had been cancelled. So back again we go to our hotel, dump the bags and off for six hours' sightseeing and shopping with Rachel and Bob. When we finally did fly out, after waiting on the runway for an hour, we went via Milan and arrived back in London at one in the morning – the end of a little trip to Venice 'to get in a fast thousand metres'.

A few days after that little episode I went to Oslo for

an attack on the world 1500-metres record. Instead, however, everyone got a laugh and I suffered my first defeat at 1500 metres or a mile since 1975. Tom Byers, an American who had been something of a front runner a few years previously before he suffered injury, was the man selected to do the pacemaking. He went off at what the rest of us, Walker, Scott, Wessinghage and Cram, thought was a suicidal stride. With each lap his lead grew as the pack stayed together. For those watching, it must have looked as though this was some sort of go-slow action by the big boys, but what had happened was that the official calling the lap times was inexplicably giving out Byers' time as we passed the lap point. Probably the official thought he was being helpful, but as far as I was concerned I thought that Byers was running some eight seconds faster and that he was either mad or inspired. By the last lap it had dawned on us that we were not running as fast as we were being told and, because I felt so easy, I too realized something was amiss. I broke at the bell from the pack and chased Byers to no avail all the way down the finishing straight, seeing I think the funny point of it all: 'don't believe all you hear' was the moral of that story. It was of course disappointing because it is such a good track for fast running and record breaking. At that point Seb and I had set five world marks there.

After helping Britain to the European Cup final by winning the 1500 metres in Helsinki, the Coe–Ovett saga took on a new twist. On 7 July Seb ran in Stockholm and recorded 3 minutes 31.95 seconds for 1500 metres, missing my world mark by 59 hundredths of a second. Twenty-four hours later in Milan I ran the same distance and finished with exactly the same time – the chances of that happening must be a million to one. Seb put his failure to break the record down to the fact that there were no lap times called which, after all the preparation, he must have found galling. It is really infuriating when meeting organisers cannot get the basic requirements correct.

In my case I should have slashed the world record down to something in the region of 3 minutes 27/28 seconds. The conditions were perfect in Milan and I had John Walker to pace me through the first two laps. But again my lack of confidence, my disbelief that I was capable of something far beyond most people's comprehension, let me down. It is very easy to sit back and analyse the performances now and wonder about the times achieved and just missed, but when Roger Bannister dipped under four minutes for the mile in 1954, was there anyone suggesting that a clutch of runners would be dipping under 3 minutes 50 seconds thirty years later?

Walker was running to a schedule of 800 metres in 1 minute 54 seconds in the Milan race, but the din of the crowd was so great that – in a similar way to Seb – I could not hear any lap times being called. In fact I thought the whole affair had been 'blown' because it seemed to me that Walker was not running very fast at all. Into the second lap I was shouting 'Go faster John, faster' every dozen yards or so, without realizing that he had in fact gone through 800 metres in the scheduled time. I was so full of running that I thought it must be slower.

As we went into the final lap I detected, by the screams and gesticulations of people on the track side, that I must still be within reach of something. I took off with 300 metres to go and felt strong all the way through to the tape. When I heard the time – 3 minutes 31.95 seconds, 59 hundredths of a second off my world mark – I was disappointed, wrongly, with John. I thought he had not done the job properly, whereas in fact I had misjudged the Master and it was my body mechanisms which were sending the wrong messages.

This race in Milan showed again how many uncovered mysteries to racing there are still. I was probably as fit physically as I had been the year before in Moscow but, without the pressure that Olympic competition brings and all the other personal worries which I carried in 1980, I was, without realizing it, in much better psychological shape. Anyway by that point it meant that I had run four of the fastest 1500-metres times in the world; and three days later back in Oslo I turned in a time of 3 minutes 49.25 seconds, again only 45 hundredths of a second off my record, to give me three of the fastest five times at the mile.

Two weeks later I raced in Budapest at one of the meetings organized by Miklos Nemeth, a man who, like his father, has done much for the sport of athletics in Hungary. Imre Nemeth won the Olympic hammer title in London in 1948 and then became manager of the Nep stadium, Hungary's largest sporting complex. Living in that sort of atmosphere, it was not surprising that Miklos became an athlete, winning the Olympic javelin title at Montreal in 1976.

When I arrived at the Nep stadium the wind was blowing a gale, the flags were stiff from their masts and I was depressed. It is always good to break new ground, to run before a crowd for the first time, but there are only a certain number of peak races in a summer. It is depressing when you travel so far for a world-record attempt and find the weather against you. Andy tried to commiserate and I remember him making the astounding remark for a former 400/800-metres runner, 'Don't worry, it will hold you back down the back straight but push you along the home straight.' I looked at him with incredulity and I think as the words came out he realized it was a senseless, if humorous remark. Miklos was a little more comforting with the local knowledge that the wind dies down there during the evening. There was a crowd of more than 40,000 watching, but in a stadium which holds over 100,000 they looked somewhat lost. They were told that the 1500 metres was going to be delayed for an hour. Still the wind did not drop, so it was put off again and then again at which point Miklos told Andy that if we did not run soon the crowd would go home because there were no more events on the programme.

Eventually we got under way and John Walker did most of the front running, taking it until the last 300 metres. He was fading at that point and I moved away midway down the back straight and still had a lot of running in me at the finish, missing the world record by 21 hundredths of a second. Many people drew the simple conclusion that Ovett missed the record because of a lack of confidence – I should have gone fractionally earlier and a new mark would have been established. But had I moved off from 400 metres, in that final 20 metres I might have slowed even further in those conditions. I was not the only frustrated Briton in the Nep stadium that night. There were, I gathered later, a lot of journalists beating their typewriters in anguish. Every time the race was put back they missed another edition and then my 'failure' only made that night's goulash and wine a little less tasty. Still, even if I had broken the world record they would not have made the front page back home – that was quite rightly devoted entirely to the Royal wedding of Prince Charles and Lady Diana. Rachel did not come to Hungary with me – there was no way she was going to be away from the television on the wedding day.

I knew that Seb had some mile races on his schedule and I was anxious not to leave him with a soft time at which to aim. However my next attempt was in Berlin, three weeks after the Budapest race, and by that time he had trimmed the record to 3 minutes 48.53 seconds in Zurich. Berlin was also not the place for record breaking – it was windy and rained as well, conditions which were no good to me but did help that hardy Scot Allan Wells to overcome the Americans and win the Golden Sprints. By now I was very tired although there were about six races before the end of the season. Fortunately, I was going back to Koblenz, where I had broken the world 1500-metres record the previous year, to a track and people I liked very much. With me went Bob Benn who had paced me in so many of my races.

Bob was another person who played a vital part in my build-up to the Moscow Olympic Games. In some respects he became quite a TV star in athletics as a pacemaker – or, as I dubbed him, 'a born leader of men'. The TV viewer would see Bob at the head of the file of runners in many of my races – he was as far as I am concerned a perfectionist in pacemaking, possessing the uncanny ability to get within a tenth of a second of the time required on each lap. There are those who decry the use of pacemakers but since they have been permitted in the rules a lot of people have run faster because of them – far better I feel in some races than a return to situations my parents told me about at the White City where the field would dawdle round three laps and pour out the speed across the last 300 yards for a winning time well outside four minutes in a mile. While the lack of a pacemaker may inhibit and have an insidious effect on the development of racing, the runner who is paced to a fast time or a record does actually have to run the time with which he is credited. He also gets the feeling of speed and is not frightened by it in championship events.

Bob's perfection of pace is but a small part of his contribution to my success. We had known one another since 1973 and met in many league matches: he ran for

Croydon Harriers, and Brighton and Hove were also in the same Southern League. By 1979 we were close friends and I would go up to Crystal Palace and meet him for training sessions during the week and at the weekends, often staying at his place in Croydon. This was a period of intensive work and Bob saw his opportunity, in training with me, to make a challenge for an Olympic place. When we went to Spain in February 1980 for warm-weather training Bob was in better shape than me. But the difference between us, as between me and a lot of my contemporaries, became apparent when we went on a trip to the United States and Jamaica. Bob was in great shape, yet when it came to the races he could not produce anything much better than 1 minute 50 seconds when, from what I had seen on the training track, he was capable of 1 minute 47 seconds which would have put him into Britain's Olympic team.

When Bob and I arrived in Koblenz the weather was balmy and still and everything was conducive to a fast time. My request to Fredy Schäfer that I would like to run a mile rather than a 1500 metres caused some problems. Fredy was quite willing to go along with the plan, knowing that I felt I could break the record of 3 minutes 48.53 seconds which Seb had set in Zurich seven days previously. Some of the athletes who were due to run the 1500 metres, such as Steve Scott, Mike Boit and Thomas Wessinghage, decided to stick with the 1500 metres but my mile still had a solid-looking field with Dave Moorcroft, Craig Masback, Tom Byers and James Robinson from the USA – and Bob to help with the pacemaking.

My friends from the press cast doubts on the competition before and afterwards because the programme was already printed and the mile did not appear in the list of events. 'Would the International Federation ratify a record?' was the question posed by some reporters on the morning after my success. It could have been a niggling dampener to the whole affair, even though I knew that I had run the event subscribing to all the technical requirements stipulated by the IAAF. I was therefore delighted when John Holt, the Federation secretary, put down this particular Fleet Street red herring by saying that the omission of the event from the programme was a pure technicality: 'The Koblenz meeting was properly conducted and, subject to the German Federation submitting this as a record, I would think that when the IAAF meet in Rome it will be recognized. We would lose all credibility if we disqualified this record.'

Bob provided his usual brand of pace to open up the race. He was in top form, for only a couple of weeks previously he had achieved a personal best of 1 minute 49.5 seconds for the 800 metres. He took us through the first lap in 55/56 seconds with me back in third place behind Robinson. Bob held the pace until close to the end of the second lap, when Robinson, who was the American 800-metres champion at the time, took over and pushed the race through the two-lap point in 1 minute 53.59 seconds with me on his heels. As we turned into the home straight I could feel Robinson was weakening and I moved by into the lead. As I approached the bell I could hear the timekeeper calling above the din 'two fifty, two fifty-one' and I knew that I had to find a final lap of around 57 seconds to break the record.

It was like the Oslo world record again, requiring hard concentration to overcome the tiredness. With the rest of the field drifting far behind, the competitiveness had gone. Having people about you racing for first place brings extra tension, but isolation on the final lap invites complacency and can break the will. As I was stepping on the track for my event, Steve Scott had walked off having just broken the American 1500-metres record, getting precariously close to taking my world record of 3 minutes 31.36 seconds with a time of 3 minutes 31.96 seconds. There was no way Ovett could follow that other than with a world record, and that thought kept me going to the final tape.

Two of the fastest middle-distance performances in history, within minutes of one another, show that Koblenz still holds athletic magic for those who run there and those who watch. In two consecutive years I broke world records on this track, a fact which was commemorated on the third year with the presentation of a beautiful bronze cast of a running spike with the times engraved and a space for the third, which Fredy said with a laugh could be filled in at the end of the meeting. Thus missing the record at Koblenz in 1983 brought greater disappointment than I normally feel over such events.

By way of celebration, and for a rest after the world record in Koblenz, Andy suggested I went to Norway to run for England in what must have been one of the most bizarre matches in the athletics calendar. England and Norway have established their own *entente cordiale* through Andy, who's wife Gard is Norwegian, and Sven Arnie Hansen and Arnie Haukvick, who promote meetings in Oslo. I think that it must have been this trio who cooked up the idea of a match in Ardal; you should get some sort of prize for just reaching the place, let alone running in it.

We went directly from Koblenz to Cologne, flew to Oslo and, then in a small biplane up to one of the Norwegian fjords. That was followed by a three-hour car journey and a four-hour boat trip, then another car journey to Ardal itself, which we reached about six in the evening. I was weary, but content to know we had reached our destination, when one of the officials said, 'This is where you run tomorrow but you are staying in a hotel another hour's drive up in the mountains.' The drive was literally up a mountain: it was rather like a Bond movie and we actually got above the snow line – and this twelve hours after being in the warmth of southern Germany. We finally reached our hotel, solitary and remote on the edge of a lake where apparently they produced aluminium. It had been built by the Germans during the war in a place difficult for the Allies to reach with their bombers; England's athletes managed it – just. I thought 1 minute 47 seconds the next day for 800 metres was a worthy contribution to this special relationship between England and Norway; the team talked about striking a badge with the legend 'I survived Ardal'. And so the trip home.

After an 800 metres two days later at Crystal Palace I recovered the frame of mind needed for a competitive race just in time for the World Cup in Rome. Remembering I ran what was described at the time as the perfect race in this event four years previously in Dusseldorf, I wanted to produce something special. As it turned out, that was necessary to put down a plot engineered by Sydney Maree and Mike Boit, who had decided that the only way to beat Ovett was to burn him off. Maree pushed the pace early on and then Boit, with 600 metres remaining, took it up. I responded and took Boit in the finishing straight with John Walker coming through to take second place. Curiously Maree finished way back in fifth place almost two seconds slower than me.

The Rome meeting had another side to it – a combination of the serious and funny. The International Federation met there to consider changing the rules on amateurism and came out with some fairly far-reaching proposals to enable athletes to benefit financially. One organization which represents many international sportsmen quickly worked out that this would turn a few athletes into very big money earners and stories were written quoting vast amounts of money. I greeted one group of journalists I met at the team hotel with a reasonable rendition of 'Who wants to be a millionaire . . .' Anyway we had apparently all got it wrong because, incredibly, twenty-four hours later the Federation stated that people had misinterpreted the rules and that there would need to be a further look into the situation. A year later in Athens they took the sensible step to ensure that their sport, as well as the individuals who make it attractive, reaped some of the financial benefit which had been generated.

Andy had once again arranged, a long time beforehand, one of those easy up-country meeting events for me two days after the World Cup in Rieti, Italy, but I had to return home to Brighton to deal with some decorating and plumbing problems at the flat I was buying prior to getting married a week later. I sorted that out and then dashed to London airport to catch a plane for Milan and a three-hour car journey to Rieti. I arrived at one in the morning for a race the following afternoon, only to find that Maree was competing – not exactly an 'easy up-country meeting'. In fact I went into the race in the wrong frame of mind. I felt much as I did when running the 1500 metres in the Moscow Games. I had won the World Cup event and that was it; I was in a dip with just a couple of races to finish off the season. However on this occasion I had promised to run and I kept to my word by trying to run hard and win. But it was clear from the outset that I was set up for defeat as pacemakers pulled Maree through. He won in 3 minutes 48.83 seconds. At least though there was something for me from the race – I learned that Rieti is a fast track and the fact was catalogued. I thought that I would go back there soon and try for a world record. But it would have to wait, for after a year with many good quality races, which were in fact a revelation to me, then getting married on 18 September, 1982 was to become a bleak struggle for my athletic survival.

Leaving home at Harrington Villas in the way I did was not one of the best ways to start life with Rachel. We knew we were going to get married long before the traumas and tensions of 1980 and if circumstances had been different we might have lived in a flat close to my parents' home as a start. We were going to live together before we got married – that I believe is the only way to discover whether you are compatible with your partner and certainly in the circumstances of our relationship it was essential. The bliss of those first months together in our rented flat was enhanced after what had gone on before. I had been preparing for the biggest event in my career, travelling constantly up to Crystal Palace to meet Harry and train after one session at Brighton earlier in the day, then going on to Maidstone to see Rachel then back home – some days I was doing four to five hours driving. How I got through this period I sometimes wonder and I know that in the run-up to Moscow I was anxious about it.

We became engaged in a similar approach to my racing programme – instant decision. My watch required a new battery and we called in at a jewellers to have it replaced. Rachel browsed and the net result was that we came out with an engagement ring – the watch is still going and so is the marriage. We decided not to get married until we had bought our own home, so the Ovett training routine was re-mapped round the streets of Brighton to take in every estate agent's office. I knew every one of them . . . and every property they had in their window displays. We just could not find the house we wanted – idealism is

I suppose a fault of the young in love. Finally it was my running, but not round estate agents, which led us to the flat we bought in Adelaide Crescent, Hove. I had some Achilles tendon problem which Bert Parker, my physiotherapist, was treating in his rooms just above the Crescent. He told me that there were several flats for sale in the area and I wandered down the slope and saw the 'For Sale' board. When we stepped inside the hallway we knew it was what we wanted. The flat had not been lived in for years and before that had been neglected, but it was the sort of place to which Rachel could bring her designing talent, with its high, well-proportioned rooms and plenty of wall space for large mirrors and Rachel's montages. In between training and racing in the European Cup and World Cup and preparing for the wedding I became decorator and restorer, working with Sam Lambourn, a marathon-running friend who is in the business.

The work on the flat went well, but then we ran into snags about actually getting married. Rachel wanted the reception at a particular hotel in Lewes because of its beautiful garden, where she could entertain the guests, so we naturally thought we could be married just down the hill at Lewes's registry office. That turned out to be impossible because neither of us were resident in the area or had been born there. So we went back to Brighton. Now I do not want to be unkind to my home town but its registry office is not very attractive. It is one of those places that goes in for plastic flowers – dusty plastic flowers – and we took one look at it and I said, 'No way are we getting married in this sort of place.' It was then I realized that the information we were given in Lewes might help us in our forlorn hope of a quiet wedding. I was after all a property owner in Hove, so off we went to its Town Hall. This is a modern building, which is not

Rachel's style, but inside we found that the rooms were pleasantly laid out. More important to our needs was a very lovely lady registrar who supported the Ovett desire for privacy and quiet up to, if not beyond the call of duty. She recognized me and immediately fell in with our scheme to try and put some limit on the attendance by the world media. By taking out a special licence the banns did not need to go up until forty-eight hours before the wedding. Our lovely lady at Hove discharged her duty, with our interests always apparently in mind, and then had to tell us of her big disappointment – our wedding day was during her holiday and she was unable to marry us, which she obviously so much wanted to do.

We invited seventy people to the reception and naturally enough the news began to leak out after the invitations were delivered. The press got wind of it and were calling at the Maidstone registry office, sniffing the plastic flowers at Brighton and finally getting round to Hove . . . and four days before the big day I began to be followed by a motorcyclist. Everywhere I went, he went and I played a few games with him, like testing his ability as a shadow by pretending that my Porsche was a Formula One car. He was even close on my heels during a training run – Bond could not have done a better job. I never did discover for which newspaper he was working. Rachel and I both knew that on the day there was no way of avoiding the media but we thought we might be able to keep the horde down to a manageable crowd.

We invited my family, but did not get a reply. Then a few days before the event we met Alan and Val Martin, friends of the family who had seen my parents. Apparently my mother and father thought it was a cheek that we had sent the invitation through the post. It was I suppose one interpretation of our action, but in view of the remoteness of our relationship I was hardly going to bowl up to the front door as though nothing had happened in the intervening twelve months. Anyway they said that they were not coming. We put that sadness aside and on the day there were the usual panics and excitements. I went off to Lewes to collect the flowers, Rachel went to her hairdresser and then I picked her up on the way home. There was a sweet touch I thought when she came to pay – her money was declined and instead all the people working there wished us both happiness. I then left Rachel at the flat to get ready with her father and drove off to the registry office with my future mother-in-law and Martin, Rachel's brother . . . with of course 'Barry Sheene' bringing up the rear. After all, he did not want to be given the slip at this, the eleventh hour.

We arrived at the Town Hall and turned into the underground car park and as we did so I could see hundreds of newsmen round the registry office door. I brought the car to a halt, looked up and saw a notice which read, 'Underground walkway to registrar's office'. I looked at Martin and said, 'I don't believe it. This is too much of a gift.' Martin could see what I was thinking, grinned and said, 'Come on, let's do it.' All those waiting newsmen, photographers and TV crews would, quite literally, then be able to report that the elusive Ovett had 'gone to ground'. Rachel's mother, however, brought a sense of responsibility to all this fun. 'No you're not. This is your big day, you're not going to start playing games with this lot now.' She was, I think, not a little furious that her only son-in-law could be so frivolous on such an important occasion. Anyway she led us through the throng to find about thirty or forty of our guests in the reception area.

When Rachel arrived she could not get out of the car. The photographers were pressed up against the door with more behind them so that no one could move. Eventually they moved aside and she came into the registrar's office. I said 'Hallo love, you look lovely,' or something like it, and she walked straight past me into a room and closed the door. There were some remarks like 'She's giving you the cold shoulder already' and I waited for what seemed like an eternity until the door opened again and a woman, who turned out to be the registrar, came out and said, 'Mr Ovett, aren't you coming in.' In all the coming and going I had been overlooked. Calm was restored and I joined my bride, whose hands were shaking, and there was a short ceremony in which our words meant so much.

Andy was my best man, which was fortunate because it needed a police sergeant and a man who knows how to organize an athletic rabble into some order to handle the photographers afterwards. I am glad that we did not know until later that, before Rachel and I arrived and just after the ceremony, there were scuffles and fist-fights as some of the photographers fought for the best vantage points. Andy organized the pictures, pointing out that it was our day and would they not behave like savages. It worked and although as usual the performance went on and on no one got hurt; there were though tears. My parents, dressed extremely casually, did turn up and appear at the back of one of the group pictures, my mother sobbing on my father's shoulder. Then, as everyone prepared to move off to Lewes for the reception, my parents apparently began to walk away. Andy, no longer in the shape he was as a 400/800-metres runner, ran after them and pleaded that they join us. They did, arriving with a formal greeting for me but thankfully a kiss for Rachel. With people like Fredy Schäfer, the promoter at Koblenz, Arnie Haukvick from Oslo, Craig Masback, an American runner and friend, and many of our English friends connected with athletics, and so many people enjoying themselves, some of whom knew the family situation, it must have been an ordeal for my parents.

A few of the photographers followed us to Lewes, but Sgt Norman appealed for privacy: my thanks to Fleet Street for at last giving us some. On reflection, I wish 'Barry Sheene' had turned up for a drink; I was beginning to miss him. We stayed at the reception longer than planned, but finally Rachel tossed her bouquet away (it was caught by Eric Nash of the Southern Counties AAA) and we drove off for the weekend to Eastwell Manor, near Ashford, only to arrive very exhausted to find that Rachel had left her case at Lewes; enter long-suffering brother who thought his sister's whims and wants were no longer his responsibility. We returned to Brighton on the Monday, moved from one flat to another, locked up – leaving the builders and decorators to get the place into shape for us on our return – and went off to Australia.

My racing programme down under in 1981 did not tax me too much. I ran four races in eleven days and finished with four victories. We returned via Singapore with the other British athletes and then said our farewells. I had planned to take my bride to Bali, a beautifully romantic idea until we reached the immigration desk at the airport. The passport official thumbed through our documents and looked up saying, 'Where is your visa?' Worldwide traveller Ovett had not bothered to discover one was needed, so somewhat forlorn we trekked into town in search of the visa office. I found it – and a very long queue – and soon discovered that once the application was made it could take three or four days for the visa to be granted. As I shuffled slowly towards the clerk in the cubby hole I was working out what we might do in Singapore for the three days' wait; at least I had to have some plan to tell the wife. Finally it was my turn to hand over the form. The clerk looked up and recognized me.

'Oh, my boss a big fan of yours, come round, come round and meet him,' he said, sliding off his seat, opening a door at the side and ushering me through. I dared not look back at the long file behind me. The boss was all gushing enthusiasm over my running, had clearly read a lot about me and seen me on television. All very nice, but he could have picked a better moment. I thanked him very much and said that I was just applying for a visa . . . and he pulled out a drawer, found a rubber stamp, smacked it on the form, scrawled a signature, stamped the passports and said, 'That's OK, you go to Bali.'

Bali turned out to be a disappointment. It was commercialized and, after spending a few days avoiding British tourists who seemed to want to do nothing else but buy Steve Ovett a drink at the pool-side bar, we gave up and returned to Brighton.

After Rachel and running, my next love in life must be cars. Through the family business there was always an involvement with cars or vans, which we serviced mostly at home. As a youngster I seemed to spend much of my time watching one of my uncles tinkering with something on four wheels and I just caught the bug. When I was old enough to drive my father bought me a Morris 1000, complete with rust. I think he paid about £110 and 40 dozen eggs, or perhaps a year's supply of chicken – some such barter. From there I graduated to a Mini, a Range Rover, Volvo, Vauxhall, Porsche, Daimler etc, etc. They were all old cars which needed attention. Although I didn't think about it at the time, getting under the bonnet in the family garage at Harrington Villas was exactly the occupational therapy I needed to keep my mind active.

When Ovett turned up at somewhere like Cwmbran stadium in a Porsche, Fleet Street would put two and two together and conclude that I was making a lot of money on the quiet in athletics. What they did not perceive was that I had just completed six months' work on the vehicle and was about to sell it and make the handsome 'profit' of perhaps a thousand pounds. I never thought of it as a business, but it did help supplement the complete support my parents were providing. The fascination grew and for many years my daily reading has been *Classic Car* or *Exchange and Mart*. I am always looking for bargains and at one point at Harrington Villas I had three cars, although my father told me to get rid of at least one because of the space they were taking up. I suppose my turnover in cars must have been fairly prolific both in number and type over the years, but I have never bought a new one – the moment you drive one out of the showroom you have lost money.

On one of my birthdays my father gave me a number plate, SJO 30, which I kept and moved from car to car. By 1981 I thought I might do a little better in the personalized number business and saw an advert in one of the papers for SJO One. I telephoned the dealer and had a long but finally rewarding chat with the salesman. Naturally I did not announce myself, but merely asked him the price. 'Well sir, I'm thinking in the region of £4000 to £5000' – which I pointed out was not my region. But he had other SJO numbers: the single-figure ones, he told me, were very pricey; even the double numbers were not cheap because, according to the voice at the other end of the phone, they are usually linked to a birthday, or a year which has some significance for the owner.

'We have got some three-figure numbers which people don't want so much of course: SJO 373, which would go well on a Volvo, then I've got SJO 800 . . . that's £120.'

The Olympic champion at 800 metres managed to contain his excitement with a drawled out, 'Oh . . . yes all right I'll have that one. It suits me.'

'All right, sir, if you would just give me the details I'll have it sent . . . your name?'

'Ovett.'

'Initial?'

'S.'

'Address?'

'Brighton.'

'You're . . . er . . . you're not that runner?'

'Y . . . e . . . s . . .'

The groaning 'Oh' that whined down the phone at me was the noise of a salesman who had just let something like £500 slip through his fingers. But to give him his due he did not backtrack. I can hardly expect the same sort of luck in finding SJO 1500 – or SOI 500 as it would have to be.

10

A Kind of Break

If you have ever struck your thumb with a hammer when driving a nail into a piece of wood, then multiply that by a hundred times and you will understand how I felt the night in November 1981 when I ran into a church railing during a training session. In that moment of impact, as the pain enveloped my leg and my body began to tremble – in shock I suppose – I thought, 'Oh my God, what have you done? What a waste of all this talent.' It happened not more than 200 yards from my home, a piece of pavement I had pounded innumerable times.

I had recently returned from Australia and was back in training after a late winter break. Sam Lambourn was helping me decorate the flat and at the end of the working day we went off together to be joined by Matt on what was a hard training run. After about seven miles, Matt left us to take his route home and Sam and I made our way downhill towards the flat. We were moving fast and nipped across a zebra crossing over Church Road. We swung round past the church and, because I was running on the outside of Sam, I took a wider course. As I went past the church noticeboard I glimpsed a poster about a carol service; I thought 'That will be nice' and in that moment my concentration lapsed and I failed to see a low iron railing, two-feet high or thereabouts, and my right knee slammed into it hard. It was as though someone had hit me as hard as they could with a hammer. I collapsed in excruciating pain.

Sam, who missed me after a couple of strides, turned back in a bit of a panic and I sent him off to fetch the car.

As I lay there I kept thinking that my career was over: how stupid, what a fool, everything lost in an unthinking moment. I felt sure I had not so much broken the leg as smashed it. I knew I had hit that railing with tremendous impact and when I examined my leg I could see it was all blue and virtually swelling up before my eyes. I lay there thinking of all the waste and how so easily it could have been avoided. Several passers-by came up and, though I could barely speak, I managed to indicate that help was coming. Sam returned, drove the car on to the pavement and I crawled on the good leg into the back seat.

When I reached home Rachel helped me to the bed-room and we sat on the bed and she cried. It was an awful feeling. We talked about what was going to happen to us, the flat, everything in the future. I really felt in those five minutes that my running career had come to an end, just at the time when it was going to be possible for us to base our whole lives on running. It was a desperate situation which I hope will never be repeated. Rachel then went up the road to Bert Parker, my physiotherapist who had helped me in the past. Luckily she caught him just as he was finishing for the day and with Sam's help I managed to get up to his consulting room. Bert reassured me that there were apparently no broken bones. He did all he could with ice packs to reduce the swelling and then strapped it up very tightly. But the next day the swelling had increased.

There was no improvement after a week and Andy almost demanded that I overcome my reluctance and get in touch with Dr Peter Sperryn, one of the British Board's doctors. He in turn sent me to see Dr David Archibald, a surgeon at the West Middlesex Hospital, who told me that an operation would be necessary. While the meeting of the Ovett right knee and the church railing had not been a bone-breaking one, the impact had torn the ligament and muscles to such an extent that the mass of highly developed muscle behind it was pushing through and herniating; it had to be put back and the 'hole' stitched up, which meant the first operation in my life. He suggested that I have it there and then, but I bottled a bit and, with an excuse about not having brought my pyjamas, went off to worry about it before returning the following morning.

The hospital staff could not have been kinder. The nurses cleared out their little side office and made it into a comfortable room for me – all courtesy of the NHS. I was apprehensive, not about the operation itself so much as the ability of the medical team to put me 'out'. After my 'pre-med' failed to bring on the expected drowsiness, I pointed out to one of the nurses that I still felt wide awake. She took my pulse and assured me that a pulse rate of 62 was that of a relaxed patient and everything was all right. I then told her that my normal pulse rate was about 39; that I was therefore in a fairly alert state; and that being the hero I am I would still be wide awake when Dr Archibald came in with the scalpel. No one seemed to share my anxiety about my warnings. I was then given an injection and told to count until I went off to sleep, which at least gave me the opportunity to prove that they were dealing with someone different when it came to anaesthetics. In went the needle and I began to count loudly and firmly, 'One . . . two . . .' – and that is as far as I reached; Muhammad Ali could not have performed a cleaner knock-out job.

If going into unconsciousness had caused me apprehension, coming out of it was a nightmare. In fact, for a few fleeting seconds I thought I had passed over to the Great Beyond for there, in the first blinking moments as I looked towards the end of the bed, were two journalists, John Rodda of *The Guardian* and David Emery of the

Daily Express. The day of retribution for my attitude towards the media had arrived. For a moment, I thought that I was facing some sort of judgement; then I thought I must be having one of those vividly real dreams. Finally I came to realize that they were in fact my first post-operation visitors. In these days of fairly liberal visiting times they had managed, with a little Fleet Street charm, to walk their way through the hospital corridors and invade my privacy. I was still very woozy but I think I treated them politely: Emery just wanted to know when I would be running again – or when I would race Sebastian Coe – but at least Rodda asked me how I felt.

I hit the railing on 7 December, underwent the operation twelve days later and I was home with the leg in plaster on Christmas Eve. But the trouble was not over, for the operation wound became infected and I had to return to hospital. I was unable to walk properly for two months and did not resume training until March.

A misunderstanding which occurred after the operation was typical of the way facts can get distorted by the media. Naturally everyone was wanting to know what Ovett was up to: would he ever run again? Neil Wilson of the *Daily Mail* suddenly had a sensational story when he saw me out training with Matt on the Worthing road, fourteen miles from Brighton, in mid May. I can imagine the Wilson reaction: 'Aha! Ovett must be fit, running all that way from Brighton!' In fact, what had happened was that Matt, training for the London Marathon, was getting fed up during his long runs by himself. I was only doing some gentle jogging at the time and could not cope with Matt's workload, but I would help him along by getting Rachel to drive me out on to the Worthing road so that I could jog with him for four miles to give him some company. When Matt turned back on the long trek to Brighton I jumped in the car beside Rachel saying, 'That's going to cause a stir, Neil Wilson saw me and I know what he'll think – that I've run from the flat on a fourteen-mile stint.'

This led to other newspapers who had missed this 'scoop' sending their reporters to sit in their cars outside my flat. That is something I've always resented. We have sometimes had groups of reporters outside my parents' home in Harrington Villas, Rachel's parents' house in Maidstone and our flat in Brighton for days on end. Opening the front door to go out, there they would be with microphones or television cameras, waiting to get a snatched picture or hoping that I would open my mouth and give them the glib one-line statement that they wanted. Driving home to Brighton on that August afternoon after the European Cup semi-final in 1975 when we decided to shut out the media, we might have thought that we somehow beat them: I quickly learned otherwise. You can put all sorts of barriers between yourself and the media, but you can never win; they are always there. Rarely do the sporting press come in for criticism of their work or even scrutiny. Unlike the athlete, there is no starting line for reporters, no finishing tape: as long as they do a reasonable job in churning out the words, they are guaranteed a pay cheque at the end of the month.

Those silent years were not completely without a word from Ovett. Usually once a year I would give an interview to *Athletics Weekly,* or a similar magazine, which gave me the opportunity to put the record straight on some things. None the less by 1980, and the height of the Coe–Ovett mania in the media, I think I had become immune to anything that was written and said about me. I even provided a butt for humour when I went down to the market and saw some of my father's friends. 'Hallo, here comes the beer-swilling, lazy so-and-so,' they would shout, referring to yet another story which compared me with the decent, academic young gentleman wearing the tie – from Sheffield.

There were many other outrageous things written about me and my family which were damaging, but the process of litigation is hazardous and can be costly. Many times there were just outright fabrications by some journalists who if they could not get Ovett 'quotes' invented them. Many of my friends, particularly, Matt, used to fume about some of the things that were said, urging me to do something about it. Rachel too was at times upset, but I just laughed about the distortions and let them wash off me; I could literally switch off from it all. The worse things became, the more I was aware that some writers were just trying to bait me into an angry response, which was exactly what they needed to stimulate their business. Steve Ovett was merely a pawn in the long-running circulation war in certain parts of Fleet Street, where standards and morality are strained in the course of survival.

The 'gentlemen of the press' are not the only people who have taken advantage of me by presenting a situation in one way and then twisting it for their own benefit. A good illustration of this occurred on the day I returned from the Moscow Games. I drove over to Rachel's home at Maidstone and we went out to dinner with Martin, her brother, and his girlfriend – on me. Rachel picked the restaurant, one which had been recommended to her in Rochester – I do not wish to give it a plug for reasons which will become apparent. We arrived to find it almost empty, took a table and studied the menu. The waiter looked at me curiously, no doubt wondering whether the man before him was indeed the same as the one he had seen on television the night before running in Moscow. He pointed out that they did have specialities of the day and they were on the board up there on the wall . . .

whereupon our eyes moved from the *table d'höte* and *a la carte*. On seeing the board we all fell about laughing, while the waiter looked bewildered. The top speciality was 'Steak Sebastian', with the Olympic rings and a medal depicted alongside. So when the waiter returned I ordered Steak Sebastian.

'How would you like it sir?' – to which of course there was only one reply.

'Well beaten.'

The waiter realized who I was and scuttled off to the kitchen. There was a great commotion, then out came another man – I think he was the chef and owner – who asked if he could take our picture for his album and children. We did not mind of course – until the following day on BBC television's *Nationwide*, Frank Bough produced a snap of the smiling Rachel and Steve in a Rochester restaurant, backed up by a film report from there which had obviously been done that day. The photograph also appeared in the London *Standard*; and we heard from friends later that the picture and the story were stuck in the window of the restaurant. The meal by the way was forgettable.

On another occasion after the Olympic Games, among the many requests to open events and make personal appearances in shops there arrived a letter from a Brighton hi-fi dealer who said his son was interested in athletics and wanted to meet me. Could I come down to the shop on such and such a day? I felt that was no more than a break in a shopping jaunt so I duly turned up, only to find television cameras and interviewers waiting for me – in other words hassle, which I did not want and had no need for. Some people would say that he and the sharp-minded Rochester restaurateur brought me exposure, but frankly I have had all I really want. Both these people gained publicity for themselves and their business and, directly or indirectly, they made money out of it – none of which came to me, or benefited athletics, or went to a charity.

Little incidents like these, and there have been several others, have coloured my attitude and probably made me less outgoing than I would otherwise have been. They make people in my position reticent if not suspicious, a side of me that I find difficult to hide even when I meet honest, genuine people.

A sociological study of Ovett's portrayal by the media before 1980 and after 1981 might give an interesting insight into how Fleet Street works. I did not flick a switch and consciously decide, 'Right, now let's show the world what I am really like.' In early 1980 when I was in Jamaica I gave Adrian Metcalfe an interview after I had run a 1500 metres, for no other reason than I knew Adrian and he had come a long way to film the race. I suppose that was in itself a weakness, in view of the position I had previously taken.

The prime reason for keeping the media at arm's length was to avoid any hindrance with my aim of getting an Olympic gold medal. Having achieved selection and reached Moscow, my family agreed that we would take the opportunity to have a platform to express my views just in case something happened involving me which needed my reply. There had been many times in the past when I had read items or reports about me which were either slanted, biased, distorted or totally wrong, but I always avoided being drawn into the news whirlpool by keeping quiet. Now I thought I could have my say, on my terms, so I took up one of the many approaches made by the papers and gave my views about running and winning in Moscow. There was nothing sensational, nor very revealing about it – but there could have been, had there been something to which I needed to respond. It was a safety valve as far as I was concerned.

After the 800 metres in Moscow there was a clamour for television interviews and since I had achieved my goal I decided that I should say something and again I accepted Adrian Metcalfe's invitation on the understanding that I would not talk about Sebastian Coe. I had never subscribed to the Coe–Ovett mania before the Olympic Games; in every race there are many other competitors and to present a race as a match between two runners was a distortion, even in the trimmed-down Games which took place in Moscow.

Certainly once the commercial possibilities in athletics emerged my approach to the media changed. At the launching of my company OVETT I was freely available to talk to people about athletics and about sportswear; in my links with U-Bix I act in a public relations capacity and that means meeting the media. Complementary to these aspects was the making of a documentary about me by ITV; appearances on *A Question of Sport* for the BBC; and my commentaries on the European Championships and Commonwealth Games in 1982. The response was resounding: 'This is not the Steve Ovett we have been reading about for the past ten years.' Unconsciously I found that I had redressed the balance.

Do not believe for one moment that Ovett presumes to have no warts and pock marks, but by presenting myself in these situations I felt at least that some people might feel that Fleet Street was not always accurate. In the hundreds of letters I received at this time (and I try to reply to every one), the majority were from the over-sixties and under-fives with some very kind remarks. I did not, as some people suggest, go out of my way to be nice, I was just myself. Of course I did enjoy the funny side of it. The bad-guy image which had been created originally was, in fact, sometimes a source of amusement. Rachel and I enjoyed it when people who we met at functions and who did not know me would tread cautiously with 'How do you do Mr Ovett . . .' expecting to get their head bitten off. Finding that I had not bitten their head off, at the end it would be, 'Thanks very much Steve.'

One thing I am still reluctant to do is the person-to-person interview, because I do not think that anyone can encapsulate me (or anyone else for that matter) in a couple of thousand words. I am still very wary about not getting into a situation where I am asked to give views on health foods, duvets, married life, dogs, children and peace; you have to have your wits about you all the time to avoid these sort of traps.

The television documentary that I mentioned earlier arose out of my fascination with the image which the media were consistently presenting of me. My thoughts reached the ears of Adrian Metcalfe, the ITV commentator whom I had known for some time, and he suggested that an in-depth documentary about me would put the record straight. Rachel and I mulled the idea over and agreed and for nine months, between December 1981 and September 1982, we were involved in a film-making operation. Rachel became an expert at producing innumerable cups of tea and coffee . . . while I became increasingly disillusioned with the process of documentary making.

I felt as we progressed that the whole operation lacked control. The crew would turn up and say 'Well, what are you doing today?' and there would be yet another session of Ovett training. What it needed was a man of direction: there seemed to be no planning and far too much waiting around for something to happen. When I think of the money that must have been involved in making the fifty-minute film the mind boggles. And while of course it can only be an opinion, I feel there was a much better programme left on the cutting-room floor. I realize that those involved did not want to create false situations, but considering the time that was spent on it I felt much more should have been achieved. For instance, it might have been better dramatically and visually to have me with disabled children at a school, but I wanted them to reflect my relationship with the youngsters in the club and what I did there on training nights. That is closer to Ovett's life than my few visits to the disabled, yet training and working with the young Phoenix athletes was not shown. I thought too the documentary missed out on the relationship between Rachel and myself. The crews spent hours and hours and in our flat yet there was very little of us filmed together in ordinary domestic situations which, I would have thought, would appeal to ITV viewers.

We did express our dismay at what had been done, or not been done, towards the end of filming and before the programme was shown. I can see from their point of view that having set up the operation it was something of a disaster when I was injured. But they did to a certain extent show the struggle I was making to recover and the final breakdown. A world record or European Championship victory might have been a better ending but injury and illness was a reality. What angered me most though was the fact that ITV decided to show the film in direct opposition to the BBC coverage of the IAC/Coca Cola meeting at Crystal Palace. Using the project as a blatant method of trying to beat down the viewing figures for the Crystal Palace meeting was a commercial abuse which I would have stopped had I had control. To add to my annoyance the film went out late at night, despite the fact that it was of great interest to younger people. Fortunately for them, it was shown again over Christmas. Overall, I was bitterly disappointed about the whole operation, particularly as I had placed the task in the hands of a man who understood the sport and was experienced in television.

Having said all that, there were moments during the making of the documentary when we all had a lot of fun. For a mixture of solemnity and hilarity, 9 March 1982 has to take some beating. It was the day I went to Buckingham Palace to receive my MBE, which for an Olympic champion and world-record breaker still takes a very high position among the Great Moments in My Life. Rachel and I treasure that day for the splendid occasion and magnificence of the ceremony – together with the hilarity which Adrian Metcalfe helped to provide. Receiving the award was a bonus for the documentary makers who were given permission to film me in the courtyard behind the main entrance to the Palace.

Adrian suggested that Rachel and I stayed in town overnight because we had to be at the Palace early. Naturally Rachel wanted to look her best and a drive up from Brighton in the rush hour might well have left a few creases in her finery. We stayed at a hotel just north of Hyde Park and I was up early for a gentle one-hour training run around the park. It was about seven o'clock and the place was quiet. There was the odd jogger or two and I remember passing the Horse Guards in Rotten Row – who later, I believe, turned out to be 'the Palace grapevine'. After breakfast we prepared for the big occasion – I wore the dark suit in which I was married, not morning dress, and Rachel wore a blue linen suit with a navy blue hat. We were naturally excited and I suppose a little animated. I looked out of the window from our fourth-floor room and saw an enormous black Daimler parked outside the front entrance. 'I wonder who that's for,' I said to Rachel, and we mused over whether it was some wealthy Arab staying at the hotel or a diplomat or some other VIP.

Some minutes later the phone rang and it was Adrian asking if we were ready. We went down, met him in the foyer, walked out of the hotel and in a couple of strides he had a hand on the door of this shining black Daimler. My heart sank and I stopped in my tracks.

'No Adrian,' I said, 'I am not getting into that.'

He was astonished, pleading that he had hired it for the day at great cost. I had to explain to him that this was a very important day, a very personal one and I did not want to go over the top. As far as I was concerned I would have walked down Park Lane and Constitution Hill had there not been the risk of the wind upsetting Rachel's hair. So, with a somewhat forlorn Metcalfe, we went in the limousine and I insisted that we park near the Palace, not inside the grounds. Adrian had passes to allow for filming in the courtyard so we all walked across together and then Rachel and I went in through the main door, whereupon guests and recipients were split up.

Once inside you are divided up into groups – knights, CBEs, OBEs and MBEs. I joined my group and of course the first thing I noticed was that most of the other people were very much older than myself. For many it was – after their wedding day – probably the greatest day of their life. There was a great deal of nervousness as we waited in what you would hardly call a room, more a chamber, with exquisite furnishings and paintings. There was small talk in which I seemed to become the centre of attention, because I was the only recognizable face. 'Thank goodness you're with us – you can do the talking,' said one.

After the sort of anxious wait which one associates with a formal job interview, we were taken out in groups of ten to an ante-chamber. There a member of the Palace staff explained in very comforting words what would happen and suggested ways of behaviour: 'Walk forward . . . stop . . . it would be polite to bow to the Queen . . . move forward again . . . she may have a few words with you . . . when your award has been presented, step back, bow and move off to the right where someone will usher you to your seat.' Everyone hung on those words, anxious not to make a mistake. As far as I was concerned, the whole affair was handled with a formal, yet light touch by people who knew exactly what they were doing and how to deal with a lot of nervous yet proud people. If you have the good fortune to receive such an honour, do not worry: they make you feel that this is your special day.

We were left again for half an hour and then came a sort of ten-minute warning. Finally we were walked through endless galleries and chambers, which left me stunned by the magnificence of the paintings, the furnishings and the proportion of the rooms. We came to an ante-chamber – the last waiting place as it were. My name was called and I walked into the ballroom, remembering to stop and bow before the Queen, then walk forward again. Like most people I suppose, I was surprised how small she is. She congratulated me, said how pleased she was to give me the award. I said, 'Thank you, Ma'am.' She then added, 'Oh, you were spotted this morning running round Hyde Park.' All I could say as I caught my breath through the shock 'Oh yes.' 'Yes,' she said, 'news got back to me that you were seen taking a morning jog.' I told her that I had done two laps of the park and that I was a bit tired because I was not in very good shape – which made her laugh. She then asked me if I had got over all my injuries and wished me all the best for the future.

I stepped back, bowed and was ushered away, musing

over how the Queen could have known about my early morning run – then I remembered the Horse Guards. Perhaps one day I will find out for sure who told the Monarch about that run. What amazed me, once I had been ushered to my place at the back of the ballroom, was the way she managed to make every person receiving an award feel it was their day. It was a remarkable performance. Rachel and I met up afterwards walking along one of those corridors and her part of the story completes the picture.

'When Steve and I were parted, the guests were taken in another direction, walking along these magnificent corridors. Most people were in twos or threes, members of families together. I was on my own and felt a bit lonely though I loved the serenity of it amongst all that beauty. We were taken into the ballroom where there was an orchestra in the gallery playing items from *The Sound of Music* and *Mary Poppins*. This seemed a little incongruous, but I suppose it was a counter to the formality of the occasion. When Morecambe and Wise received their awards they played their tune 'Bring me sunshine'. I had a seat right in the front, the perfect place, and I was absolutely in my element looking at the hats, the mirrors, the various people coming in who helped in the ceremony, the Queen's bodyguard in their full regalia. One man's job was to place and remove the kneeler when those receiving knighthoods came forward to kneel and be touched on the shoulder with the sword.

'Before all this we had the procedure explained. "The national anthem will be played when the Queen arrives at eleven o'clock. There will be no clapping and no one may leave." As eleven approached, other people who were involved in the ceremony came in to take their places. Then at eleven, what I thought was a very long mirror parted and there was the Queen – demure and, because she was in such a simple pink dress, the most striking woman in the place, a contrast to all the hats and hairdos in front of her.'

Afterwards we walked out into the courtyard, everyone sharing their own moment with other members of their family, when suddenly the photographers were on us like a pack. Having been part of that wonderfully quiet, dignified world inside the Palace, I was now Steve Ovett the runner again. It was 'Steve, show your medal . . . Steve, kiss Rachel: no, the other cheek . . . Steve, thumbs up . . . Steve, wave; no Steve, someone walked by, let's do it again . . . Steve, one more . . . Steve, look this way; Rachel, look at Steve; Steve, look at Rachel . . .' It went on and on and on. Television cameras moved in, the men behind the mikes asking me what I thought of it.

I was conscious that a lot of other people were watching us and I became acutely embarrassed. All around me were people who had received awards and probably worked all their lives in some job or service; yet here was Ovett, a young runner, getting all the attention. I said 'That's enough' several times and was only glad to break off and pose for mums and dads who wanted a photo with me in it for their family album. Finally we walked out across the courtyard in front of the Palace, pursued still by the 'one more' brigade: 'One with the Palace in the background, Steve; one with the policeman, Steve.' One of the funnier moments in the documentary came when we were running across that wide stretch of road between the Palace and the Victoria Memorial pursued by a photographer, clicking away – at our backs.

We rendezvoused at the discreetly parked limousine and out came a battered, but welcome thermos flask with the coffee, when suddenly we had one of Metcalfe's 'instant' stunts. As we were standing by the car, Adrian leapt out and chased after a jogger who was pounding by on his lunchtime run.

'Excuse me, excuse me,' Adrian called, bringing the poor man to a stop.

'Yes?' replied the runner, a bit breathless and perplexed.

'Do you know, Steve Ovett has just got his MBE?'

'Very nice, what's it got to do with me?'

Whereupon Adrian asked me to jog along the Mall with him – a case of Adrian going overboard. I turned down that gimmick, but Adrian, not beaten yet, said, 'Well, let's have a shot with him.' I turned to the runner and said, 'Sorry, but do you mind?'

The cameras went into action, which immediately brought the news photographers back, and before long this NatWest bank clerk, as he turned out to be, was enjoying the fun of it all and we had our arms round one another. At least he had a tale to tell them back at the bank . . . though I do wonder whether they believed him. Eventually we slipped into the limousine and went off for a champagne lunch to be regaled with Metcalfe stories.

Adrian had not yet wrung every ounce out of the occasion for the documentary, for speeding homeward down the M23 he installed a camera crew next to me and tried to get me to recount the morning's experience and the feelings I had about it. It was though a wonderful day. Rachel had enjoyed herself enormously. With the run in the park, the limousine, the splendour of the Palace, the Queen's words – it was a memorable event.

11

In Step with Seb

The phenomenon of Sebastian Coe and Steve Ovett began for me in the depressing weather conditions of Prague in 1978 at the European Championships. Ever since then, the 'contest' between these two native athletes has consumed the media's attention in a manner that has never been seen before by the British public. It is of course highly unusual to find two sportsmen from the same country and during the same era dominating the same events to such an extent. The Swedes had Gundar Haag and Arne Anderson immediately prior to and during the Second World War, but they did not make the same impact in championships or on the record books as we have done.

Over the past six years, particularly during the period 1978 to 1982, the media were keen to portray the contrasts between the two of us. On the one hand, Seb was projected as the clean-cut young gentleman, the academic who spoke well; on the other hand, there was this vaguely artistic character of less intelligence with rough edges, a natural result of being the son of man whose livelihood came from a market stall. Add to this a concocted long-running 'feud' between the two of them and you have the ideal ingredients to keep Fleet Street fuelled.

The media never missed the opportunity to elaborate and embellish their theories, though I gave them little to go on. Sometimes there were situations that fell into Fleet Street's lap. After I had won the inaugural Golden Mile event in Tokyo in 1978 I declined the invitation to defend my title because the race was going to be staged in Oslo. I felt that with all the middle-distance talent Britain had we should have staged the race in London. I was asked whether in fact I felt that the event in Oslo would be a hollow one without me, to which I replied, 'Yes, I think so.' Subsequently, Seb ran, broke the world record and so my words naturally were rammed in my face.

My family and I could not have guessed back in 1975 that the two greatest middle-distance runners would emerge in Britain but I am glad the Ovetts took the course they did as far as the media were concerned, for in the run-up to the Moscow Games the clamour for interviews was reaching absurd proportions. American and Japanese reporters and television companies wanted my services and seemed nonplussed at my refusal to go along with their conception that they had a right to interview and I had a responsibility to respond. I was ruining their programmes, their articles, by not giving them the material to match up to their Coe–Ovett ideas.

Seb took the opposite view and co-operated although much that was said at the time came from his father, which I supposed eased the burden. But by the time he arrived in Moscow the pressure must have been reaching alarming proportions, an indication of which was a press conference held by him which drew a staggering six hundred pressmen.

While the media have always been quick to point to the differences between us, no one has ever drawn attention to the uncanny parallel of our lives, largely because they were missing some of the facts. The main aspect which strikes me is that Seb has a dominating father, while the strongest influence in my family came from my mother. In both instances, you could argue that their parts in our lives went beyond that of normal parents. Seb's father took a very public part in the affair

– in fact my first memory of Seb is not so much of him but of Peter, this rake-like figure with angular, gaunt face and eyes peering over the top of his glasses, ushering and fussing around Seb in almost the manner Zola Budd suffered when she arrived in Britain in 1984.

Fathers who coach their sons are fairly prolific in athletics, but no one has attended to the needs of the athlete with such constant attention as Peter Coe. He always seemed to be on hand, with spikes and track suit at the ready, before and after races and attending press conferences. That sort of proximity, which you normally associate with ice dancers and their coaches, would embarrass me. I am sure Seb must have suffered from athletic claustrophobia at times, living at home amidst much athletic talk and then continuing the saga on the training track with his father. In my case, while the controlling influence and support came from within my family, particularly in the early days, at least they were divorced from my training. When Seb went to Loughborough University and was helped by George Gandy things must have changed a bit; but still his father's presence was a strong one. The similarities in this area are well illustrated by what happened in Moscow. Between the 800 metres and 1500 metres Seb was castigated, in public, by his father for his performance in what was his prime event; at the same time I had a private row with my mother over Rachel.

In some minds Moscow proved nothing, yet it was uncanny that each athlete had won against all odds the other's prime event. It was understandable that, after we had both taken gold medals and I had then gone on to break the world record at 1500 metres, there should be a worldwide clamour for us to meet the following season. In the eyes of the public it would have been simple for us just to turn up at the same meeting and race, but it was far more complicated than that and I must take a share of the blame for not fulfilling that simplistic understanding of so many people.

I was aware, as was Seb I am sure, that if we did race then a lot of money would be generated – one figure quoted was a quarter million pounds. At the time, none of it would have gone into the Coe and Ovett bank accounts; neither did the laws of the International Federation even allow us to nominate a charity or a good cause – like the AAA or the Southern Counties Coaching Fund or the English Schools AA – organizations that would have made good use of the money for *athletics*. One or two people came to me with suggestions about how the rules might be circumvented, but that was not what I wanted; and I most certainly did not want to run in circumstances that would have allowed agents and television companies, as opposed to athletes and athletics, to have collected the lion's share of the money generated by the contest. I knew that the sport was changing fast, that commercial avenues were opening up for competitors and that rule changes would not be long in coming – so I preferred to wait.

Many people saw the end of amateurism as the beginning of professionalism and that is why the Establishment of athletics resisted change for so long. Amateurism was an English way of life created to protect gentlemen from the artisan. It was there to preserve the class distinctions of another century and is wholly unrelated to the society in which we live today. It was never very honest and 'shamateurism' appeared long before athletes took double air tickets to meetings as a way of benefiting. Over the years, accusations of 'shamateurism' were cast in my direction because I was not working and my parents decided to sacrifice all so that their son could aim for an Olympic gold medal. If that is 'shamamateurism', so too must be the case of somebody like Lord Exeter, who was also provided for by his family thus enabling him to concentrate on athletics and win a gold medal in the 400-metres hurdles in the Olympic Games of 1928. The short-lived professional circus in the seventies, in which people like Kip Keino of Kenya and Britain's David Hemery took part, reinforced the Establishment's resistance to change, although in more enlightened quarters it did serve as a warning of what might happen if the sport did not move with the times.

As very much part of the Coe–Ovett phenomenon I wanted to ensure that the sport as I knew it was preserved; that I and people like myself could benefit from our talent yet still have the fun of running for a club such as Phoenix AC. I have seen other sports tear themselves apart through trying to stick religiously to the amateur principle. In rugby union, for instance, you have the ludicrous situation where a player has only to write a book on the game and be paid for it directly to be dubbed a 'professional'. The consequences are that he is banned from playing and can take no further part in the coaching and administration of the sport – an utter waste of talent. What I, and I believe Seb and others wanted was for us to remain very much part of the present framework of the sport so that we and athletics might *mutually* benefit financially. I could see that shaping after the meeting of the International Federation in Rome in August 1981.

At the meeting the IAAF considered proposals for allowing athletes to earn money through advertising but in a confused debate the majority of the Federation members believed that the income would go to Feder-ations. Alarmed by newspaper reports that this money would go to athletes, the Federation's lawyers combed through their constitution and decided that it required several rule changes to make this permissible. It was not until 12 months later in Athens, just before the European Championships, that the Federation met again to consider new proposals. They must have looked revolutionary to many of the Old Guard, but Andy Norman, speaking as a delegate of the British Amateur Athletic Board, called for an end to the hypocrisy to the double standards and to allow the sport, through its competitors to generate the money that was available. In true Andy style it was forthright and forceful and helped push through the proposals for the setting up of Athletes Funds into which money from advertising and sponsorship would go to be used through trustees by the athlete until he retired and then the remainder, less a percentage which the Federation had taken, would go to the competitor. In addition it was agreed that appearance money could be paid to athletes – through their federation and into his fund – at specified meetings. It was the first sensible step towards the realism of athletics in the eighties.

Back in 1981, one of the outcomes of that confusing meeting in Rome was that athletes could now be represented by agents. Seb already had links through his father with International Management Group, Mark McCormack's organization which represents many of the world's leading sportsmen and sportswomen, and it was natural that they would be acting for Seb in the future. By the end of the season the clamour for Coe and Ovett to meet had become almost a daily conversational topic and it was quite obvious that IMG, in their wish to promote Seb, were also keen to lay on such an event. I had no objections in principle now that changes in the amateur rules were materializing, so discussions took place in the autumn between IMG and representatives of the AAA who acted on my behalf and Seb's.

I had made it known before an approach was even made that I did not want to join IMG. If I had joined this particular company they would have been in a position to exert a strong control over the sport. Whether it was them or one of the other commercial organizations involved in sports promotion, with Coe and Ovett on their books they could have put undue pressure on British and international governing bodies, dictated to meeting organizers, even used us if they wished as a lever to get other athletes to join them. I am not suggesting that this was or is the motive of IMG, but it was a possibility and I was not prepared to take the risk. By having the AAA conduct negotiations, I felt it gave the governing body an opportunity to become involved with a commercial organization in a way that was likely to be a blueprint for the future. The end result of the discussion was an agreement that Seb and I would race each other three times in 1982. The money accruing from the races would go into a training fund from which Seb and I could benefit until we retired. After that the fund would be used to provide training grants for others, Seb and I acting as two of several trustees.

The announcement of the three-race series was made in May 1982. Rachel and I went up to London and stayed overnight in a hotel near Hyde Park and on the morning of the press conference I went for a run in the park . . . and there, in the same part of that very large park, was Sheffield's world-record holder. It was yet another of those uncanny situations in which some unseen magnet seems to be at work on Coe and Ovett. In June 1981, within twenty-four hours of each other, we both ran the 1500 metres in exactly the same time, to the hundredth of a second. Seb in Stockholm and me in Milan – incredible. Later that year we had broken the mile record three times in the space of nine days. Now, in Hyde Park, we found ourselves running together for the first time since our contests in the Olympic Stadium at Moscow. Here were two men who were supposed to hate each other's guts, passing joggers and office workers who looked on in disbelief. We ran for a while, both staggered by the coincidence, wondering what a photograph of us together in that situation could have been worth in Fleet Street. Seb asked me how married life was; I wanted to know what he was doing at Loughborough. Then we went off . . . to appear smart and clean for the press conference.

The reality compared with all the hopes and prognostications which came from that press conference was bleak. In addition to looking forward to the three-race series – 3000 metres at Crystal Palace on 17 July, 800 metres in Nice on 14 August and the mile in Eugene, Oregon, on 25 September – Seb and I were both intending to win gold medals in the European Championships and the Commonwealth Games. After the vacuum following the Moscow Games it suddenly seemed that the summer and autumn of 1982 would be full of races between Coe and Ovett; but it was not to be.

Whatever you may feel in training there is only one place to test your fitness and that is through competition. You cannot hide from that; a race is a race is a race. But if you cannot actually hide it is possible, even for someone like Ovett and Coe, to draw the curtain a bit. I chose the Southern Championships – always, I feel, staged too early in the season – the heats of which at Crystal Palace on the evening of 20 June followed a rather dismal match between Britain and the German Democratic Republic. The run restored my confidence and really confirmed all that I had learned from training which was that I was getting myself fit for the European Championships and Commonwealth Games, the build-up to which included two of the three races against Seb.

Having lost so much time through my injury I was trying

to sandwich about five months' work and competition into two. Six days after the Crystal Palace meeting I ran at the Bislett Stadium, Oslo, in a 3000 metres and was beaten by Tanzania's Suleiman Nyambui, who lives in the United States and benefits from the collegiate system there. It was just the sort of run I needed. I wasn't quite sharp enough to hold Suleiman in the final 300 metres, but my time of 7 minutes 43.87 seconds was the fastest by a British runner for four years. There was a good class 2000 metres in Budapest three days later but the wind ruined any chance of a fast time, so a week later I found myself back in Oslo racing the same distance again. Although you will not find 2000-metres races in international and championship programmes, it is a useful distance to run because it tells an athlete something about his form and straddles the move from longer distance work to the speed I would need for 800 metres and 1500 metres. Remember, I had to turn out a lively 3000 metres at Crystal Palace on 14 July in one of the so-called Coe–Ovett clashes. So the Oslo 2000 metres provided another boost to my morale when I beat Thomas Wessinghage, who was in fact later to win the European 5000-metres title. Thomas tried to shake me off with a lap to go; not only did I hold him but I also managed to recall the feeling of what sprinting meant by passing him on the final 150 metres. It felt good and the time of 4 minutes 57.71 seconds was a British record.

I felt so good that I asked Andy if he could get me into the Paris meeting two nights later. He arranged it and Rachel and I were joined by Maurie Plant, one of my Australian friends, on a smooth flight to Paris; it was the last thing to go right for the next three days. The idea was to have a little spending spree, a good restaurant that night and shopping for Rachel, after she had called in at her Paris agent's office to collect £800 they owed her. She had not heard from them for a while and when she went round to their office she discovered why; they were bankrupt – end of shopping spree. Paris was warm and the reception for the athletes on the evening before the meeting was a barbecue in which the victuals comprised bread, wine, spicy sausages and lamb. One of the sausages I ate, or perhaps all of them, was to have an untimely effect on the Ovett racing career.

I went for a jog the following morning and returned from it ominously pink and very very hot. I was sweating profusely, which ought to have been a warning sign that something was wrong. We went to the stadium early and sat in the shade of some trees, watching Mary Decker break the world mile record and Mel Lattany win a sprint. Then I started to warm up and immediately felt a need for liquid. Maurie managed to get me some lemonade, which quenched the dryness, and I remember feeling very strong as I went to the starting line. But within 200 metres there was a sharp pain in the pit of my stomach. I continued, thinking that it was only nerves, but I was mistaken. The pacemaker had dashed off but I was not really keeping up with the pack. As I was running down the home straight for the third lap the pain was intense and I thought that I might do more harm continuing, so for the first time in my life I dropped out of a race. I ran on to the infield and bent forward, which immediately started the stomach muscles cramping. I put my hands on my knees and it became worse and I dropped on to all fours. I vaguely remember people around me helping: Andy trying to get medical services; someone massaging my stomach (Pat Connolly, the coach of the American sprinter Evelyn Ashford); someone else draping their track suit over me (Jacek Wszola, Poland's Montreal Olympic high-jump champion). I became cold and shivery and was finally taken away on a stretcher and off to hospital in a police car because the ambulance did not arrive. I remember thinking that it might be a burst appendix and that would be the end of my running again, for some time. But after lots of questions at the hospital, and some medicine to ease the pain, I was allowed back to the hotel.

In the morning I felt fully recovered and rather embarrassed about all the fuss the incident had caused. I later found out that the poor media had got into a bit of a state about it. The first Coe–Ovett race, due in a few days' time, had already lost Coe because of shin soreness which kept him out of training and competition; now they thought it might also have lost Ovett. There were, however, more important things on my mind that morning in Paris. All the others contracted laryngitis (and there is no more pitiful sight than Walker without his voice), and Maurie, had stayed behind to ensure that I was all right. Like several other athletes, he had had some travellers' cheques stolen from his room while he was at the meeting. Worse was to come – an air strike, so we could not get a flight back to London. We hired a car and made a mad dash for Dieppe. Unfortunately, whoever was navigating gave Maurie, the driver, the wrong directions and we took the road to Bordeaux, which is, if you look at a map of France, roughly ninety degrees out. The time we lost in that detour was costly because we arrived at Dieppe just after the last ferry had departed at 11.00 P.M. We decided to spend our last few francs on a meal and a half bottle of wine between three and wait for the ferry, which departed soon after 3.00 A.M. The dawn at Newhaven was welcome – until we discovered that British Rail also had a strike. As it was too early to call out friends from Brighton, we started trundling into the town to find somewhere which would take a credit card for breakfast. Fortunately, a man driving a caravanette, who I might say did not recognize me, stopped and gave us a lift back to Brighton. Overall, the Paris trip was an experience I could have done without.

I rested for a couple of days, but as is usual did not bother to have a check-up to make sure that the Paris bug had left me. The 3000 metres at Crystal Palace on Friday created by entrepreneurs for Coe and Ovett, without the former and with only a little contribution from the latter, did none the less turn out to be a magnificent race, one of the best seen in Britain, with Dave Moorcroft breaking the European record and beating Sydney Maree, John Walker and yours truly.

My hopes of defending the European 1500-metres title and then going on to Brisbane to compete for the first time in the Commonwealth Games finally came to a painful halt one cool August evening at Withdean Stadium. Two weeks before I was due to go to Athens for the European Championships I decided to put my body to a severe test in a 500-metres time-trial. Coming round the last bend my left hamstring tore, sending me leaping in the air with pain. After pulling myself into some sort of shape following the confrontation with the church railing then having stomach problems in the Paris race, my body finally rebelled and I ran into an athletic brick wall. It was a sickening blow, showing me that my body was still not properly balanced for the top-class racing programme ahead. It was depressing, but not nearly so depressing as I suspect many people may have thought. Obviously I was disappointed at missing the events in Athens and Brisbane but to me there are always other races, other events and I knew that a torn hamstring would mend.

Andy came to see me and told me not to sit on my backside. I was going to be busy working for my company OVETT which I had planned to do when I came back from

Australia. With a technique he used frequently, Andy saved the real purpose of his visit until he was almost on his way out. He had been approached by the BBC who had asked if I would do some commentary work for them from the London studio during the European Champion-ships and Commonwealth Games. In effect, what they wanted was me to watch what the viewers were seeing and add my comments and opinions to the descriptions which the team in the stadium was providing. I did not immediately jump at the idea because I knew that such a task is extremely demanding. I was also worried that after a couple of days my lack of expertise might come through in the form of repetition. After mulling it over for a bit I told Andy that I would do it.

I enjoyed the role because I like working with people who know their job and do it well. I admired the professionalism of Frank Bough and Desmond Lynam, with whom I worked in the London studio. Watching them at close quarters, their reaction under all kinds of pressure and their care for detail impressed me. For the European Championships I would be in the studio soon after lunch and go through heats that had been recorded. They seemed surprised that I could forecast who was going to do what in which heat, but having run against many of the athletes, or watched them compete, you do get to know roughly what is going to happen. For exam-ple, runners who do not have a sprint finish are bound to run a fast early pace in their heat because that is the only way they are going to qualify. I soon settled into the pattern of making a quick comment in the middle of David Coleman's race description. 'You've got fifteen seconds from now, Steve,' the producer would say into my earpiece, and when I had had my say back we would go to Athens and David's commentary. If there was not too much excitement going on during the race I would use the time to point out certain things like the duties of officials on the infield, judges who were stationed round the track looking for infringements. They are the people I have to keep an eye on; if I'm using my elbow to fend someone off, I have to make sure they're not looking or that I take their name and send the cheque in the post if they are!

I dealt with some of the field events, such as the triple jump and the javelin, which of course is not really my area, but the one event in which the watching millions became aware of Ovett's fallibility was the 800-metres final; trust Seb to drop me in it.

After his early season shin soreness, Seb had marked his return to the track a few weeks before the Championships under the disguise of a 'demonstration' at a Loughborough coaching course which the National Director of Coaching, Frank Dick, managed to turn into a race; complete with appropriate, graded timekeepers. By the time he got to the Championships he was looking good and we were naturally covering this race, one of the major events of the Championships, live from Athens. In the run up to the race I was asked who was going to win and of course said: 'There is no doubt that Coe will win it. He is the best in the world, he's alone and if you look back in his heats he was the only man to cruise through, while others were having to race. The evidence is there, there can be no doubt about it . . . He is a class apart.' My words were subsequently used in a news bulletin, for reasons that will become obvious.

Coleman commentated on the entire race and Frank and I just sat back in the studio and watched. We had a few moments of Peter Coe before the start – 'We are quietly confident,' he said – and then the gun went and they were off. Wishing that I was out there racing too, I began to drift into a sort of wistfulness and felt really depressed when they passed the bell in 52 seconds. It was just the sort of first-lap pace that would have left me with all the sprinting power I needed to get rid of my rivals round the final bend. Seb then hit the front and I felt, 'Well there it is, it's all over.' Suddenly, like a thing possessed, Hans Peter Werner of West Germany broke from the pack and caught up with Seb with over 40 metres remaining to race. There was still time for Seb to find another gear, but he had nothing left; meanwhile Coleman was going berserk, reflecting the shock which must have been hitting millions of viewers.

Thinking about my pre-race prediction I then began to wake up. 'What have I said?' were the words going through my mind as I started to smile to myself – a smile that was picked up by the studio camera and which half the nation took as a somewhat ungracious attitude towards Seb being beaten. It was very easy to translate it that way and that is just what one of the Fleet Street papers did the next day, showing a picture of Seb being beaten with an insert of me smiling. I think I was still blinking at one of the biggest sporting upsets for years when Coleman asked from Athens, 'Well Steve, what do you think?' My response probably reflected the feelings of millions of others: 'I am absolutely flabbergasted. I don't know really what to say,' which I suppose for a television commentator is the last thing you should say. 'As far as I'm concerned Seb can run seconds faster than this. His running in the semi-finals has shown that he is in the shape to run much faster. After all he ran 1 minute 43 seconds in the world-record relay run at Crystal Palace. It is just inexplicable. Something is wrong.' At least I got one forecast right that day, because Seb withdrew from the 1500 metres and returned quietly to London to have tests at Charing Cross Hospital. He was eventually diagnosed as suffering from 'low-level glandular fever'.

The Commonwealth Games was harder work. Starting a programme at 6.30 A.M. seemed grim enough, but then I found out that some days they needed me there at 4 A.M. to watch races that had been taped earlier in the night. After the breakfast programme I would be back in the studio sometimes twice during the day, so I earned every penny of the money that went into my trust fund. Again, I enjoyed the experience of working with the likes of Bough, Coleman and Ron Pickering. They are constantly criticized by people but their unbounding enthusiasm for what they are doing amazed me. Throughout the programmes I tried to be honest, saying exactly what I thought, and no one tried to interfere. I had hundreds of complimentary letters about my part in the two programmes, and there were even letters from old-age pensioners saying that they had begrudged the licence fee until I came along!

My commentary experiences for the BBC; being involved with the making of the television documentary; settling down to married life with Rachel; launching my own company . . . all of these kept my mind occupied in a year which had promised so much on the track yet came to so little. That none of the Coe–Ovett 'clashes' took place was surely a timely warning that athletes are only human and that the sport must not rely solely upon 'staged' events such as these to generate the income to support its many ventures. The fact that Seb and I did not meet did not, I believe, do anyone any harm; rather the reverse. The fascination, the question mark over who would win meant that the focus worldwide on British athletics was maintained. Had we raced several times after Moscow, that interest might well have faded. As it turned out, the next time we were to race each other was in the Los Angeles Olympics . . . and by then there were others such as Steve Cram on the scene.

12

Another Personal Best

The year of 1983 began with another nightmare of injury and ended with a world record. While hitting the church railing had been painful and well reported, the setback of 1983 was hardly less damaging to my running in the short term. In January I developed a pain in the right knee and had some physiotherapy treatment. It did not help; in fact I could not run for more than half a mile before the pain became excruciating. I tried to keep fit by doing exercises involving stretching. I did press-ups, squats, sit-ups, sprints on the spot – intensive stuff which, unbeknown to me, led the people in the flat below to conclude that either we had a tremendous sexual appetite or I was decorating furiously. I had kept the injury to myself as much as I could because early on I did not think it was very serious; then, as time dragged on, I did not want to give the impression of crying 'wolf' all the time. But the pain did not stop and the weeks were beginning to slip by, so I went to several doctors until finally one told me the cause of the injury: the alteration of the balance in one knee, caused by the operation, was being compensated for in the other and the knee cap had moved and was rubbing against ligaments.

The doctor said that a cortisone injection might be necessary, but tried remedial treatment first. I was keeping fit but still doing no training for racing and suddenly I realized that we were just coming up to the World Cross Country Championships – mid-March – and I had not started preparing for summer. If something drastic did not occur then I could see that I would have to call a halt and forget about the season altogether. The doctor could see my predicament and understood that either by stopping for a long period, or by having a cortisone injection which went wrong, I could miss the season. We opted for the injection and hoped that we had made the best choice. Even the Ovett streak of fear about needles and injections ebbed away; I screamed blue murder when the deed was performed but after the soreness wore off I tried some gentle running, tried it again the next day and for the first time in ten weeks the pain had gone completely. It was magic, as though someone had waved a wand. My first reaction was anger at myself – I had wasted all this time when I might have had the injection of cortisone immediately and been back in training so much earlier. That reaction though did not fully take account of the fact that there was a risk and it was better to try the other long-term treatment first. There followed an intensive training period, working three times a day and taking two trips to Portugal to get the benefit of warmer weather. It was a reasonable job of patching up but you really cannot rush the business of getting racing fit and my reward did not come until almost the end of the summer in Rieti.

I am a market boy at heart and there are many times when I find it difficult to believe that what is happening, is happening to me. The beginning of my international season was almost a disaster, yet I tend to remember the better side to it. Sitting outside a café in the square of the ancient Italian town of Udine in the middle of June, letting the Gelati slide down slowly (was that the cause of tomorrow's problems?), watching the most spectacular fireworks display I have ever seen, the dark night sky just filled with sound and everchanging colour – who could ask for better? We count our good fortune and savour and appreciate moments like that evening in Udine.

When disaster comes I accept it, almost as a way of paying for the good times. On this occasion, it was the quick-change act to Italy which meant so much.

I had returned to a chilly England from training in Portugal, felt in reasonably good shape and decided to get in a fast 800 metres to drive home to the selectors that I wanted to tackle that event as well as the 1500 metres in the World Championships in Helsinki in mid-August. I telephoned Andy to find out where I could race; Andy suggested the Italian meeting, which was being staged in connection with Udine's 1000th anniversary – hence the fireworks. We flew to Venice and were driven the eighty miles inland to the north east. The day of the race, Sunday 12 June, was extremely hot and the event was in the afternoon. I wanted a run out in the morning and spotted from my bedroom window what appeared to be the only green patch in the town, a walled-in football pitch with one tiny stand. John Robson, a Scot who was also running in the meeting, and I found our way into the ground and began to do some striding and exercises. No sooner had we started than a frowning groundsman came rushing over, gesticulating that we should not be there. We pleaded for another five minutes but he shook his head in disagreement. We carried on until suddenly over a crackly loudspeaker came rousing music and out across the pitch two teams. Then I saw there were about fifty people in the stand and I realized we were interfering with Udine's Match of the Day. We retired quietly. After lunch we went off in a bus to the stadium and arrived at this magnificent arena, capable of holding 60,000 people – Udine are in the higher echelons of the Italian soccer world. There were about 10,000 spectators in the stadium. By now it was baking hot and neither Robson, Paul Forbes, (another Scot who was to race in my event), nor myself had thought about packing drinks with our running gear.

I warmed up with Paul who had run 1 minute 46 seconds a few days before in Rome and was keen to get down to 1 minute 45 seconds. I was looking forward to a good run, but being the first race of the year I was not quite sure what was going to happen. As we went to the starting line all I knew of the pre-race planning was that an Italian runner would take the field through the first lap in about 52 seconds, comfortable enough for my requirements. The gun sounded and as I went round the first bend I felt terrible – I knew it was one of my red-face days when I seem to overheat. Nothing was flowing, nothing was moving right. I thought 'I'm in terrible trouble here. I'm going to have to dig deep' and reaching the bell I heard an official calling, 'fifty three, fifty-four'. I was off the pace by about five yards and in third place. Down the back straight I concentrated on the job, rather than on what had gone wrong, and closed the gap on the Italian leader. Coming off the final bend I kicked, or what I thought was a kick – looking at the TV replay later, it was nothing more than a desperate attempt to get in front. I won the race but only by the skin of my teeth in a sluggish 1 minute 47.8 seconds.

As I pulled on my track suit, thinking how glad I was it was over, I saw Paul bent double on the track. He was complaining of feeling unwell, and all I could say in consolation was that I had not felt very happy either. Later, John Robson suffered in similar fashion and dropped out of the 5000 metres after only three laps. Looking back I think it was a case of not paying attention to detail and forgetting that, in switching from one climate to another, we ought to have been taking more fluid. There was nothing to drink for the competitors at the track and after the long journey back to the hotel we had to wait for the post-meeting reception at which of course wine was the main drink. By then, I think the three of us had become dehydrated.

I returned to England feeling very tired but I kept the training going and decided to simulate four races in two days by running both events for which I had entered in the Southern Counties Championships the following weekend. I had to run the 800-metres and 1500-metres heats on the Friday evening and both went well – there was only about an hour between the two but it was a smooth, satisfying run in both instances. Rachel and I stayed at a small hotel in Hendon not far from Copthall Stadium where the meeting was held and after a good night's sleep I felt ready for the two finals. The day was probably the warmest we had had at home so far that year, but I paid particular attention to my warm-up. I went into the 800 metres feeling comfortable and with no signs at all of a Udine 'hangover'.

The first lap was untidy, a lot of bumping and pushing. I was spiked and I realized that I was being pushed around, which I normally avoid – I fend off people who come within my space yet for some reason I was not doing it. Thus into the final back straight someone went berserk and took off, thus putting some space around me. I eased up a gear, comfortably ready to touch the accelerator round the final top bend. Instead, as I made my effort – 'Bang', a shooting pain up my backside as though someone had stuck a needle into me. My immediate thought was 'Oh no, a bloody hamstring' – the pain was severe and although I didn't really know what it was I thought it must be something serious. I slipped quickly on to the inside of the track and was immediately overcome with a feeling of annoyance and then depression that something had gone wrong again. All that work . . . and now this.

Harry Wilson was the first to come over to me. I told him that I did not know what was wrong but I thought it was a pulled muscle. I took his handkerchief and dipped it in the cold water of the steeplechase water-jump and made a compress for the area where the pain was hitting me. Then I said to Harry, 'Let's get out of here before the world's press is on my back' – I could see them homing in from all points because the Hendon track is not the sort of place where they are contained in a press box. We went back to the dressing rooms to discover that not only was there no physiotherapist at the meeting but there was also not even a St John ambulance representative: a very black mark for the Southern Counties who do so much good for the sport. Harry rubbed the painful area at the top of my leg and it began to ease, making me think that it was, after all, only cramp. In fact that was what I wanted it to be because all those in the crowded dressing room – Harry, Andy and Eric Nash of the Southern Counties – were saying in varying degrees that I should pull out of the 1500-metres final. However, I was determined to run – and if it was a pulled muscle I would soon know because it would get worse.

I went out on to the grass area behind the stand with Harry who watched me striding out and going through a warm-up for the race. It felt alright, just a little sore, and I went ahead and ran. The race turned out to be an altogether gentler exercise than the 800 metres. Surprisingly, no one wanted to take the race out and put pressure on the one-legged Ovett, so I just took it gently and kicked on the final straight, not on a bend which requires a different technique because the body is not so well balanced. My time was 3 minutes 46.5 seconds but that was of no consequence: I had run safely and won. All those people who had tried to stop me racing because they thought I had pulled a muscle were wrong – or so I thought. The soreness subsided after a few days and I considered further diagnosis and treatment unnecessary.

After the Southern Counties near-disaster and my form in Italy I really needed to get the feel of good running, without encountering too much pressure. That I thought would be provided by a 1000-metres race, in which Garry Cook and Peter Elliott were running, at the Tarmac Games in Edinburgh on 26 June. As soon as we were off, into the first bend, I felt good. The movement was flowing nicely: I was a little behind the leaders, whipping out a fast pace, but I was completely in touch with the running. Then, yet again, disaster struck. As we went into the second bend, there was some bumping up in front of me and someone stumbled and went down. My next stride was going to finish with the spikes of my running shoe planted somewhere in his body – that flashed through my mind and I instinctively kept my leg going through the air a lot longer than it would normally have done and I managed to miss him. It was weird because everything seemed to go into slow motion with my concentration on the race broken. I turned to see that the runner who had fallen, Geoff Turnbull, was alright and as I did so someone else came over the top and hit the track with such a crunch that I thought he must have done some damage. By this time, without realizing it, I had stopped with my back to the way I should be running. I helped Geoff to his feet, turned and started running again, moving quite well, knowing that I was out of the race but determined to use the event in some way. Having given the leaders at least four seconds I made up a lot of ground to finish fourth. The fact that I ran the final 200 metres in 26.4 seconds pleased me, but really it amounted to another frustration, another wasted day. The World Championships were creeping up, selection day was drawing closer and I did not have the qualifying times.

Three days later I went to Oslo for a race and achieved 3 minutes 33.81 seconds, inside the necessary qualifying standard for the World Championships but not without controversy. To get that time I had to push my way through a wall of runners. In doing so I knocked into Ray Flynn of Ireland; he in turn lost his balance and knocked over Jose Abascal of Spain, who landed on his face. Some journalists accused me of being responsible for the incident, but I was not. This was not just another Bislett Stadium time trial. Jose Gonzales, the Spaniard who had just beaten Seb Coe in Paris, was out for my scalp and I am sure the Spaniards were working for my downfall. The early pace was lively with the 800-metres mark being passed by the leader, Mark Fricker of America, in 1 minute 53 seconds. It was in the back straight for the last time that I think I let my concentration slip and a couple of people passed me; that is how the wall formed ahead. I was running strongly as we reached the home straight and realized that the men ahead of me were slowing down as I was starting my kick. The result was a collision of bodies but I did not knock the Spaniard over, I just brushed Ray Flynn. It was my first serious 1500-metres race of the year and I needed to win it in order to qualify for Helsinki; both were achieved.

After a run over 1500 metres for England at Birmingham, I became embroiled in another controversy when the newspapers tried to turn Steve Cram and myself into enemies over a meeting at Hengelo in Holland in the run-up to Helsinki. Following my injuries I was desperate for races. Anyone who understands the sport would appreciate that if I were going to race over 800 metres and 1500 metres in the World Championships I needed competition at the longer distance first, before some sharpening work for the 800 metres. I knew too that I had to run the latter distance before the selectors at the

AAA Championships and my only way to guarantee being chosen was to win that title. There was the opportunity to race at Hengelo where there were likely to be good conditions.

I asked Andy to make the arrangements and he pointed out that Cram was in the 1500. I told him that my need was a 1500-metres race; I did not have time to worry about Cram and if he was in the race that was alright by me. The promoter thought heaven had sent him a package because I indicated that I needed a fast race and he turned that into a headline for his local paper: 'Cram versus Ovett in World Record Bid'. When Steve heard about it he was I think a bit upset and moved to the 800 metres, which did not worry me one way or the other. I do not think it was fair to call him 'chicken' as some people did. He was preparing for the World Championships his way and that did not include a contest with Ovett; had I been in better shape I might have taken a similar view. There was though never any malicious intent on my part to kick anyone out of a race. After all that, it was windy and the pacemakers were a couple of jokers so no one benefited – except perhaps the media who contrived three or four days of stories out of it and justified their expense accounts to Holland. After a first lap in 52 seconds I switched off and won in 3 minutes 38.96 seconds.

A packed Crystal Palace, a glorious summer evening – thousands of athletes would have jumped at the chance of running; but on this occasion (the Talbot Games on 15 July, three days after the Hengelo meeting) I have never wanted to turn my back on the track as much as I did then. Yet I knew that I had to run.

I was down to take part in a 1000 metres and there was a fleet of cars going up from Brighton with Phoenix Club members. Joyce Bigg was taking her three boys and a couple of other youngsters in their Rancho, and one of them was due to drive back with me because Joyce's husband, John, was joining the family from work in London and there would not have been enough room in their vehicle. Rachel and I left on time in the late afternoon with Rachel doing the driving. As we reached Bolney there was a queue of cars crawling along and I knew there must have been some kind of accident. When we got over the brow of a hill I could see a coach pulled in with lots of children on board; then, amidst glass and metal, I saw the Bigg's white vehicle – I knew the registration number – an absolute write-off. As we drew closer, sickened at the sight, Rachel pulled the car over and I jumped out to find an ambulance with three of the boys inside wrapped in blankets. Someone said they were badly shaken but not badly hurt; I could not see Joyce and I dared not ask. I wandered about looking for her amidst the other cars involved and then I saw her walking towards me. She urged me to get back on the road to Crystal Palace to be in time for my race, the last thing I wanted to do at that moment. She and the boys implored me and one of them, the least badly shocked, joined us for the rest of the journey.

Joyce told me exactly where she was due to meet John and when we arrived I saw him sitting on the grassy verge at the back of the main stand looking through the programme and clearly anticipating the night's sport. I told him what I had seen and heard, assuring him that his family were not badly hurt but that he should go down to the accident site and then on to the hospital. He took my car and eventually found his wife and boys back at home with no more than cuts and bruises and shock. As he told me later, it was a weird feeling for him to watch the meeting on television after having been at the stadium and bought the programme. I found it extremely difficult to concentrate on my part of the meeting, at that point not knowing the outcome of the accident, yet I had to run because if I had missed the race the Bigg boys would have believed it was their fault. It was an unpleasant experience, but thankfully no one that I knew was badly hurt. The accident was caused by an overtaking car coming from the opposite direction failing to get back on its side of the road in time. The driver was drunk.

Nine days later in this incident-packed year the Ovett career was brought to another juddering halt. This time it was at the AAA Championships during the 800 metres in what was my final touch, I believed, to winning a place at that distance at the World Championships. In the final I suffered two injuries, one bringing on the other. It was a slow, rough-run race and towards the end of the first lap someone's shoe came down on mine, a spike went through my upper and into my foot. Momentarily I was 'pinned' to the track and the rhythm and cadence of my movement was broken. Instead of going forward my body went up in the air, jarring the leg and stretching the muscles beyond their natural tension. I could feel the blood flowing from the wound in my foot and down the back straight I moved out to kick for home. As I did so the pain struck where it had hit me in the Southern Counties race five weeks earlier – right in the buttock. It was not as bad, but there was that same feeling of cramping up so I stopped and stepped off the track. The spiking, with all the blood, looked dramatic but I knew that was not very much to worry about; but the 'cramp' was a concern. It was soon after, lying face down on the physiotherapist's couch beneath the Crystal Palace stand, that I learned the truth from Helen Bristow, one of the AAA physios, and Dr David Archibald. It was not cramp that I had suffered from in the Southern Counties meeting but a pulled muscle. The pain that I had now was coming from the damaged muscle, which had not healed properly and of course had not been treated.

My attitude towards injuries and seeking treatment can be no help to those who wish to set up sophisticated medical arrangements for competitors. Up to the point when I ran into the church railings in 1981 I had been seriously ill or injured only a couple of times in my whole career and the last thing I want to do is go to a doctor. My attitude has brought me arguments with Rachel, Harry, Andy and others close to me, but I do not think I will change – I certainly have no intention of doing so. There are hundreds of athletes like me who will run on with injury until they drop. I suppose in all of us there is that deep-down worry that a doctor might start probing about and find something else wrong. Anyway in this instance Dr Archibald sent me to Bert Parker, my physiotherapist, and he cleared up the trouble – yes, after asking me why I had not gone to him in the first place – within a week. The immediate consequence of my injury was that the selectors omitted me from the 800 metres and so denied me the opportunity of becoming the first British athlete to achieve a double victory at the World Championships. Rarely have events in athletics upset me as much as that decision, a decision which showed that our system of selection is wrong – a subject I discuss further in chapter thirteen. The selectors were fully aware of my position from two people – Frank Dick and Andy Norman. But it was clear from the reaction of the women's associations on the committee that they regarded Andy as pushing for 'his friend'. If they had set aside the personal aspects of the matter and looked at the facts it was difficult to leave me out.

I had of course been injured, then there had been problems with the leg-muscle pull, not properly detected.

But at the AAA Championships, just before team selection, they had seen me run 1 minute 46 seconds in a heat easing down; they had seen me injured in the final but knew from their own doctor that the matter could clear up quickly. They knew too that I have a record of doubling up and using the 800 metres as a run for the 1500 metres. In 1978 I took the silver in the shorter event and the gold in the longer at the European Championships where I was Britain's only winner, and in 1980 my warm-up went so well that I won the Olympic title at 800 metres. In choosing Garry Cook for the event in the World Championships they completely overlooked that he does not train for a three-race event in the way Seb and I do; Cook is a one-off race man. I know the people who voted against my selection and I conclude their action to be vindictive. Being omitted left me depressed, a state further compounded when Coe dropped out too late for me to be included, although new countries in the Championships, by way of encouragement, were allowed to nominate competitors at the last moment; alongside this dispensation the Olympic champion could not take a vacant place.

After all my setbacks, I went into the first World Championships in Helsinki apprehensive and very depressed. My training sessions up to the Championships indicated that not all was well and that compounded psychological problems. I was worried about my state of fitness and when I arrived in Helsinki I gave a press conference in my hotel and saw, I thought, a few looks of disbelief when I said that I was not absolutely fit. That was confirmed in my first-round race. I really had to struggle to qualify, finishing in second place in a very slow time. I thought at the time, 'That was really hard.' Breathing was a problem, I felt headachy, the whole performance was a real labour of work rather than being enjoyable and I do not like running like that. If it had been during the middle of the season in a race of less significance I would have called a halt there and then and taken a month's break to find out what was really wrong. But that of course was not possible. After a day's rest I felt a little better and in the semi-final I faced Steve Cram and just eased round the top bend and qualified. It felt much easier, my confidence was lifted, and I thought that if this was the sort of improvement I could produce then maybe it was races I needed.

In the final I did feel a lot better, but unfortunately I ran like an absolute fool. I found myself in situations which I would normally avoid and doing things that I would not otherwise do in racing. Looking back, I think I was worried about the fact that I was not fit enough for such an event. Added to that, perhaps because I had been in two Olympic Games and won a gold medal, I did not approach this new event in the same frame of mind as many of my rivals. The Americans, for instance, regarded it as the most important event in their calendar for seven years, which it was since they missed the Games in Moscow; others held the view, which I did not share, that the World Athletic Championships would soon overtake the Olympic Games in importance. Yet to me it was just another concoction by the IAAF – for British athletes at least there is the Olympic Games, World Cup, European Cup, European Championships, Commonwealth Games and now, without any of the others being dropped, a World Championships. I found it difficult to attach to it the importance which perhaps I should.

Lacking the urgency of purpose which I would otherwise have brought to a major event, and concerned about my fitness, I went into the final worrying more about how I was going to feel rather than what was going on around me. I was concentrating on myself rather than the opposition. When the break occurred – Cram followed Said Aouita with a lap to go – I was thinking about saving energy and moving on to the inside. I was trapped anyway, which I should not have been, by a wall of runners and there was no way of going round the outside. With 300 metres remaining I was waiting for a gap to open up, but with everyone running fast that was not going to happen. Meanwhile the real contenders were getting away. I kept to the inside track and when there was a clear space I accelerated and tried to get through on the inside lane, something which, just as on a motorway in Britain, you should not do. I came alongside Jan Kubista of Czechoslovakia going very fast and he moved to his left and hit me – it was my fault – and being big and heavy he knocked me on to the infield. I stepped back on the track and ran round him thinking that this was one of the most bizarre races in which I had ever run. I began to make up ground but it was clear to me that I had made an absolute mess of things and I was out of the hunt. I really lost that race a long way before the last lap started, but there was no excuse for getting into the position of being so badly trapped.

I was not particularly disappointed by the outcome of the race, a sure indication that I was not in the sort of racing shape needed for an important event such as this. The fact that I ran so badly in the final yet still finished fourth provided a certain consolation: Sydney Maree, Tom Byers and Graham Williamson failed to get into the final; Seb did not start, and here I was running a very poor race indeed missing a medal by one place.

The depression of Helsinki evaporated within a few days of returning to Brighton and I quickly regained my form. Without being called up for duty in the European Cup at Crystal Palace I had a longer break from racing than I anticipated, but I knew that I was ready for something special when I went to Oslo for a mile event on 23 August. Sydney Maree, who had also run badly in the World Championships, was there to find his form again so it was a competitive event. I knew as the first lap unfolded that I was back to record-breaking form – the sense of well being was marvellous. We passed the 800-metres mark in 1 minute 54 seconds and I felt as though I was just strolling behind Sydney as we went into the final lap. Down the back straight I took off with the smooth acceleration which I had not felt for a long time. My winning time of 3 minutes 50.49 seconds convinced me that I could break the world mile record, or my own for 1500 metres. In fact I was so convinced about it as I ran down the home straight that I looked up at the press box and lifted a finger to alert them. I think it took some of them aback that within minutes of finishing I found my way up to their working area and announced that I was going to Koblenz the following week to break a world record. I have never done that before, because I have been careful about not letting people down, but that night in Oslo I felt utterly confident. Perhaps it had something to do with all the setbacks of the year.

Before I arrived in Koblenz seven days later, Sydney lowered my 1500-metres record from 3 minutes 31.36 seconds to 3 minutes 31.24 seconds in Cologne. I reached Koblenz in good fettle, feeling that my announcement in Oslo was not overoptimistic. It had certainly surprised me, after having beaten Sydney there by 20 metres, that he should be able to take my record. But all that feeling of well being, heightened by being back on the track where I had broken two world marks and being with old friends, plummeted in the first lap. Pat Scammell of Australia, who had done such a good pacemaking job at Crystal Palace a few days previously, inexplicably took the field through the first lap in 58 seconds: all chances of a world record had gone. I buried some of my frustrations in a last lap of under 55 seconds, but a time of 3 minutes 32.95 seconds, which looked alright to many people, was certainly not what I wanted.

My athletic frustrations never last long. I can be an angry man of the track, but it only lasts about an hour and in a place like Koblenz with people I like my annoyance at missing the world record did not last. I then asked Andy when and where I could get back my 'property' and the alternatives were the Coca Cola meeting at Crystal Palace or a meeting at Rieti in Italy. The first had all the attendant English weather risks and the second meant a day's journey, much of it on windy roads, with the memory of defeat there by Maree in 1981. I chose the latter. Although we tried to make special travel arrangements, there were delays and we ended up arriving at one in the morning – not, I felt, the best way to prepare for a world-record attempt.

The following morning I got up and went for a jog with Rachel, did some striding and then went back to bed for another sleep. We were driven to the stadium and it was a lovely day – except that it was blowing a gale. Rachel looked at me, could see my depression and was close to tears: everything had gone wrong in Koblenz, then I lost the record and now this. I went on to the infield with Andy, who had travelled with us, and was treated to one of the classic Norman remarks, which I collect: 'It's funny, you know. Although it's blowing you don't feel it.'

At least that changed my mood and started a laugh. 'Andy,' I said, 'you may not feel it walking around – but try running and you'll feel it.' That remark of Andy's comes back to me every time I see a clip of the race: while I am running down the home straight you can see in the background the ornamental palms around the prize podium being bent over by the wind.

Andy told me that David Mack, the American who had agreed to do the early pacemaking, was still prepared to take the race out. I tried to go along with Andy's optimism but I felt it was hopeless. He started to talk about the Coca Cola meeting: 'Perhaps the weather will be right . . . and what's happening with your meeting in Germany with Thomas . . .' He was referring to a race I was to run in Engleheim, Thomas Wessinghage's home town – it was doing a friend a good turn and no more; it would certainly not be a world-record attempt.

The wind had not eased very much by the time I lined up for my event, which was not just a record attempt – there was racing to be done as well with Pierre Delize of Switzerland, Jose Abascal of Spain, and Louis Gonzales of France. We set off with David taking it hard down the back straight and even behind him I could feel much of the wind's force. He quickened the race out of the wind and we went through the first lap in a nippy 54 seconds. Up against that 'wall' again he plugged it hard and we reached two laps in the very fast time of 1 minute 51/52 seconds. Then, not surprisingly, he began to weaken. As we came to the end of the straight – and the end of the wind tunnel – I moved ahead on the inside and strode out round the bend into that comfortable home straight. Then came that tough grinding stretch, but as I turned into the wind for the last time I heard the time as I finished the third lap: 2 minutes 49 seconds.

That was fast and it lifted my spirits. But the wind was fierce and I was digging in hard at every stride, thinking 'Just the end of this straight and it'll be all right . . . keep digging, keep digging.' As I turned at the 200-metres mark it was like closing the door against the cold. I felt good. I was running well and I was getting it going right through the line, oblivious to what had happened to the opposition. As I stopped my instant thought was 'What a shame about the wind' and then I turned to see the crowd jumping up and down. (This was in complete contrast to the actual race when they were so subdued that I could hear the announcer giving the details about the 400 metres. It had been odd, but I suppose it was because no one had been encouraged to think that a world-record attempt was possible in this gale.) Then suddenly Sandro Giovanelli came screaming up to me, picked me up, gave me a kiss and yelled 'You've done it. You've done it.'

I turned and saw the electronic scoreboard – 3 minutes 30.77 seconds – and really couldn't believe it. Andy came over and could see I was a bit bemused. I knew that I was fit enough and ready to take the record, but in those conditions I thought it was beyond my reach, even when I passed the three-lap mark in such a fast time. Being buffeted down the back straight and then having a marvellous sense of well-being running to the finishing line, your judgement can become blurred and it took me some moments to put together the fact that I had actually achieved it. Italian euphoria then followed but I sought out Andy to ensure that I could undergo a dope test, which is now required for all world records. That took a couple of hours while I kept filling myself with drinks and talking to the only British journalists there to watch the event, David Emery of the *Daily Express* (that man at the end of my bed) and Vic Robbie of the *Daily Mirror*. They seemed taken aback that I was going to race in the mile at the Coca Cola meeting against Steve Cram. After my run in Germany a couple of days later I went home very weary and took a day's rest before the meeting at Crystal Palace.

Steve took over in the North East of England, on Tyneside, where Brendan Foster left off. I watched his progress from the year of the Moscow Games, where he and Graham Williamson were forced into that ridiculous sudden-death race behind me when I set a world record in Oslo. His success in 1982, in the European Championships, the Commonwealth Games and the World Championships of 1983 was gained, not only because he did everything right, but because of a lack of commitment by other people. Without Seb, and with me less than a hundred per cent at Helsinki, I think he realized his good fortune. After his world title he ran an 800 metres in Oslo in 1 minute 43 seconds and a 1500 metres in Brussels in 3 minutes 31 seconds, then took a rest prior to the Coca Cola meeting.

The mile was one of the best and most satisfying races I have run – definitely my number-two performance of the season even though I was beaten. It was a tremendous race from start to finish. Maybe if I had made my effort a little earlier there might have been a different result; maybe I should have anticipated earlier that Steve was going to weaken in the last few strides. It does not really matter because it was such an exhilarating race in which to take part. I was not in the shape I would have wanted, but that doesn't matter: I was beaten by the better man on the night. If we can produce a few more races like that mile the followers of the sport will be happy – it is the sort of competition on which our sport flourishes.

13

Sergeant Norman's Law

My biggest problem with Andy Norman, as far as this book is concerned, has been how to describe him, what in fact to call him. Over the years since that abrasive encounter on the patio of the Rome hotel in 1974 he has been many things to me – adviser, coach, financial assistant, bag carrier, minder, air ticket supplier, best man, counsellor. But above all he has been one of my very best friends – Andy.

As in my Rome experience, he does often seem to leave a bad impression with people after first meetings. I always remember introducing Rachel to him and later, driving home in the car, asking her opinion of the man and getting the reply, 'I do not like the man and I never will like the man.' My wife is not alone in changing her mind about Andy. Many officials resented this rough-diamond upstart when he turned his skill and energy to the administration of athletics. Even his first contact with the Minister of Sport, Neil Macfarlane, ended in a blazing row in the Commonwealth Games Village in Brisbane; but the Minister revised his views on the man like so many other people who have come to realize that Andy has done more for the sport of athletics in the last decade than most people achieve in a life time. He is the architect who redesigned and shaped the sport – in Britain and to a certain extent internationally – to fit more closely with the present-day needs.

I find it uncanny that Seb Coe should arrive on the scene to join Steve Ovett; surely it is serendipity too in the manner that Andy came into the sport with

administrative ideas to match the quality of our performances in the ensuing years. As a sportsman he still had
plenty of active years ahead when he ruptured his Achilles
tendons playing basketball in his early thirties. That injury
brought a dramatic change in his life so he directed his
physical and mental energies to galvanizing the sport into
a new shape – surely a case of 'Cometh the Hour,
Cometh the Man'. At the time when Britain had a sudden
resurgence of talent, here was the man to ensure that
talent flourished and developed.

Unlike many people, whose services have been recognized with various awards, he has no title, no letters after
his name, but in my opinion he has done an immense
amount for the sport in a vast number of areas. There
has been in the past criticism in athletics that too many
people wear too many hats; Andy is guilty of that but
to good effect. Promoting Metropolitan Police events,
running a Southern Counties team, organizing coaching
for British competitors abroad, taking athletes to overseas
meetings, obtaining the best possible fixtures at the International Calendar Congress, finding the sponsors, not
only for matches but for individual athletes, and spelling
out the realistic worth of athletics in television terms –
Andy has done all these and much more. He is also the
man responsible for taking athletics to such a healthy
financial position that if it chooses it could now be
independent of government support. With that sort of
future the sport should be reorganized so that people
like Andy will not have to take on board too many
responsibilities, which would inhibit the more valuable
aspect of his work in dealing with policy and the financial
structure already created.

From the early seventies he, more than anyone, understood the benefits yet appreciated the dangers which
commercialism and the move away from amateurism

was having on athletics. Through his close contact with athletes at all levels he understood changing attitudes: the grateful, touching-forelock era towards the administrators, sustained I believe by people such as Lord Exeter, Harold Abrahams and Jack Crump who were running the sport in the post-war years, was fading. The pre-war order of things which carried on into the fifties was not really acceptable to young people living in the more materialistic world of the seventies. It seemed incongruous to many – and I was among them in my early years – that a packed stadium, a sponsor and television could generate so much money, yet the competitors were often regarded as second-class citizens. It was as though they were the supporting cast to the stars of officialdom, being given the minimum of expenses and little or no support individually to help them progress. I was extremely fortunate in my circumstances, having the support of my family and excellent training facilities close to my home. But there have been hundreds of stories of budding young prospects having to travel many miles to train and unable to afford the petrol money. Somewhere between the old order of 'Take it or leave it and be grateful that we are allowing you to run' and making our athletes soft is a sensible approach and Andy has, I believe, bridged that gap more than anyone else in Britain.

He was in fact one of those instrumental in pushing through the changes at the IAAF conference in Athens in 1982 in a blatantly provocative speech. He warned that if the national governing bodies continued to shut their eyes to under-the-counter illegal payments and inflated expenses, then some promoter or entrepreneur would come along and offer the alternative of a professional circuit. He clearly upset many of the representatives at the Congress and caused a dilemma among the Eastern

European countries, who are of course against any structure linked with capitalist ideas. But he convinced the majority that he was merely trying to rid athletics of its anomalies and hypocrises. He knew what athletes wanted, and how it was obtainable.

Andy has always been very conscious of the fact that administration is only the working arm for the athlete. Perhaps because of the complex administrative framework of athletics in Britain, too many officials have become immersed in administration and have lost the vital link with the competitor. There have been many mistakes in the way sponsors, in particular, have been treated, where promises about events and competitions were given without taking cognizance of the athlete or his programme. However as Andy assumes more responsibility, particularly in the international field, one of his failings has emerged – his inability to delegate, born of the mistrust of other people's capabilities. The net result could be the materialization of one of his greatest fears, that he too will lose touch with the feelings and needs of the athletes.

There have been in the past far too many half-truths, 'misunderstandings' between the administrators of athletics and sponsors and the long list of companies which have come and gone from athletics to other sports is evidence of it. Andy, however, understands the requirements of sponsors. If a sponsor puts thousands of pounds into a meeting it wants something for its money – the days of patronage are long gone and if the rules of the sport cannot provide a sponsor with the exposure of its name or product, then either the rules should be changed or the sponsor should be told. The sport is after all dependent upon sponsorship to survive; and Andy, who is always looking ahead to see the way in which the sport is moving and how best to develop its growth, is partly responsible for turning the recent success of our athletes into money and goodwill – or, as they say, the bottom line.

Many people feel that he is abrasive but I have always felt that he is a straightforward, honest person who gets down to the basics quickly to eliminate misunderstandings. Perhaps these are a reflection of the fact that he earns his living as a desk sergeant at a police station. There he has to deal with a multitude of different situations in which he has to take decisions quickly, acting sometimes with compassion and sympathy and at others with a tough firmness. I think his abrasiveness comes down to no more than honesty in a sport that is full of inflated egos; he tells you in straight words how bad you are as well as how good you are.

Sergeant Norman has been greatly involved in many areas of my success. Over the years he has got me into the right sort of races at different periods during the season; he has helped build my confidence; and now with the changes over the last few years in the amateur rules we discuss business situations which affect both the sport and my personal life. Since I do not have an organization like IMG managing me and there are obviously people and organizations who wish to contact me, they usually find their way via the AAA to Andy who knows almost exactly what is happening in my racing life and my situation outside athletics. As a friend he does not try to do the 'hard sell' which is the job of an agent, acting instead as an intermediary where business and other opportunities come along. As there is no contract between us I can always say 'No'. He acts in this capacity not only for me but also for many other athletes. His involvement with the AAA administration means that when companies and other organizations approach the association for the services of athletes or the sport in general, Andy is the key link between both sides.

When the IAAF changed their rules on amateurism so that it was possible for athletes to have commercial links, through advertising and representation, I, together with a few other athletes in Britain, received approaches. Seb, whose father already had an association with IMG, joined them and subsequently appeared in a commercial on television for Horlicks and was advised and guided by them in other areas. I was never actually approached by an agent but several firms wanted my services and at a meeting with representatives of U-Bix Copiers I agreed to act in a Public Relations capacity for them on a consultancy basis. For them it was a natural link with their increasing involvement in the sponsorship of athletics although I made it clear from the outset that their sponsorship of meetings was no guarantee of my appearance. In fact in the first two years I missed meetings under their sponsorship through injury; and, to my obvious embarrassment, I missed their major venture, the European Cup at Crystal Palace in 1983, because I was not selected!

My work for U-Bix involves attending many of their functions – management meetings, seminars, trade fairs and the like – to promote their product, but at the same time I promote athletics because they are one of the major sponsors. While it is not part of my job description I can and do advise both sides on how to get the best return from their partnership. While the AAA have their committee structure and U-Bix have their PR organizations to promote their name through the sport, there are many times when I can play the role, in a minor key, of trouble shooter, helping to avoid difficult situations and taking the steam out of others. I think it could be a crucial role for leading athletes in the future. It would seem a bonus for companies involved in the sponsorship of the sport to 'adopt' a leading competitor who can be of value to them not only through advertising, or in the PR role I play with U-Bix, but also as a go-between from association to company in the area of sponsorship. While some officials might think this is cutting across the democratic processes, I would regard it as merely a positive extension of commercial involvement in athletics.

I was also approached by a number of sports goods clothing manufacturers with ideas about endorsing their products. That would have been alright for a few years until I faded from the limelight. What I preferred was having a part of a new small company, which bears my name. We design and market sportswear clothes, particularly running gear, with the aim of fulfilling the sort of practical requirements I know runners want. We do not subscribe to the fashion changes which the big manufacturers have adopted. Sportswear selling is a jungle and a considerable challenge. One day I will be able to take more of the responsibility of meeting that challenge than I am able to at present. I am the company's chief 'test pilot'. Rachel is a working partner in the business, bringing her expertise from the world of clothes as a model with ideas about materials and colours.

Someone once said that Andy Norman does not suffer fools lightly, which unhappily he does because in the sport of athletics he is surrounded by people who neither understand nor have the time to really appreciate the changing mechanics of the sport. There are too many people in the sport who attend the committee meetings, are party to the decisions, but do not then go away and do the work. Andy cannot be away from the *work* of athletics. You will not see him in the VIP box at a major

Crystal Palace meeting – somewhere he has a job to do. When the England team manager (which is one of his jobs) visits Phoenix AC at Brighton (he is an Honorary Life member) he will be standing in the finishing tunnel taking down the numbers. His attitude there is no different to when he sits down with the Mark McCormack management, or NBC television who wants to beam an AAA Championships race to the States – it is a job of work.

Andy's work – and that of other more enlightened administrators – would be made considerably easier if some of the anachronisms in our sport were abolished once and for all. I am not the first person to utter the plea for 'one person and one organization'. That would be the ideal situation for the administration of British athletics. I realize that we are not going to achieve the ideal but we can go a long way towards it. The Great Britain team, or the United Kingdom team – whatever it may be called – should be selected by one person who is identifiable and accountable and who will stand or fall by results. The selectors serve on the British Amateur Athletic Board as administrators and selection is a very small part of their task. In my estimation, it should be no part of their role; selection should be left to if not one person, then to a group of no more than three, which should include a professional such as Frank Dick, the Director of Coaching, a man who is constantly involved with international athletics and athletes and has an understanding of what athletes have been doing and how that will relate to what they can achieve in the near future.

The present system of selection dates back to a time when the British Amateur Athletic Board was a necessity since the International Amateur Athletic Federation, the world governing body, required affiliations from one political entity. So did the Olympic Games – you had to have a British team in the Games; it was not possible, because of the rules, to have teams from Northern Ireland, Scotland, Wales as well as England. At the moment a committee of eight (ratified by a council of sixteen), drawn from the men's and women's associations of the four areas of the United Kingdom, decide who or who should not go to the Olympic Games, World Championships and international matches. But what can the women's associations of England, Scotland, Wales and Northern Ireland know about Steve Ovett or Dave Moorcroft or Sebastian Coe? Apart from Marea Hartman I do not think I have met any of them; and none of them know what I am doing as far as training or competition is concerned.

The Women's AAA has shown over a long period a reluctance to have anything to do with the men, resisting a merger of associations and the sharing of a Championships, yet they still send people along to the committee meeting which decides which men, as well as women, are to be selected. They wiped me out of the 1983 World Championships 800 metres because of an accident which occurred in the AAA Championships, when I was spiked and pulled up with muscle trouble. In spite of the arguments of the English representatives, who knew what I had done and of what I was capable – I did after all win an 'Olympic title at the distance, suffered a bad injury and then recovered from it – the combined voting power of the rest put me out. Fortunately I have not suffered very often from this system but many have and it is time it was changed. The trouble is that, as with so many other bits and pieces of the administration of athletics, people in committees are not just going to wind themselves up. No one is going to vote themselves out of office.

Selection should not be a matter of bartering between

the representatives of Scotland and Wales, or Northern Ireland and Scotland, or England and Scotland, to get their athletes in the team; it should never be a matter of balance between the countries or the associations. It can only be a question of choosing those people who will do well in the event for which they are being selected. It is not simple. It is often complicated and demands an appreciation of training, coaching and racing programmes, which, with respect, the eight or the sixteen may not possess. They are responsible for areas of administration within the Board and within their own associations which cannot possibly leave them all with the time to deal with the vast amount of detail required in assessing competitors for the events which make up a full Championship programme. It is therefore understandable that when it comes to selection, those selectors apart from the English are fighting for their own native representation in the British team; England may provide ninety per cent of the UK team so the Scots and the Welsh and the Northern Irish have to push for their people to maintain their credibility.

We have to realize that in the space of ten years athletics has grown to a very high position in national sport ratings. Attendances at Crystal Palace meetings have been at capacity when people like Sebastian Coe, myself and other leading runners are competing. The stands have not been full when Great Britain meets Sweden or the East Germans or some other country; people are interested in watching the personalities, not the teams.

The administrators are aware of it, but some are reluctant to recognize it. Fortunately the Amateur Athletic Association, the oldest governing body in Britain, seems to be moving with the times and they have a much better consultative arrangement with the athletes than

anyone else. Even now the British Board selects Great
Britain teams for away fixtures, which have no right to be
called Great Britain because they are full of third- and
fourth-string competitors. Athletes no longer want those
matches when there is plenty of alternative competition.
The AAA have their England fixture list and the Board
have their Great Britain matches and the result is a tug of
war for the services of the competitors which does the
sport no good.

The idea that one person can select an athletic team of
seventy might sound revolutionary but it is not. Seventy-
five per cent of the teams select themselves. There is the
evidence of time, distance or height which can be used
sensibly – or as in the case of the committee system can
just baffle. Without personal knowledge of the athletes
selectors I know tend to rely on the evidence of the
statistician; if someone has run 10.41, 10.45 and 10.46,
then he must be better than Charlie Bloggs who won in
10.64. The Selection Committee cannot get the instant
answers to some fairly obvious questions, but The Selector if he is doing his job properly would seek out the
background to that particular situation and select whom
he thought would be the best person. Notice I wrote
would, not *is*. There is a myth in some selection bodies
that you pick the best people in the trial or championships. It is time we got away from that mistake. People
should be selected not because they win a trial or championships but because they will do well in that international event for which they are chosen. Trials can often
destroy, not make, and we need to learn far more about
the athletes' training programme, what type of work
produces what type of conditions, peaks and lows. No, I
will not try to sell that one to any committee in which
selection is merely a small part of their valuable administrative work. Some of them may know nothing about

coaching or training, or if they do it is related to a time past. But my selector would have knowledge of coaching and training, and have integrity; and he would think United Kingdom – not Scots, Welsh or English. He would of course have the support of the national coaches and the ability to see athletes in action without being burdened with too many other jobs. Above all he would talk to athletes and their coaches.

Pre-selection, which I know is opposed by some of the old guard in the Establishment, has shown benefits. In 1974 it was used by Britain for the first time when in the February Ian Thompson the marathon runner was pre-selected for the European Championships in September – he won. Two years later he had a bad run in the trial for the Montreal Games and was not picked – the three men who did go finished nowhere. I feel sure too that a change in the system would benefit our women and give them greater confidence, for at the moment most of them are frightened of their part of the Establishment.

If we cannot move immediately towards a selection supremo in Britain, or a group of three people, solely charged with the business of choosing teams, then I would suggest that the present system is changed to give each association voting power related to the number of athletes in its organization; that of course would weigh heavily towards the English. We must select teams aiming to win medals, not, as we have so often done in the past, to keep everybody happy.

Testing for drugs, the system under which it is managed and the penalties for those who are caught, adds up to hypocrisy. The desire to win, to succeed, is something on which people become 'hooked' and, as in every other facet of life, even though it may be physically damaging and morally questionable, someone is going to come along and offer you ways to satisfy that need. The idea that a better performance might be possible after some little pills or an injection is not new. The Greeks were probably up to it in the Ancient Games; while there are suggestions that when Dorando Pietri tottered into the White City Stadium, London, at the finish of the Olympic marathon of 1908 and became famous because he was disqualified a few yards from the line, his final shaky steps were probably due as much to a dose of strychnine as exhaustion after the 26 miles 385 yards from Windsor Castle. Substances like strychnine were not illegal in those days.

Now, unhappily, the sport seems to be fighting an undeclared war with the pharmaceutical industry and losing the battle, but it is unwilling to admit it. The system testing for drugs and the imposition of penalties for those who break the rules appeared, when it was set up, to be an admirable attempt to deter, but it was limp in its understanding of human nature. The British have been at the forefront of the campaign to eradicate drug taking from athletics and other sports. Sir Arthur Gold, the president of the European Athletic Association, has been one of the most fervent campaigners over the past ten years. The fact that he has failed to achieve a 'clean' sport is not a criticism of him, more a plaudit for a man who has shown the world the hopelessness of trying to break the human will. The failure of the campaign does, I believe, add up to a hypocritical attitude on several counts.

The sport, which in spite of recent increased funds is still run largely by amateurs, is never going to be properly equipped to beat the commercial chemists and scientists who are working constantly at producing more refined drugs, even adapting human substances such as natural-growth hormones. The pharmaceutical industry regularly produces new products which in the remedial sense are used in some cases to stimulate quicker muscle growth. Adapted by some sportsmen the enhanced muscle growth provides a so-called short cut to success. Due to the inevitable lack of finance of sporting bodies those doing the testing are never going to catch up. They are trying to find substances in athletes' urine samples which may no longer be used or which are out of date. But when they do catch people, occasionally in athletics, they are suspended from the sport and then, in most instances, have their appeal to be reinstated upheld eighteen months later.

A few days before I won the European 1500 metres in Prague in 1978, Gold walked out of the VIP box at the stadium when Ilena Slupianek of the German Democratic Republic was presented with her gold medal for winning the shot. She was one of several athletes who had been found to have taken drugs but had had their appeal upheld for reinstatement so that they could compete in Prague. Gold was not a member of the IAAF committee which reinstated the athletes and I can understand him demonstrating in the manner in which he did. I can equally appreciate the attitude of those who gave Slupianek her chance to win again – it was an attitude which mixed compassion with their own failure to have a system which was fair.

That leads me to another point of failure in the system. The majority of the drugs which are taken have a long-term effect, in muscle building. It is more effective to take a course during winter or spring training and then come off them before the time of competition. After a few weeks the substance disappears from the body and cannot be detected, but their effect remains. Thus it requires testing to be done all the year round and not just at competition sites. The Amateur Rowing Association use a 'flying squad' to test British competitors during winter, a system which still continues. Gold has suggested that British sportsmen (not just athletes) should go on a voluntary register for testing. But what about the rest of the world? There have been suggestions that the IAAF should have a team of doctors ready to fly anywhere in order to surprise people, but the problems of entry into certain countries and the impingement upon freedoms means that this is a forlorn hope. It would anyway, with so much more sophistication in the number and kind of drugs being used, only compound the hypocrisy.

I believe that the sport of athletics and in fact all sports must take a fresh look at drug taking and relate it to the world beyond the confines of their own responsibility. With certain reservations, I think that taking drugs to aid performance should be a matter of personal choice, just as it is in other aspects of life. We take drugs when we are ill to aid our recovery to full health and we use them for minor ailments, such as headaches and sleeplessness; but from there we move across the spectrum, begin to touch on the area of morality associated with taking drugs for better sporting performance. Many people take sleeping pills and tranquillizers to aid their performance at work the next day and no one questions the morality of drugs used in this area. Drugs are used to enable people to cope with increasing pressures of life. In moderation these do no harm but assist by alleviating a condition which would make life more difficult. So the moral question in our everyday life is a difficult one to answer and becomes even more complex in the area of using drugs for enhancing sporting performance.

I am not suggesting that we wipe out all drug testing. I realize that there are existing drugs, or maybe new ones, which are harmful, possibly lethal. I think the greater dangers may lie with the pain-inhibiting drugs, substances taken to cover the pain so that an athlete may continue or get back to competition more quickly. Should not the medical profession and the sport be looking more closely at the dangers inherent in this area of 'help' for the competitor? There have been rather woolly claims that drugs on the banned list are damaging; when anabolic steroids were first used there were stories about possible cancer, impotency and other claims but it seems to me that these were childish deterrent methods used by administrators to frighten athletes.

We need to have a more honest attitude from the medical world and the administration and a completely new approach towards drug taking. There should be more information made available to deal with the problem of ignorance so that athletes do not take drugs or, worse, are led to do so by other people who know little about what they are doing. We have to this day a rather Victorian attitude towards drug taking. It is something that is never openly discussed, and when there are instances of people taking drugs everything is brushed under the carpet. There should be, in my opinion, open discussion about drugs at all levels, about how taking drugs might damage health, what the long-term effects might be. The reason that there is no discussion about banned drugs is because of the very fact they are banned; but that does not stop people taking them. What it does do is to suppress the spread of knowledge about new substances, new dangers. Bring the subject out in the open so that if an athlete is offered something by his coach he can find out more about it, discover whether it is a vitamin pill or something which may be dangerous. In twelve years as an international athlete I have never come across documentation about drugs and their dangers.

It is impossible to trowel the cement over the whole of

athletics and produce a smooth surface. I am not suggesting that. There are different moral standards in different countries. In some places opium is legal, in some states of America the use of cannabis is permitted. There are probably many anomalies. What I want is a much wider awareness of what is already happening. I accept that when I go to the starting line in some races there are competitors who have taken drugs. Other athletes I know are aware of that situation and accept it. Let us now move to the position where that is made known and everyone can make their own judgement.

We must thank people like Sir Arthur who has campaigned vigorously for the eradication of drug taking by the imposition of sanctions. He has shown however, courageously at times, that such a course is hopeless. In Britain we have the Sports Council putting a lot of money into supporting drug testing at Chelsea College while around the world the number of registered laboratories for drug testing in our sport is increasing. But it is false to draw a sense of well being from these developments because testing for drugs at a major athletics meeting is confined to really only a small random sample. During the European Cup at Crystal Palace in 1983, for instance, of approximately 250 competitors twelve were picked at random for testing; then the two women who broke the world high-jump record, Ulrike Meyfarth of West Germany and Tamara Bykova of the Soviet Union, were added. Drug testing in sport needs changing radically. Certainly there must be testing for substances which could prove lethal; otherwise let the money which is now spent on drug testing be supplemented by other funds and used to tell sportsmen that taking drugs is not good for their health and that it is not good for fair competition. The British Government's anti-smoking campaign is having effect. The number of smokers has dropped dramatically;

more important, the attitude towards smokers and smoking is changing. In the long term I believe a similar attitude towards those who take drugs in sport would evolve; they would gradually become outcasts, unacceptable. I do not suggest that this is going to solve the problem of drugs overnight. I just think that it is a more honest approach and ought to be looked at more closely by administrators, very few of whom were competing at a time when drugs were in sport, at least in Britain. Let us leave it to the individual.

As I have written elsewhere in this book, I am blessed with my athletic talent. I have never taken drugs, never needed them. I may have been beaten by someone who has taken drugs, but when I retire I will be able to live with my conscience over this question. I sincerely hope all other athletes can do the same.

14
Almost Spiked on Bondi

My planning for the 1984 season took into account that in a normal year my best running comes late, in September. For the Olympic Games I needed an earlier peak so, in addition to the usual two or three weeks' winter training in Portugal, I went to Australia in February and March to step up the training. This meant that I was able to dovetail the work I would do normally in the English spring with the faster work that I would be undertaking in May. It was a scheme that fitted neatly with my domestic arrangements, for just before Christmas we sold our flat in Adelaide Crescent, Hove, a place of many happy memories, and bought a dilapidated house in Brighton. There seemed to be workmen everywhere and living in a couple of makeshift rooms soon began to get on our nerves. By then it was time for the trip to Portugal, after which we had little more than time to pack our cases again for the flight to Australia. Matt, who had a year's sabbatical from his post of assistant headmaster at Patcham Middle School, came with us, his company and his constant reassurance that all was going well making the training so much easier. In just about twenty-four hours we travelled from Brighton to Brighton Beach, Melbourne, where we rented a small house. It was quite a contrast to my home town – there was so much more space and the weather, which is what we went out for, was sometimes a little too hot for comfort.

I had of course been to Australia in 1981 and I liked the place. Australians are so outgoing, so untrammelled by tradition or convention, and leave the impression that they would get up and have a go at anything – without being restricted by petty rules and regulations. The politeness of the young people surprised me. On many occasions, I found Australian children greeting me as 'Mr Ovett' and wishing me all the best in the Olympic Games – even a handshake was in order. It was a refreshing contrast to some of the behaviour I encounter in Britain, where I have come to expect being shouted at by youngsters. I realize that after a seven week stay, when we were travelling round enjoying a holiday-style visit as well as training, one can only make a superficial judgement, but I did come away feeling that Australia is my kind of country and Australians are my kind of people.

I had hoped to have three races near the end of the trip, when I knew there would be sufficient speed in my legs to cope with Australians who were at their peak, but unfortunately the races came early on. The first was in Melbourne and the second in Sydney and on both occasions I managed to take second place – it was extremely satisfying. I was expecting to do something around 3 minutes 37/38 seconds and in the first one Pat O'Donoghue, a New Zealander seeking the Olympic qualifying time, sprinted past me in the home straight and I recorded 3 minutes 37.52 seconds. A few days later Mike Hillardt, Australia's leading middle-distance runner, ran 3 minutes 34.20 seconds and I followed just under a second behind. Looking at the video of those races they showed that all that was missing was an ability to match the sprint finish of the winner – in the middle of the English winter, it was an extremely healthy state to be in.

The training went well and we enjoyed our travelling around, seeing the Admiral's Cup and going to Sydney Opera House. One of the more relaxing trips took us to that place synonymous with the great Australian outdoors, Bondi Beach – and nearly brought to an end my

Olympic challenge and possibly an abrupt end to this book. I have read about fatal swimming accidents occurring a few yards off shore and wondered how it could have happened – now I know.

The surf off Bondi is much bigger than that around the British coasts; the water is rougher, the waves larger. My swimming capabilities lie somewhere between that of a lead weight and the Titanic, so it was gingerly that I walked in up to my neck – and was knocked over by a breaker. As I swam to the surface another roller crashed over me and then the undercurrent dragged me down. Again I surfaced, this time having swallowed water. Seeing Maurie Plant about fifteen yards away I called to him to give me a hand. Knowing my love of a practical joke, he laughed and did not understand. The next wave hit me with such force that I was dazed. I suppose I was beginning to panic, physically resisting rather than relaxing the body. When I came up, this time sucking in air desperately, Maurie spotted that something was definitely wrong, swam over and lifted me up so that I could breathe normally. I told him I was alright, swam a couple of strokes back to find a footing, then walked out of the sea.

All this had happened no more than fifteen yards from the edge of the water. Two massive Australian life savers spotted that there was trouble and walked towards me. 'Are you Steve Ovett the runner?' one said. 'Yes,' I replied, 'the runner but not much of a swimmer.'

I told them that I was alright, signed my autograph and went back to Rachel for a little feminine sympathy. She had missed the drama, sleeping, and I tried to convince her that I had come close to drowning. Exhausted, I reached her place on the beach and said, 'I nearly drowned' – which brought the drawled, sleepy reply 'What . . . ?'

'I said I was almost gone, out there.'

'Oh don't be stupid . . . sit down.'

Half an hour after the drama Matt and I were back in the water, but this time on a section of the bay that had a shallow run into the water and therefore less of an undertow. By the following morning the incident had suffered Australia's Fleet Street treatment: apparently I was rescued by the life savers a hundred yards out or somewhere near the shipping lanes in shark-infested waters. Anyway, my running was little affected because it was on that day that I had my best performance of the trip, 3 minutes 35.36 seconds.

After that race I had my longest run on the Australian trip, courtesy of Matt. We sought a fresh route for our usual morning five-mile run to break the monotony and, with Matt navigating, certainly found no man's land. We ran lost for ten miles, which was alright; but after fifteen we were beginning to panic, particularly as it had started to rain. Finally, we found someone who knew where we had come from and pointed us in the right direction. After a few more miles we spotted a landmark, which was on the very fringe of our training runs. I think I did a personal best for the marathon that day and was grateful for a long hot shower when finally we arrived back at the house two and a half hours later to find a very worried Rachel peering through the window in disbelief.

Overall, my seven weeks in Australia provided me with probably the most concentrated period of training I have ever undergone. The best possible test of my fitness and form came in a road race over a mile in Paris at the end of April, not long after my return. It was an opportunity not only to get the feel of racing without being pitched immediately into something fierce on the track but also to see how I fared in such a short distance on the road. There is a vast difference between training on the road at a steady pace and racing on that surface. I was anxious to get the feel of it because these sorts of road races are, I suspect, going to become popular events in the future. They are designed for television consumption and through that medium they promote athletics.

The idea of having city miles through some main thoroughfare was regarded, when the idea was first mooted, as a rather frothy piece of show business which does help to publicize the sport, but nothing more. In fact they are ideal vehicles for sponsors – they have impact and identity, yet the sponsor does not have to put on all the other events in the athletic programme. In the United States road running is an industry and some organizers and sponsors have been flouting the International rules relating to cash prizes and the amount of advertising athletes may carry on their vests.

The Paris Mile seemed a typical television production for we raced down the Avenue Foch, with the Arc de Triomphe and the plane trees as a backcloth to the contest. This particular package for television was not very good – the race was over a French bank holiday so the course was not lined with crowds, and the motorcycle carrying the TV camera seemed to have no shock absorbers so the runners appeared to be jumping up and down on the spot rather than running.

My initial feeling was one of apprehension because, when we set off, most of the run was slightly downhill. The pace seemed so slow, yet men like Sydney Maree and Jose Abascal were soon breathing hard. I felt perfectly relaxed and my only worry was that, if it had been raining, running on the smooth tarmacadam surface with this steep camber could have been extremely hazardous. I went into the lead at a roundabout which left us with about 300 yards to go, slightly uphill. I pushed hard, indicated that I was turning right, and when I reached the finishing line I could not hear anyone behind me. My time of 3 minutes 56.12 seconds must not be taken too seriously: a mile in these circumstances cannot be measured as precisely as a distance on a track, and of course there was the downhill stretch. Nevertheless it was revealing as far as my fitness was concerned in relation to other people like Maree, Abascal and Thomas Wessinghage, who were all due to be in Los Angeles.

Soon after my return, the illness which was to lead to my demise in the Olympic arena began. A cough which kept me, Rachel and our dog, Jazz, awake through a couple of nights was the start of all the problems. I was still training and not feeling very much discomfort, but the nights were wearying and I was becoming more and more tired during the day. Eventually – again – I went to my doctor and saw a locum who diagnosed a bronchial infection which had all but passed but she gave me a course of antibiotics. I lost two weeks of training, in the middle of May, for I was only able to do some light jogging and striding.

The break was particularly galling since Matt and I had worked on an experiment which was going really well until the coughing started. I came back from Australia feeling fit and knowing that all the basic preparation had been done to such an extent that I changed my spring and summer regime. We had been thinking about the plan for some time and the success of Australia convinced us that this was the time to experiment. Instead of the normal morning training run of several miles which served to keep up the basic training input, I was doing quality work twice a day – a hard session in the morning and another session in the evening. It was exhausting, yet I felt that the power and sharpness that I was building up for racing was there as never before. The old cliché 'I've never felt fitter' was utterly appropriate. Perhaps then it was driving my body to a new limit which exposed me to the bronchitis.

After losing a fortnight's training, I suffered a further setback over the Bank Holiday at the end of May when I chose to stay at home for some uninterrupted training instead of going down to Cwmbran with Matt for the UK Closed Championships in which some of the Phoenix members were taking part. I did some short-distance repetitions at the track in miserable rainy conditions, thinking more about the effect it would have on my chest than anything else, when I felt a slight pain in the left leg. I drove on through it and was not really concerned – as quickly as it came it disappeared. The following morning I went down to Withdean Park to do some thousands. On the first stride there was a twinge, it was worse on the second and after the third I came to a halt. Turning to Rachel, who had brought Jazz for a run in the park, I said 'It's a hamstring.'

Back home, out came the ice packs and towels. I then rang Bert Parker, knowing that he would fit me into his appointment list, only to discover that he had just had open-heart surgery and would be away for quite some time. I saw the person who was looking after his practice but it was obvious that she would not be able to cope with all of Bert's and her appointments and treat me. I then went to see John Allen, a physiotherapist in Guildford who has had much to do with many international athletes' problems, and he confirmed what I already really knew: I would not be competing in the Olympic Trials in the early part of June. My plan had been to win automatic selection for the 800 metres by taking first place in the Trials, rather than to leave the decision to selectors who might do as they did the previous year in the World Championships team and omit me. Now though there had to be a complete rescheduling of plans.

I could not go three times a day for treatment to Guildford, particularly as at that time, when I was not involved in training, I was working on transferring my company from London to Brighton. The problem of how to get the sort of intensive treatment I required was certainly worrying me as I drove back from Guildford to Brighton, but fortunately the first phone call on returning home led me to the solution. Keith Hayman, my new manager of OVETT, rang with some business news and then mentioned he was off to Sussex University for some treatment for a sports injury. I asked him to find out if there was anyone there who could help me. Two hours later he called again having found a physiotherapist who was working at Brighton General Hospital and would help out. I went through the proper channels of getting a letter from my doctor, then Barbara Turner put Ovett back on his feet after five days' treatment.

I resumed sprint training and then did a time trial in the week that I was due to race at Loughborough. Fate seemed to be against me again because it suddenly turned cold and blustery and the small group of Phoenix club people who knew me well realized that this particular evening was a very important point in my Olympic preparation. I ran 1 minute 48.6 seconds which doesn't sound very good but within me I knew that it was all that could have been expected.

There was though the problem of convincing the selectors that the Olympic 800-metres champion was capable of defending his title. I wanted to provide an absolutely convincing performance of which I knew I was capable – but not just at that moment. If I had been told that I was picked then I could have concentrated on rehabilitation. By the beginning of July I think I would have raised a few eyebrows by getting down to 1 minute 44 seconds for 800 metres. I knew from the work that I had been doing that this would be the sort of run I would achieve before very long – it would be a performance to give me confidence as well as the selectors. That though was not going to be possible because I had to concentrate on two races, one at Loughborough the other in Belfast, within a few days of one another. I needed to win those races in reasonable times and beat people whom I was aware the selectors were considering, Rob Harrison and Ikem Billy – all of this in the attendant glare of television exposure.

I achieved what I knew was required. At Loughborough I came out of the last 200 metres with plenty in hand, eased off near the finish and recorded 1 minute 47 seconds, the Olympic qualifying standard, with Billy and Harrison in my wake. At Belfast a few days later I was faster, 1 minute 46.15 seconds, with Ikem Billy again behind me. As far as I was concerned that was sufficient evidence for the selectors and I certainly had no intention of running the AAA Championships which, through some popular clamour, was turning into a second Olympic trial. I could ill afford to race in Loughborough and Belfast for it was eating into valuable preparation time after my two setbacks, so there was no possibility of my competing in these Championships even though they were sponsored by U-Bix Copiers. I know they were disappointed but they understood my position and were only concerned that I should be fully and properly prepared for Los Angeles.

I regret that the notion that the AAA Championships was in fact a further Olympic trial was nothing more than a ticket-touting operation. The AAA wanted a big crowd and so did television, who went in for some overemphasizing, stating in my event, for instance, that if someone did something reasonable Ovett's position could be vulnerable. The event reached its most absurd proportions when Seb's position in the 1500 metres came into question when he was beaten by Peter Elliott. Some people – and there were selectors among them – said Peter, with barely any experience at the distance, should have the remaining 1500-metres place in Los Angeles, rather than the Olympic champion. No doubt those of that opinion conveniently forgot it several weeks later when Seb won the 1500-metres title in a manner which brilliantly surpassed any of his predecessors. All of this underlines the need to reshape completely the way we select our athletes, a subject I have discussed elsewhere.

I had always had the hope of starting my 1500-metres competition in Oslo at the end of June. With the problems of selection for the 800 metres out of the way, I could now concentrate on sharpening up. The Oslo race may have looked impressive, as some reports said, but it did not, in retrospect, satisfy me. I was in a 'drifty' mood, responding to those about me in a lazy manner. I was not running my own race and ought to have been more commanding. After a very quick first 1000 metres courtesy of the pacemaker, James Mays, he stepped aside and I was left in front. I slowed so that the others caught me, took six yards off them again and then allowed them to catch up before just winning on the line from Gonzales of Spain. It was the wrong attitude to take to some of the world's best 1500-metres men and the time of 3 minutes 34.50 seconds, then the third fastest of the year, only glossed over a performance which was less than adequate at that point in the season.

Oslo marked the end of a phase. The house into which I moved at Christmas was at last getting into some state of readiness. I had worked at many of the alterations and decorations, and Rachel and I had been living for many months in conditions which were for us not normal. The carpets were down, there were home comforts and I felt more relaxed now that some of my domestic problems were diminished.

The second stage of the season's preparation began in Stockholm on 2 July. I was tired when I arrived, but I needed the race and it was a pleasant evening in an atmosphere created by people who understand the sport of athletics. The Olympic Stadium has thankfully been changed very little from when it was used in the 1912 Games; it still has the copper, tent-shaped canopy in the middle of the main stand where the King of Sweden greeted Jim Thorpe, the legendary Olympic decathlon champion. A month before the Los Angeles Games, the Olympic 800-metres champion felt good, the track was fast and the competition worthwhile. I found myself boxed in the first lap as the leaders took it through at a cracking pace, close to world-record schedule up to 800 metres, but I felt relaxed and fully in control. When I took up the lead in the final lap I said to myself, 'Steve, you're not working very hard are you?' I looked back and saw that others were pushing hard to catch me but not making any impression, so down the long home straight I accelerated right to the line and took another half second off Pierre Delize of Switzerland and two seconds off Chuck Aragon of the United States. I felt much more comfortable in the Stockholm race than I did in Oslo and very happy that I could take off in the way I did and sustain the pace.

I returned to Brighton with a sense of well being that I certainly had not experienced before that year. I was getting into racing shape and the competition I had pencilled in up to my departure for Los Angeles was proving useful. But I should have known that once things start going well for Steve Ovett disaster is not far away – and it was ironic that I should encounter my next niggling setback in the city of the Olympic headquarters, Lausanne. It was extremely hot when we arrived and on the night before the race I developed a rash, which became worse. I ran and won in what was fortunately not a very demanding race, but that night one side of my body was covered in the rash and I had an upset stomach. Various suggestions as to the cause – Swiss water, strawberries, the heat, worry about the Olympic Games – were offered but I saw a specialist who said that it was a viral infection which would get worse before it got better. He was right. I missed two more races which left me with little time and choice about competition before I departed for Los Angeles.

After a week of rest following the virus, in which I did little more than jog, I went to Edinburgh for a 1500-metres race. The opposition was modest and I won comfortably, although I did not feel as good as apparently I looked. I understand that from the television pictures of the race a lot of gambling people immediately put money on me for the Games. I felt in fact a little jaded in the first couple of laps, but once I got into the rhythm of the run I was fine and I certainly felt in control of the race in the last lap – but so I should have been, that close to the Games, in a race run in 3 minutes 36.90 seconds.

The second part of this final competitive fling was something of a disaster. Andy wanted me to run in Larvik, Norway, which I thought was geographically close to Oslo. I left Edinburgh on an early morning flight to London, waited an hour for the Oslo flight which took two and a half hours, waited in Oslo to be picked up for a two-hour drive to Larvik and arrived about an hour before the race. After that I felt I ran reasonably well over 800 metres, but I was beaten by Ikem Billy who did 1 minute 46.10 seconds. My own time was three-tenths of a second slower which was, of course, a disappointment but in the circumstances I was not too displeased. I returned to London the following day, a hectic one of packing and tying up some business arrangements, and the following morning I flew to Los Angeles.

The British athletics teams had two homes for the Olympic Games – in the Village at University College of Los Angeles, about sixteen miles from the Coliseum, close to Beverley Hills and away from the smog; and a holding camp down on the Pacific Coast at Point Loma, San Diego. It was a good piece of planning by the British athletic officials – distinct from the British Olympic Association – which allowed the athletes to complete their preparation in a restful, relaxing atmosphere, away from the high-powered and often intimidating atmosphere of an Olympic Village. The facilities at Point Loma College were adequate and there was a running track in the complex which was new and very hard but met my needs.

When Matt, Rachel and I flew in to San Diego we were due to be met but there was no one at the airport. In a way that was a blessing because it meant that I could have a quiet look at the College facilities – there was absolutely no one about. I decided to stay in a hotel near the Harbour. I do not want to give the impression that I am an anti-team man, but now that competitors are permitted to stay outside the Village or team accommodation I was glad to take the opportunity to be with Rachel and Matt. It recreated to some extent the living environment I have in Brighton, and must have helped to relieve the pressure slightly on those who had to stay with the team because the College soon became overcrowded.

Many leading athletes, like Seb, Carl Lewis and others, did not stay in the Village. They used its facilities during the day, but lived elsewhere, thus reducing the pressures on themselves. When I heard that it would be four living

in an apartment on the UCLA campus I decided logically
to share Rachel's hotel room. But when we arrived in
Los Angeles, two days before my first race, there was
panic because her booking at the hotel had not found its
way through the computer and there were no rooms
available. I went off to the Village, discovered it was now
seven to an apartment, and then found that Frank Dick,
the British Director of Coaching, had a list of houses
which were available. I rented one in a pleasant suburban
district off Wilshire Boulevard out near Beverley Hills.

The house was within reasonable reach of the Village
and only half an hour's drive from the Coliseum. It meant
too that I could be left in peace just prior to the Games.
The world's media had joined the intensely competitive
news-gathering world of California and many of them
had me on their shopping list for exclusive interviews.
There were 9000 people from the media accredited to
cover the Games; while the majority of these were
backroom boys in television, there were still 3000
reporters and photographers looking for stories. In the
quiet of the Wilshire area of Los Angeles I was never
discovered, not even after my dramatic trip to hospital.

15

'Have a Nice Day'

Los Angeles left me with memories that no sportsman would want: illness and defeat in the 800 metres and then, after the struggle to fight back, those chilling initials by my name in the 1500 metres – DNF, or 'did not finish'. It was a bleak and depressing Olympic Games for me except for one factor, the overwhelming warmth and goodwill which came from people all over the world.

I do not think that I will ever fully comprehend why an athlete collapsing on the track in Los Angeles and being carted off to hospital should command the attention of millions when there was so much else going on in the Olympic arena. That Ovett's medical condition should be number-one item on BBC television news, ahead of the Miners' Strike and other events far more important to people's lives, leaves me just a little frightened – after all, it is only a sport. Yet since my return, and even now in writing this final chapter of my autobiography, I am beginning to touch on the feelings which my part in the Games created. The cards and letters pour in to my home at Brighton with messages wishing me good health and wanting me to get back to racing. In many ways I seem to have won more than I lost in Los Angeles.

There were though people who felt that, after the 800 metres and a day in hospital being monitored by some of the best medical gadgetry in the world, I should have gracefully bowed out and left the combat to others. Among them were my wife, Rachel, and my training partner, Matt. The combination of their argument was strong, the one wanting a healthy husband, the other wanting a friend of long standing not to be humiliated in the greatest sporting arena. I could appreciate and understand their concern, but Steve Ovett could not walk away from that situation. People have said that I displayed courage by my actions but I truly believe that I acted with stupidity – no one should have run in the condition I was in. True courage was displayed by Rachel and Matt, who knew their own feelings yet had to sit in the stand and just watch.

That I was able to defend my 800 metres title at all is due entirely to the disorganization of the athletics programme on the first few days. Fifteen minutes after I was due to report in for my heat at the warm-up area, I was walking about a street near the Coliseum in a desperate panic asking 'Where is the warm-up track?' of people who were polite but had no idea where to send me. They always seemed to finish their response with that strange Americanism 'Have a nice day', which added to the nightmare of it all.

If I had gone from my house to the Village and down to the Coliseum by bus then the problem would not have arisen but, in order to avoid that hassle and remain as relaxed as possible, I chose to get Matt and Rachel to drive me in the car. We allowed an hour and a half to do what was a half-hour journey and when we arrived at the Coliseum we were snarled up in the traffic nose to tail.

'Can you tell me where the warm-up track is?' I asked of the officials in their green and orange tracksuits.

'Warm-up track?'

'For the athletes.'

'Athletes?'

'Oh, I mean track and field competitors.'

'Oh no – I don't know that I'm afraid.'

There were similar abortive conversations with a blue-jacketed official, then more orange and green ones. Time went by until finally I came to a check point where there were several officials and a telephone. At last a ray of hope . . .

'No, we can't ring for information. That's not our job.'

This went on and on for half an hour. We tried everyone including policemen. The inflexibility of the system and their paranoia with keeping everything compartmentalized was getting to me. I then spotted a sign 'Athletes Report Area' and I breathed a sigh of relief and told Matt to pull the car in to the side. I jumped out, they wished me good luck and I went up to the official.

'This is the report area? I'm in the 800 metres.'

'Oh, this is the report area for ceremonies,' was his reply, plunging me back into panic. At least this official directed me to a transportation point.

I got on a Press bus going to the University of Southern California campus, though the driver did not know if that was near the warm-up track which seemed to be slipping further and further from my reach. The bus was held up while more pressmen piled in, then again while some procession went across its path. It was then that I noticed Matt's car just four vehicles ahead. I jumped up and told the driver I wanted to get out.

'I can't let you out,' she said, obviously quoting from her Olympic training manual. But when I calmly threatened to break the door of her bus she did let me out. I banged on the car window to the astonishment of Matt and Rachel and they drove me to a checkpoint at USC. One of perhaps twenty officials announced that she knew where the warm-up track was situated, but when I asked that she take me there – about half a mile away – I was met with the predictable response: 'Oh no, I can't leave my post.' I followed her directions and jogged the half mile to find Harry Wilson waiting anxiously in the warm-up area. I then had a little over five minutes before checking-in time.

I changed quickly, jogged a few laps of the track and then got to the bus which was supposed to take two minutes to get to the final checking-in point. In fact it took over fifteen minutes, by which point I was over my time. At any other international meeting, the World Championships or the Olympic Games in Moscow, I would have been out. I arrived thinking that it was all over, what a farce; then I realized the area was more crowded than it should have been. In fact they had been allowing forty minutes call up, when only thirty minutes was needed, and my heat had not 'closed' but was delayed. Luck at last.

Apart from my hunt-the-warm-up-track game, the time from warming up to going out on to the track, a period of an hour, was one of exposure to the heat. The tented area by the Coliseum was about half the size of a hockey pitch and when I was there it had about two hundred people in it. Let me assure you there is no political connotation in my comparison, but when one sets it alongside the Moscow operation, Los Angeles was a mess. In Moscow there was a special traffic lane, all the officials understood the business of athletics and the structure of the warm-up and call-up areas were based on accepted standards for athletes that have been tried and tested over many major international meetings in the past. Having said that, when the Americans got into the swing after a few days things relaxed a little and some of the major problems were ironed out.

After the confusion before, the race itself provided a welcome relief although I did not expect to have to run the first round of an Olympic 800 metres in 1 minute 45.66 seconds. Looking back, the first signs of serious trouble were looming, but in the circumstances of the event they did not seem as such. Since moving up from San Diego I had noticed a deterioration in the quality of the air. Smog, which none of the American officials or media wanted to talk about, was definitely there, worse on some days. I had been suffering from a rasping throat, shortness of breath and sometimes my eyes were smarting; but worst of all was the intense heat in the Coliseum. While the official result sheets of the events were carrying temperature figures of 78 to 80 degrees, down there on the floor of the Coliseum it was in the nineties; one day Seb told BBC viewers that a temperature of 102 had been recorded – that certainly did not surprise me. At the end of my first race my fingers and arms were tingling, but I thought that it was a natural symptom of the heat. I knew that in spite of pouring in fluids I was dehydrating.

The second round brought no respite and I thought it odd that I should again have to face Joachim Cruz of Brazil, the winner of my first heat. Cruz again took it out, running the first 400 metres in 51.26 seconds, faster than the first round, and into the second lap I realized it had gone quiet behind. I looked round and found a big gap, eased down along the home straight and finished second in 1 minute 45.72 seconds, my fastest time for quite a while. Having to produce this type of performance in the second round indicated the consolidation of the event. With a lot more talent in the field, survival meant we had to find much greater speed.

Before the race I had a tightness in the chest and slight difficulty with my breathing, but at the finish, as Johnny Gray of America slowed down and I passed him to finish second, my forearms were numb, paralysed almost, and my thumb and forefingers were locked together. It was a weird feeling and when I turned to shake hands it was like offering a stump. I was also feeling very lightheaded and my breathing was very shallow, which is unusual for me. In character, I suppose, I did not do anything about it apart from mentioning it to Matt and Rachel, who suggested that it had something to do with the heat and I had better take some more fluid. I was in fact pumping fluids down me as if I was a fish.

It has been suggested that if I had been living in the village all this would have been monitored, but I am afraid I would still have kept it to myself as nothing very much to worry about. Some athletes are like that: if you think there is something wrong, then your concentration on the business of running and winning is diverted. However, it was worrying and Harry mentioned it to one of the doctors who stated that the trouble was probably caused by the heat and nervousness together bringing hyperventilating and that deep breathing should relieve the condition. It did not of course because part of the problem was related to the aftermath of my previous bronchial condition which left me on about seventy per cent efficiency.

By the semi-final I was beginning to think that there was some skulduggery going on in the seeding room. Did they think that Ovett had the finishing kick of 1980 and were trying to blunt it by pitching him into fast preliminary races? I am sure that it was not really as sinister as that but how I managed to draw Cruz, the fastest qualifier, in each of the first three rounds I do not understand.

The semi-final was much faster than I anticipated, but it was Edwin Koech of Kenya, not Cruz, who did the damage. To qualify I had to run my fastest time for six years, which seemed absurd. Moreover, the normal facility in an international meeting for runners – lap times being called – was not available. The main digital clock was high up at the end of the stadium, not on the track where it is usually placed, and to see the lap time one would have had to look up turning into a bend which would have broken concentration. In many ways it was probably a good thing not to know how fast I was running in that semi-final as I would have been frightened out of my wits; or perhaps it would have reassured me – I don't know. I thought the race would be run at around 1 minute 45/46 seconds and when I went through the back straight, trailing fifth, I thought 'I must be feeling terrible. Something's wrong.' I went past halfway in fourth place, Koech, the leader, having run 49.61 seconds with me on 50.50, the fastest first lap I had run since the European final of 1978 in Prague. But I was unaware of it at the time.

In the back straight I began to feel very tired and I lost a couple of places as Cruz took over the lead. Going into the final bend I began to think that there was something really wrong, but I tried to shut the thought out and concentrate. 'Keep pumping, keep pumping,' I kept trying to think. I knew that I was not catching them, that I was running out of space and I needed to make up two places. Then I felt that Omar Khalifa of the Sudan, just in front, was dying. But so too was I. 'I'm not going to make it' I thought, and then in the last couple of strides I pushed as hard as I could and lunged for the line and collapsed on the track. As my body went down I knew that I had won the last qualifying position. Then I thought, 'What am I doing on the track like this? What has it come to when I have to lunge for the line?' I was alright, not breathing heavily, and I tried to get up, but as I did so two guys came over and held me.

'Stay down buddy,' one said, holding my shoulders.

'I'm alright,' I replied.

'Stay there until we get a doctor.'

'Look,' I said, 'I'm alright.' I was having to turn my head and speak out of the side of my mouth, because they were pinning me down.

'Don't move you could have broken something.'

'No, I'm OK, I know I haven't broken anything.'

'No, don't move.'

I began to wonder whether they were joking or doing this for television, but in the end they let me get up and I was just badly bruised on one side with friction burns as well. As I stood up they were replaying the race on the big video screen. They showed the first three – Cruz crossing the line in 1 minute 43.82 seconds, followed by Koech and Jones, the American – and then they stopped. Whereupon the eighty thousand people in the Coliseum began to shout 'Go on, Go on'. In the end they moved the picture on frame by frame until you see that my dive for the line had enabled me to qualify. The crowd erupted when they saw that the Olympic champion had survived.

It was not until I had walked back and was in the tunnel that I heard the times and that I had run 1 minute 44.81 seconds, my second fastest 800 metres. Had I been in the other semi-final and run that pace I would have won, beating Seb by about five yards!

The effort did of course exhaust me, but under normal circumstances I would have recovered quite quickly. On this occasion I did not. My breathing was short and the pains in the arm were still there so that evening I went up to the Village to see the Doctor. I was referred by Dr Archibald to Dr Harries, a pulmonary specialist. He said that my condition was probably caused by the smog. The hockey players had been suffering and they had found some relief in using an Intal spray, normally used by asthmatics.

Again, for the final, the weather was extremely hot. Half an hour before the warm up I took the spray and concentrated on the deep breathing, but as I was warming up the cramping in my arms came back. There was a pain down one side and my fingers stiffened to the point that I had to push them into the shape that I wanted for running. I think, for the first time, I became really worried, but I felt that I was doing all that the doctors had said and there was no question of pulling out.

I thought the final would be run fast and on reflection I think I ran it like a sprinter would race 100 metres. Drawn in lane seven, I went hard in the first lap, almost without taking a breath, on anaerobic capacity. I ran the first 400 metres as though I were going flat out and I was dying on my feet from there on because my body was not taking in any oxygen. I just could not breathe. The whole function had broken down for the sort of running I was doing. In the last lap I felt I was running in an almost unconscious state. I felt very lightheaded as though I was going to faint. I could see the field going away from me but there was absolutely nothing I could do about it. I remember thinking, 'Don't drop out, don't drop out.' As I went into the final bend all I could do was to hold my concentration together in my effort to stay upright and get to the line. When I did, I thought 'Thank goodness'.

I stepped on the inside and put my hands on my legs. I was panting I tried to control my breathing but couldn't. I began to walk back to the tunnel midway down the straight, which was the only way off the track, feeling unsteady. I thought if I get there I can sit down and I'll be alright. I kept thinking that I mustn't faint in front of all the people. But when I reached the tunnel I felt worse. It was hot, with lots of people, and I was overcome with a feeling of claustrophobia as I sat on a bench and tried to rest. Seb handed me something and said, 'Here, drink this' – which I did and immediately vomited. From then on I was in a state of semi-consciousness until I found myself in bed in hospital an hour later.

I am unstinting in my praise for the medical service which I received at the Los Angeles Orthopedic Hospital. I underwent every possible kind of test – blood, urine, cardiac. Rachel, Matt and myself were questioned thoroughly about everything I had done over the past few months. They wanted to know about the bronchitis, the rash, the hamstring injury; they also wanted to know why I did not have these matters more thoroughly checked out. I was given a scan; I saw my heart under sonar X-ray; I was put on a drip; a nurse took my temperature and blood pressure regularly throughout both nights I was there. What I did feel was that they were looking very hard for a cause which would exonerate smog, a word that was hardly used in all the many conversations I had with the doctors.

It was a strange period for me – one moment I was in an Olympic final, the next in a hospital bed. My mind was, in a strange way, detached from what was going on with my body. The medical fuss and testing must have been too absurd for me to come to terms with. It seemed like some strange daydream, with my mind unable to relate to the reality of things. I remember sometimes waking to find Rachel crying or Matt just sitting in my room, and yet there was little or nothing I could do to change the situation. Emotionally, things were uncertain and clinically, the doctors could not guarantee that after three rounds of the 1500 metres the same thing would not occur again; but as far as they could see, as a result of their exhaustive and meticulous examinations, I would not do myself any serious harm. They did add the proviso that if I felt any discomfort during a race not normally associated with running then I should stop immediately.

Dr Archibald visited me and hinted that he thought it best that I should not run, but did not actually say so. Then in the evening Nick Whitehead, the British athletics team manager, came and said that the general feeling was that the administration etc did not want me to run. I pointed out that the doctors had said that, as far as they were concerned, there was no reason why I should not take part. Then, just as he left, he turned to Rachel and said to her – not to me but within my earshot – 'We don't want any heroics out there.' That incensed me; I saw her calm expression change back to that of worry. If the management thought I was just doing this for heroism then they should have said so to *me*, which would have given me the opportunity to take them through an explanation in simple, clear words of the real reason why Steve Ovett runs. The odds were of course stacked against me after illness, two days in hospital, lack of proper rest; but that did not douse that simmering belief that I could win a medal, a belief which ultimately many people shared until 1150 metres into the Olympic final.

I left the hospital after two days and told the world's media that I was going to try and run. Only then did I learn that some of them had been found wandering the hospital corridors in white coats and others, on the pretext of visiting the children's ward, had tried to infiltrate my privacy. I intended to talk about my illness and what had happened and I was eager to offer my thanks, through the media, to the magnificent medical set up through which I had gone, but I wanted to do that properly and when I was ready, within the Olympic orbit, not on a hospital doorstep with one or two glib statements.

I returned to the house with just twenty-four hours to rest before the first round of the 1500 metres. I was determined to give it a go, and my mind was locked into the belief that I should at least try. Although I sensed that Rachel and Matt were apprehensive, they did not say I should drop out.

Frank Dick, the British Director of Coaching, came to the house, obviously as an emissary, to try to persuade me not to run. It was felt in certain quarters that I should not run but he could give me no specific reason. The

British Olympic Association, as far as I could establish, had not been informed of the medical reports from the hospital and I could only deduce that they were taking the soft option: if I withdrew, then no one would get hurt or ruffled apart from Ovett, who would only have missed an opportunity. I sensed, as I had done during Nick Whitehead's visit to the hospital the previous night, that they did consider just striking out my entry. Without specifically expressing my suspicions to Frank, I made it abundantly clear that, since the American doctors had given me the go-ahead, I could not understand why the athletic officials and the BOA were taking the view he was putting before me. The words 'legal', 'court' or 'lawyer' were not, I think, mentioned in the conversation, but I know that I got the message across that Steve Ovett was intending to race and that no one should attempt at this point to risk the humiliation of making that decision for me. If there was one thing at that moment I liked about America, apart from their medical services, it was the ease and swiftness with which their courts can act. Had I been informed that my entry for the 1500 metres had been struck out I would have taken the BOA to court long before I was due in the warm-up area.

That statement may sound dramatic and slightly excessive, but in the circumstances the only way I was going to get anything out of myself in the 1500 metres was to let my mind control my body; to tell it that it could run. Any extraneous thoughts about whether I was even entered for the event had, therefore, to be crushed in the same way that I had dealt with doubt in my own mind.

Happily all such thoughts were washed away and I went out into that burning cockpit of Olympic competition. My first-round race was fortunately slow and all I needed was a sprint for the finish to win in 3 minutes 49.23 seconds. The semi-final was much faster and I qualified for the final in fourth place with a time of 3 minutes 36.55 seconds, but I was in a bad way again. The breathing was difficult and there were pains in the arm – although it was not as bad as in the 800 metres, it was there again.

As I turned to go back after the race I realized I was unsteady. I was weaving and I knew that certain people would be watching and all I wanted to do was to get to that exit tunnel. I hated its claustrophobia, its memory, but I wanted to get off the stage and it was the only exit. I flopped down on to a bench and put my head in my hands. My breathing just wasn't functioning properly at all and I sat there for about half an hour trying to get back to normality. I was then taken back to the medical centre and was given fluid and checked over thoroughly. One of the doctors who had attended me in the hospital was there and there was never any suggestion from him or anyone else that I was unfit to race.

What I failed to do after the race was to walk right into the tunnel. I had flopped on to a bench too near the entrance and at least two pairs of binoculars were able to focus on me from the other side of the arena. Rachel and Matt had been watching the slow process of Ovett's recovery and when I finally joined them at the car they had come to fairly definite conclusions. Watching me in the tunnel and waiting for me to come from the medical centre, they had, understandably I suppose, come to the conclusion that I would be incapable of running in the final. They assumed that I would join them having already resigned myself to that fact. They expected to have the problem of coping with a man who would be physically and mentally exhausted and very depressed and disappointed. They were worrying about coping with that situation when a tired-looking but reasonably bright Ovett arrived back at the car. They were a little perplexed, but the puzzlement evaporated as we started the drive back to the house and I mentioned the following day's final. Rachel turned and said 'But you're not running tomorrow.'

'Yes, I am – I'm all right,' I replied.

There was silence and the first of many tears to be shed that night rolled down Rachel's cheek. Reasonably cheerful, I said that it would be alright, that I was not going to do myself any harm.

'How can you be sure?' was Rachel's response, with an anger I have rarely seen in her. She said that the race didn't matter, that my health came first, and asked me whether I was worried that my father had had a series of heart attacks when he was very young and this might be something hereditary. Her attitude, through all the words, the appalling atmosphere of the evening and then on through a very sleepless night, was a reflection of her very deep love for me.

Matt was also upset and soon started to shift his tack from trying to persuade me not to run, to telling me what Coe and Cram were going to do and that I would obviously embarrass myself by competing. I could appreciate their feelings and concern, since they had seen me in the tunnel. Had they just watched me walk off the track and then appear, nothing more than a little tired at the car an hour or so later, then their attitude would I am sure have been different. I had hoped for that.

In all this there was one area of agreement: I had reached the Olympic Games superbly fit; never before had I been in such a physical condition. Matt and Rachel agreed that the training sessions which I had done at San Diego were phenomenal. I knew that I was in tremendous shape when I arrived in Los Angeles and then it fell apart. But I knew that after all I had gone through there was still a shadow of a chance that I could run and it would be OK and that I would be in with a chance. I felt that I needed just a twenty per cent improvement on my running in the 800 metres and the heats of the 1500 metres and I would be OK. I wanted to gamble, wanted to take the chance and get out there and give it a go. Obviously I could appreciate that Rachel and Matt were concerned, but the way I saw it was that if I ended up in hospital again then I had four years in which to recover.

I woke on the day of the final feeling tired, but with no other aches or pains to cause worry. Breakfast time was amicable. The arguments of the previous night had been won and lost and Rachel accepted that I wanted to run. She was now absolutely behind me.

I arrived for the warm up feeling good but annoyed. When I went through the field and saw the people against me it was irritating because I knew that a fit Ovett would have a very good chance of winning. It looked to me like no more than a good field for a race at Oslo or Crystal Palace. I could not of course completely shut out of my mind my condition. In fact, one of the doctors told me that if I was to feel that pain again I should drop out; I promised Rachel that if that happened I would stop.

With my longstanding connections with the medical unit I decided that instead of leaving my kit-bag at the starting blocks I would pop it in the tunnel on the way down. A premonition of what was to come perhaps? No, I don't think so, just cold logic. Whenever I had been carted into the medical room before it seemed to take a long time for them to find my bag. When I reached the starting line round the back straight I realized I still had my watch, so I asked Seb if he would pop it in his bag. 'I've left mine with the medical people,' I said, which must have been just the psychological boost he needed to put him in gold medal running shape! But we both laughed.

As it turned out, of course, I only saw the crucial part

of his run on the video later, but what a tremendous piece of running it was. At least I take pride in being part of – for most of the way – one of the greatest 1500-metres races ever run. Running in his seventh Olympic race, the conditions were all against such excellent competitiveness and speed.

During the race I felt really fine, bubbling along and thinking as we went into the third lap that Seb was having a good run: he was well positioned and never got into any trouble. I could feel people around me breathing heavily, yet I wasn't. I would have preferred being closer to the leaders but I didn't want to drive hard and provoke something until the last lap. As I approached the bell, Steve Scott, who had inexplicably taken the race out early on and made it easier for Seb and Steve Cram, was beginning to come back so I decided I would go past Scott and go hard. As I started to surge I had a pain in my chest and my arm and as I pushed it became worse. I worked for another 50 metres and although something inside me said 'Keep going', another part said 'Don't be silly'. I then moved to the inside.

I am left forever with the unanswered question: If I had gone on, would the pain have subsided; in the last home straight of the 1984 Olympic 1500-metres final, would there have been three men in Great Britain vests coming down the straight for the medals, as I had always believed and hoped? That, in the circumstances, is a regret I know I share with millions of people.

When I bent down on the side of the track all I wanted was to get my breath and for the pain to subside, but there were people fussing around me and wanting me off the track as soon as possible. I was not unconscious but they insisted on putting me on the mobile stretcher; it all looked far more dramatic than it really was. The pain in my chest and arms soon subsided but I was overwhelmed with depression. That passed – it never lasts very long with me in any circumstances – but Rachel and Matt were very upset. They both knew how hard I had worked and none of us could really understand what went wrong. All the questions about my health were then still to be answered.

Neither Rachel nor I quite appreciated the manner in which all this was being presented and projected back home. Rachel did manage to speak to her mother over the phone on one day, and was taken aback by the fact that, with so much happening in the Olympic arena, Steve Ovett's health seemed to be the number-one concern of the nation. It was that which I think persuaded me after the first heat of the 1500 metres that I should try to speak to the media and explain what was happening. I was not trying to dramatize the affair. I was merely trying to show people that even if I was not very well it was not as bad as those stretcher pictures and medical statements to camera might have indicated.

After being let out of hospital once more, we spent the night in a hotel in Los Angeles and enjoyed the coolness of the air conditioning. We were anxious to get back home to Brighton so that I could follow up as quickly as possible the medical advice to have further tests carried out in Britain.

My plane home had almost crossed the American continent by the time Carlos Lopes had won the marathon and the closing ceremony was under way. It was a timely victory by the Portuguese runner as far as I was concerned; with my relish for running, it would be nice to think about winning when I am his age, thirty-seven. The razzmatazz of the Hollywood-style finale I did not miss. In terms of the Olympic Games, particularly in my state of mind, it was not what I would call my cup of tea.

My concern as we made the journey home was of

course about the future – the future of the sport which I practise, as much as my own. With new commercial involvements and the ten and a half million pounds contract signed with ITV, those who administrate the sport now have vital and massive resources at their disposal. Sadly I do not see, within their ranks, men and women to match the needs. I thought too about Britain's success, more medals having been won in athletics than the bumper haul at the Tokyo Games of 1964. The sport in Britain did not profit much then from the success of Mary Rand, Ann Packer, Lyn Davies and Ken Matthews; will, I wonder, athletics be able to use properly the medal-winning investment of Los Angeles?

In two years' time, amidst the new projection which ITV will provide, comes the first real test, the European Championships at Stuttgart in West Germany when the power of Eastern Europe will be aligned against our Olympic élite in a championship programme. There is therefore no time to rest, little time to reflect on the glories of Los Angeles, for the immediate future of athletics has more challenges, not only for Britain but in international terms as well, than at any time in its history.

Coming into Heathrow airport I looked across to Rachel and Matt who were both asleep with exhaustion. How difficult it is for those who sit and watch. In athletic terms, Los Angeles was a failure and the competitor in me cannot accept that; but if I am to reflect on it logically, I tried my best and was beaten by better. There has again been speculation over my future by the Ovett 'experts' and, of course, the usual definite predictions. But what the future actually holds, thankfully no one can predict. One thing I can be sure of is that if it involves me in any shape or form it will be unpredictable.

Checklist of Races

Checklist of Races

Date	Meeting/Venue	Event	Pos	Time etc
21 Mar 1970	English Schools CC C'ships (jnr), *Blackburn*	CC	37	–
5 Apr	*Crawley*	800m	1	2:09.0
18 Apr	*Epsom*	800m	1	2:07.0
25 Apr	*Brighton*	800m	1	2:01.6
3 May	*Crawley*	800m	1	2:00.1
16 May	*Walton*	800m	1	2:00.0
18 May	Brighton Schools C'ships, *Brighton*	800m	1	2:04.0
21 May	Brighton Schools C'ships, *Brighton*	400m	1	52.2
3 June	*Crystal Palace*	800m	2	2:02.9
13 June	Sussex Schools C'ships, *Brighton*	400m	1	51.6
14 June	*Aldershot*	100m	1	11.9
14 June	*Aldershot*	200m	1	23.8
28 June	Young Athletes, *Thurrock*	100m	1	11.9
28 June	Young Athletes, *Thurrock*	200m	1	24.1
10 July	English Schools C'ships, *Solihull*	400m-heat	1	52.7
10 July	English Schools C'ships, *Solihull*	400m-semi	3	53.7
11 July	English Schools C'ships, *Solihull*	400m-final	1	51.8
15 July	*Crawley*	800m	1	2:09.0
15 July	*Crawley*	100m	1	11.8
21 July	*Crawley*	800m	1	2:07.0
21 July	*Crawley*	100m	1	12.2
6 Aug	*Brighton*	200m	1	24.2
9 Aug	*Crawley*	1500m	1	4:43.0
9 Aug	*Crawley*	800m	1	2:18.0
9 Aug	*Crawley*	Long jump	1	20' 02½"
15 Aug	*Feltham*	400m	3	52.4
22 Aug	*Epsom*	200m	1	24.1
23 Aug	*Crystal Palace*	400m	6	52.6
30 Aug	*Walton*	100m	4	12.1
30 Aug	*Walton*	200m	3	24.3
5 Sept	*Brighton*	400m	1	51.9
5 Sept	*Brighton*	Long jump	1	20' 06"
9 Sept	*Walton*	400m	1	53.7

18 Apr 1971	*Maidenhead*	1500m	1	4:17.6
24 Apr	*Brighton*	800m	1	2:01.3
1 May	Pollitt Trophy, *Brighton*	800m	2	1:56.8
19 May	*Crystal Palace*	800m	1	1:57.8
27 May	Brighton Schools C'ships, *Brighton*	400m	1	51.5
5 June	Sussex County C'ships, *Crawley*	800m	1	1:59.3
5 June	Sussex County C'ships, *Crawley*	400m	1	53.8
19 June	Southern Youth C'ships, *Crystal Palace*	800m-heat	2	1:59.9
20 June	Southern Youth C'ships, *Crystal Palace*	800m-final	5	2:00.9
22 June	*Brighton*	100m	1	12.0
26 June	*Brighton*	400m	1	51.3
9 July	English Schools C'ships, *Crystal Palace*	400m-heat	2	51.7
10 July	English Schools C'ships, *Crystal Palace*	400m-semi	1	50.4
10 July	English Schools C'ships, *Crystal Palace*	400m-final	3	50.4
17 July	*Brighton*	100m	2	12.1
17 July	*Brighton*	200m	1	23.7
20 July	*Brighton*	200m	1	23.5
20 July	*Brighton*	Long jump	1	20' 07"
20 July	*Brighton*	High jump	1	5' 05"
24 July	*Brighton*	400m	1	51.1
24 July	*Brighton*	Long jump	1	20' 07"
24 July	*Brighton*	High jump	1	5' 03"
25 July	*Crawley*	400m-relay	–	49.8
28 July	*Crystal Palace*	400m	1	50.0
31 July	*Brighton*	400m-relay	–	49.8
7 Aug	AAA Youths C'ships, *Wolverhampton*	400m	1	49.8
14 Aug	*Bracknell*	400m-relay	–	49.7
18 Aug	*Crystal Palace*	400m	2	51.8
22 Aug	Invitation, *Crystal Palace* *UK age fourteen record*	800m	1	1:55.3*
22 Aug	Invitation, *Crystal Palace*	400m-relay	1	50.0
19 Mar 1972	*Crystal Palace*	1000m	1	2:34.5
20 Mar	*Crystal Palace*	1000m	1	2:29.2
25 Mar	English Schools CC C'ships (inter), *Hillingdon 1st – K. Dumpleton, 10th – S. Coe*	CC	2	–

26 Apr	Newham Games, *Newham*	600m	2	1:19.5
	1st – M. Winbolt Lewis 1:18.7			
10 June	Sussex County C'ships, *Brighton*	800m	1	1:53.3
10 June	Sussex County C'ships, *Brighton*	1500m	1	4:09.7
17 June	Sussex Schools C'ships, *Brighton*	800m	1	1:52.5
7 July	English Schools C'ships, *Washington*	800m-heat	1	2:00.2
8 July	English Schools C'ships, *Washington*	800m-final	1	1:55.0
22 July	AAA Youth C'ships, *Kirkby*	400m-heat	1	50.9
23 July	AAA Youth C'ships, *Kirkby*	400m-final	1	49.1
— Aug	Southend Club match, *West Germany*	400m	1	48.9
— Aug	Southend Club match, *West Germany*	800m	1	1:53.6
20 Aug	Youth Invitation, *Crystal Palace*	400m	1	48.4*
	UK Youth record			
20 Aug	Youth Invitation, *Crystal Palace*	400m-relay	1	49.4
10 Sept	*Newham*	1500m	1	4:01.5
20 Sept	Southern Counties AAA Open,	200m	2	23.0
	Crystal Palace 1st – G. Doerr 22.9			
20 Sept	Southern Counties AAA Open,	400m	1	50.8
	Crystal Palace			
24 Mar 1973	English Schools CC C'ships (snr),	CC	2	–
	Swindon 1st – K. Steere			
2 May	Golden Wonder Floodlit, *Newham*	600m	1	1:20.0
19 May	Sussex County C'ships, *Brighton*	1500m	1	3:53.4
23 May	*Crystal Palace*	400m-relay	2	47.6
	1st – Alan Pascoe 46.8			
27 May	Inter Counties C'ships, *Warley*	400m-heat	4	48.0
28 May	Inter Counties C'ships, *Warley*	400m-final	6	48.4
	1st – J. Aukett 46.9			
2 June	*Newham*	200m	1	22.8
2 June	*Newham*	800m	1	1:54.4
15 June	Southern Counties AAA Jnr	1500m-heat	1	4:04.2
	C'ships, *C. Palace*			
16 June	Southern Counties AAA Jnr	1500m-final	1	3:51.6
	C'ships, *C. Palace*			
22 June	Southern C'ships, *Crystal Palace*	800m-heat	1	1:57.0
23 June	Southern C'ships, *Crystal Palace*	800m-final	2	1:48.4
	1st – P. Browne 1:48.3			
13 July	AAA C'ships, *Crystal Palace*	800m-heat	2	1:47.5
	1st – M. Winzenreid 1:47.3			
14 July	AAA C'ships, *Crystal Palace*	800m-final	6	1:47.3
	1st – A. Carter 1:45.1			
25 July	City Charity, *Motspur Park*	Mile	2	4:00.0
	1st – N. Rose 3:58.4			

4 Aug	UK 'A' v France 'A', *Sotteville, France*	800m	3	1:49.6
	1st – Sanchez 1:48.9			
17 Aug	London Fire Brigade, *Crystal Palace*	1000m	1	2:20.0
19 Aug	Junior Area match, *Crystal Palace*	1500m	1	3:55.7
24 Aug	European Jnr C'ships, *Duisburg, W. Germany*	800m-heat	1	1:51.6
25 Aug	European Jnr C'ships, *Duisburg, W. Germany*	800m-semi	1	1:49.6
26 Aug	European Jnr C'ships, *Duisburg, W. Germany*	800m-final	1	1:47.5
14 Sept	IAC/Coca Cola, *Crystal Palace*	Mile	9	4:09.2
	1st – B. J. Jipcho 3:56.2			
19 Sept	UK v Sweden Jnr International, *Warley*	1500m	1	3:54.9
29 Sept	England Commonwealth Games, *Crystal Palace*	800m	3	1:48.4
	1st – C. Campbell 1:48.0			
12 Jan 1974	Midland Counties AAA Indoor, *RAF Cosford*	800m	1	1:52.8
1 June	British League, *Edinburgh*	800m	1	1:53.7
1 June	British League, *Edinburgh*	1500m	1	3:46.2
15 June	Southern Counties AAA Jnr C'ships, *C. Palace*	400m-heat	1	49.7
15 June	Southern Counties AAA Jnr C'ships, *C. Palace*	400m-final	1	47.5
21 June	Southern C'ships, *Crystal Palace*	800m-heat	1	1:52.7
22 June	Southern C'ships, *Crystal Palace*	800m-final	1	1:47.6
30 June	UK v Poland v Canada, *Warsaw*	800m	1	1:46.8
12 July	AAA C'ships, *Crystal Palace*	800m-heat	1	1:48.8
13 July	AAA C'ships, *Crystal Palace*	800m-final	1	1:46.9
17 July	*Haringey*	Brigg Mile	1	3:59.4
27 July	UK v Czechoslovakia, *Edinburgh*	800m	1	1:48.8
3 Aug	Gateshead Games	1000m	2	2:20.1
	1st – A. Carter 2:18.5			
10 Aug	*Crystal Palace*	Mile	5	4:03.8
	1st – F. Clement 3:57.4			
2 Sept	European C'ships, *Rome*	800m-heat	2	1:47.0
	1st – G. Ghipu 1:46.9			
3 Sept	European C'ships, *Rome*	800m-semi	1	1:47.2
4 Sept	European C'ships, *Rome*	800m-final	2	1:45.77
	1st – L. Susanj 1:44.1			

31 Jan 1975	AAA Indoor C'ships, *RAF Cosford*	1500m-heat	1	3:48.9
1 Feb	AAA Indoor C'ships, *RAF Cosford*	1500m-final	5	3:45.9
	1st – P. Banning 3:42.6			
16 Feb	Cross country (10.2 km), *Dieppe*	CC	1	–
	1st equal with P. Standing			
1 Mar	English CC C'ships (jnr), *Luton*	CC	1	–
17 May	National League, *Brighton*	1500m	1	3:54.6
31 May	*Crystal Palace* Emsley Carr Mile	6	4:00.1
	1st – F. Bayi 3:55.5			
21 June	UK v GDR, *Dresden*	800m	3	1:47.6
	1st – H. Ohlert 1:47.0			
22 June	UK v GDR, *Dresden*	1500m	2	3:43.3
	1st – H. Ohlert 3:42.1			
30 June	Invitation, *Stockholm*	Mile	9	3:57.0
	1st – J. Walker 3:52.2			
4 July	Invitation, *Crystal Palace*	800m	3	1:49.3
	1st – M. Boit 1:48.6			
5 July	National League, *Kirkby*	400m	1	48.7
5 July	National League, *Kirkby*	800m	1	1:52.3
13 July	Europa Cup semi-final, *Crystal Palace*	800m	1	1:46.7
26 July	National League, *Barking*	200m	1	21.7
26 July	National League, *Barking*	400m	1	48.7
1 Aug	AAA C'ships, *Crystal Palace*	800m-heat	1	1:49.5
2 Aug	AAA C'ships, *Crystal Palace*	800m-final	1	1:46.1
7 Aug	Southern Counties AAA Open, *Crystal Palace*	800m	1	1:47.7
17 Aug	Europa Cup Final, *Nice*	800m	1	1:46.6
19 Aug	Invitation, *Stockholm*	1500m	9	3:45.9
	1st – J. Walker 3:35.6			
29 Aug	Coca Cola, *Crystal Palace*	Mile	8	4:01.3
	1st – J. Walker 3:53.6			
1 Sept	Manitou Games, *Gateshead*	300m	6	35.3
	1st – D. Jenkins 32.9			
17 Jan 1976	South of Thames CC C'ships	CC	1	–
18 Jan	Cross Country, *Wingen, Belgium*	CC	3	–
	1st – K. Lismont			
12 May	Southern Counties AAA Open, *Crystal Palace*	600m	1	1:18.5
12 May	Southern Counties AAA Open, *Crystal Palace*	400m	1	48.9
15 May	*Crawley*	400m	1	49.0
22 May	*Liverpool*	800m	1	1:52.7

26 May	Borough Rd. Coll. v AAA, *Crystal Palace*	400m	7	48.63
30 May	Inter-Counties C'ships, *Crystal Palace*	800m-heat	1	1:51.7
31 May	Inter-Counties C'ships, *Crystal Palace*	800m-final	1	1:47.3
4 June	Olympic trials, *Crystal Palace*	800m-heat	1	1:48.6
5 June	Olympic trials, *Crystal Palace*	800m-final	1	1:46.7
11 June	Olympic trials, *Crystal Palace*	1500m-heat	3	3:44.4
12 June	Olympic trials, *Crystal Palace*	1500m-final	1	3:39.6
18 June	Southern C'ships, *Crystal Palace*	400m-heat	1	49.0
19 June	Southern C'ships, *Crystal Palace*	400m-final	4	48.17
27 June	Invitation, *Saarijarvi, Finland*	800m	1	1:50.1
3 July	UK v Poland v Canada, *Crystal Palace*	800m	1	1:46.7
23 July	Olympic Games, *Montreal*	800m-heat	1	1:48.3
24 July	Olympic Games, *Montreal* 1st – Juantorena 1:45.8	800m-semi	3	1:46.1
25 July	Olympic Games, *Montreal* 1st – Juantorena 1:43.5, 2nd – Van Damme 1:43.86, 3rd – Wolhuter 1:44.12	800m-final	5	1:45.4
29 July	Olympic Games, *Montreal*	1500m-heat	1	3:37.9
30 July	Olympic Games, *Montreal* 1st – J. Walker 3:39.65	1500m-semi	5	3:40.3
6 Aug	IAC/Coca Cola, *Edinburgh*	800m	1	1:46.9
7 Aug	Open, *Coatbridge*	1000m	1	2:21.0
10 Aug	Invitation, *Helsinki*	800m	2	1:46.1
13 Aug	AAA C'ships, *Crystal Palace*	800m-heat	1	1:50.0
14 Aug	AAA C'ships, *Crystal Palace*	800m-final	1	1:47.3
16 Aug	Invitation *Nice*	1000m	2	2:19.2
18 Aug	Invitation, *Zurich*	800m	2	1:45.5
21 Aug	*Edinburgh*	800m	1	1:48.2
7 Nov	Mike Sully CC Race, *Bath* 1st – A. Simmons	CC	7	–
16 Jan 1977	Cross Country, *Wingen, Belgium*	CC	1	–
22 Jan	Inter Counties CC C'ships, *Leicester* 1st – D. Black	CC	2	–
5 Mar	English CC C'ships, *London, P'ment Hill Fields* 1st – B. Foster	CC	13	–
30 Apr	National League, *Brighton*	800m	1	1:53.9
30 Apr	National League, *Brighton*	1500m	1	4:04.0
30 Apr	National League, *Brighton*	3000m	1	8:18.8

3 May	Invitation, *Kingston, Jamaica*	1500m	2	3:39.8
	1st – S. Scott 3:39.8			
8 May	Philips Night of Athletics, *Crystal Palace*	3000m	2	7:53.4
	1st – F. Bayi			
1 May	National League, *Brighton*	1500m	1	3:53.4
1 May	National League, *Brighton*	400m-relay	–	48.5
8 May	*Belfast*	Mile	1	3:56.2
1 June	*St Maur*	1500m	1	3:39.8
2 June	UK C'ships, *Cwmbran*	1500m	1	3:37.5
6 June	*Crystal Palace*	Mile	1	3:54.7*
	UK record			
2 July	British League, *Keele*	1500m	1	3:52.0
2 July	British League, *Keele*	400m-relay	–	48.3
5 July	Invitation, *Cork*	Mile	1	3:59.1
7 July	Invitation, *Middleton, Eire*	5000m	1	
6 July	European Cup semi-final, *Crystal Palace*	1500m	1	3:39.1
0 July	Gateshead Games	5000m	2	13:25.0
	1st – M. Yifter			
4 Aug	*Bideford*	800m	1	1:58.1
4 Aug	*Bideford*	1500m	1	3:50.0
4 Aug	*Bideford*	3000m	1	8:22.2
3 Aug	European Cup Final, *Helsinki*	1500m	1	3:44.9
0 Aug	Half-marathon, *Dartford*	13.2 miles	1	65:38
9 Aug	*Crystal Palace*	800m	1	1:48.3
3 Sept	World Cup, *Dusseldorf*	1500m	1	3:34.5*
	UK record			
9 Sept	IAC/Coca Cola, *Crystal Palace*	Mile	1	3:56.6
3 Sept	Invitation, *Wattenscheid*	3000m	1	7:41.3
4 Sept	Invitation, *Hanover*	2000m	2	5:04.7
	1st – T. Wessinghage			
4 Jan 1978	Inter Counties CC C'ships, *Derby*	CC	1	–
4 Jan	Cross Country, *Belfast*	CC	1	–
4 Mar	English CC C'ships (snr), *Leeds*	CC	4	–
	1st – B. Ford			
2 Apr	Five Mills CC, *San Vittore, Italy*	CC	4	–
	1st – W. Polleunis, Belgium			
9 Apr	*Brighton*	1500m	1	3:59.7
9 Apr	*Brighton*	3000m	1	8-16.6
3 May	*Crystal Palace*	3000m	1	7:57.8
5 May	*Hendon*	1500m	1	3:52.2
6 May	*Hendon*	400m-relay	–	47.4

21 May	Invitation, *Milan*	2000m	1	5:10.6
24 May	Philips Night of Athletics, *Crystal Palace 1st – H. Rono 7:43.8*	3000m	2	7.48.0
26 May	*Belfast*	800m	1	1:49.0
3 June	*Crystal Palace* *UK record	2000m	1	4:57.8
10 June	UK v GDR, *Crystal Palace*	1500m	1	3:53.8
4 July	Invitation, *Cork*	Mile	1	4:08.2
11 July	Invitation, *Dublin*	Mile	1	3:55.7
22 July	*Parliament Hill*	400m	1	48.4
22 July	*Parliament Hill*	400m-relay	–	47.3
26 July	Invitation, *Malmo*	1500m	1	3:37.6
27 July	Invitation, *Turku, Finland*	800m	1	1:45.4
3 Aug	Invitation, *Oslo*	1500m	1	3:35.8
19 Aug	National League, *Brighton*	100m	2	11.5
19 Aug	National League, *Brighton*	200m	1	22.9
19 Aug	National League, *Brighton*	1500m	1	4:08.1
19 Aug	National League, *Brighton*	400m-relay	–	47.4
23 Aug	Rotary Watches, *Crystal Palace*	Mile	1	3:57.7
29 Aug	European C'ships, *Prague*	800m-heat	1	1:47.8
30 Aug	European C'ships, *Prague*	800m-semi	1	1:46.5
31 Aug	European C'ships, *Prague* *UK record. 1st – O. Beyer 1:43.8, 3rd – S. Coe 1:44.8	800m-final	2	1:44.1
2 Sept	European C'ships, *Prague*	1500m-heat	1	3:42.9
3 Sept	European C'ships, *Prague*	1500m-final	1	3:35.6
15 Sept	IAC/Coca Cola, *Crystal Palace* *World outdoor best	2 miles	1	8:13.5
20 Sept	Invitation, *Oslo* *UK record	Mile	1	3:52.8
25 Sept	Invitation, *Tokyo*	Golden Mile	1	3:55.5
3 Mar 1979	English CC C'ships, *Luton* 1st – M. McLeod	CC	6	–
1 Apr	Five Mills CC, *San Vittore, Italy* 1st – L. Schots, Belgium	CC	6	–
20 May	*Tullyease*	2000m	1	5:20.8
26 May	*Crystal Palace*	1500m	1	3:53.1
26 May	*Crystal Palace*	400m-relay	–	48.0
9 June	National League, *Enfield*	1500m	1	3:40.8
9 June	National League, *Enfield*	400m-relay	–	47.8
23 June	UK v W. Ger. v Poland v Switzerland, *Bremen*	1500m	1	3:41.7
24 June	Invitation, *Nijmegen*	1500m	1	3:37.7
10 July	Invitation, *Dublin*	800m	1	1:46.2

3 July	AAA C'ships, *Crystal Palace*	1500m-heat	1	3:44.6
4 July	AAA C'ships, *Crystal Palace*	1500m-final	1	3:39.1
9 July	National League, *Hendon*	1500m	1	3:46.2
9 July	National League, *Hendon*	400m-relay	–	47.3
7 Aug	Invitation, *Gothenburg*	1500m	1	3:36.6
8 Aug	*Crystal Palace*	1000m	1	2:23.4
5 Aug	*Crystal Palace*	600m	1	1:16.0
7 Aug	Invitation, *West Berlin*	Mile	1	3:54.1
8 Aug	Invitation, *Crystal Palace*	800m-relay	–	1:49.8
9 Aug	Invitation, *Cologne*	800m	2	1:45.0
	1st – J. Robinson			
7 Aug	*Crystal Palace*	800m	1	1:49.6
7 Aug	*Crystal Palace*	400m-relay	–	47.0
1 Aug	Rotary Watches, *Crystal Palace*	Mile	1	3:49.6
4 Sept	Ivo Van Damme Memorial, *Brussels*	1500m	1	3:32.11
5 Sept	Invitation, *Koblenz*	1000m	1	2:16.0*
	**UK record*			
9 Sept	Gateshead Games	Emsley Carr Mile	1	3:56.6
4 Sept	IAC/Coca Cola, *Crystal Palace*	Mile	1	3:55.3
9 Apr 1980	*Crystal Palace*	400m-relay	–	48.2
8 May	Invitation, *Houston, Texas*	3000m	1	7:52.44
9 May	Invitation, *Kingston, Jamaica*	1500m	1	3:38.7
8 May	England v Wales v Hungary v Holland, *Cwmbran*	800m	1	1:49.17
8 May	England v Wales v Hungary v Holland, *Cwmbran*	400m-relay	–	47.6
May	Philips Night of Athletics, *Crystal Palace*	Bannister Mile	1	4:00.6
4 June	Invitation, *Bergen*	800m	1	1:46.6
June	Talbot Games, *Crystal Palace*	1500m	1	3:35.3
July	Bislett Games, *Oslo*	Mile	1	3:48.8*
	**World record*			
July	Invitation, *Gothenburg*	800m	1	1:48.16
July	Open Meeting, *Welwyn Garden City*	3000m	1 eq.	8:24.6
	1st eq. – J. Espir			
July	Oslo Games, *Oslo*	i500m	1	3:32.09*
	**Eq. World record*			
July	Olympic Games, *Moscow*	800m-heat	1	1:49.4
July	Olympic Games, *Moscow*	800m-semi	1	1:46.6
July	Olympic Games, *Moscow*	800m-final	1	1:45.4
	2nd – S. Coe 1:45.9			
July	Olympic Games, *Moscow*	1500m-heat	1	3:36.8

31 July	Olympic Games, *Moscow*	1500m-semi	1	3:43.1
1 Aug	Olympic Games, *Moscow*	1500-final	3	3:39.0
	1st – S. Coe 3:38.4, 2nd – J. Straub 3:38.8			
8 Aug	IAC/Coca Cola, *Crystal Palace*	5000m	2	13:27.9
	1st – J. Treacy 13:27.9			
11 Aug	Invitation, *Budapest*	5000m	1	13:31.9
15 Aug	Invitation, *Lausanne*	1500m	1	3:35.4
25 Aug	British Meat Games, *Crystal Palace*	Golden Mile	1	3:52.8
27 Aug	Invitation, *Koblenz*	1500	1	3:31.3
	World record			
5 Sept	AAA C'ships, *Crystal Palace*	Mile-heat	1	4:07.9
6 Sept	AAA C'ships, *Crystal Palace*	Mile-final	1	4:04.4
19 Apr 1981	Road Race, *Vigerano*	Road	1	–
26 Apr	Road Race, *Oslo*	Road	1	–
3 May	Nike Grand Prix Road Race, *Oslo*	Road	1	–
24 May	UK C'ships, *Antrim*	1500m-heat	1	3:45.1
25 May	UK C'ships, *Antrim*	1500m-final	1	3:42.8
3 June	Philips Night of Athletics, *Crystal Palace*	3000m	1	7:54.1
7 June	Citizen Games, *Gateshead*	Mile	1	3:57.92
17 June	Invitation, *Venice*	100m	1	2:21.8
26 June	Bislett Games, *Oslo*	1500m	2	3:39.53
	1st – T. Byers 3:39.01			
4 July	Europa Cup semi-final, *Helsinki*	1500m	1	3:46.47
8 July	Invitation, *Milan*	1500m	1	3:31.95
11 July	Dulux Oslo Games, *Oslo*	Dream Mile	1	3:49.25
14 July	Invitation, *Lausanne*	Mile	1	3:49.66
26 July	Gateshead Games	800m	1	1:47.96
29 July	Invitation, *Budapest*	1500m	1	3:31.57
31 July	Talbot Games, *Crystal Palace*	1000m	1	2:20.67
3 Aug	Invitation, *Bergen*	1500m	1	3:34.63
21 Aug	Invitation, *West Berlin*	Mile	1	3:55.58
26 Aug	Invitation, *Koblenz*	Mile	1	3:48.40
	World record			
29 Aug	England v Norway, *Ardal, Norway*	800m	1	1:47.0
31 Aug	Amoco Games, *Crystal Palace*	800m	1	1:46.40
5 Sept	World Cup, *Rome*	1500m	1	3:34.95
9 Sept	Invitation, *Rieti*	Mile	2	3:50.25
	1st – S. Maree 3:48.83			
11 Sept	IAC/Coca Cola, *Crystal Palace*	2 Miles	1	8:25.52
3 Oct	Commonwealth Games Preview, *Brisbane*	800m	1	1:49.13
7 Oct	International, *Adelaide*	1500m	1	3:42.6

10 Oct	International, *Sydney*	Mile	1	3:59.8
13 Oct	Burnside Games, *Adelaide*	1500m	1	3:42.68
19 June 1982	Southern Counties C'ships, *Crystal Palace*	1500m-heat	1	3:47.61
26 June	*Oslo*	3000m	2	7:43.87
	1st – S. Nyambui, Tanzania, 7:43.12			
30 June	*Budapest*	2000m	1	5:05.75
7 July	*Oslo*	2000m	1	4:57.71
9 July	*Paris*	1500m	DNF	
17 July	*Crystal Palace*	3000m	10	7:48.07
	1st – D. Moorcroft 7:32.79			
31 July	England International, *Edinburgh*	800m	1	1:47.59
7 Aug	*Crystal Palace*	1500m	1	3:38.48
11 Aug	*Viareggio, Italy*	800m	2	–
	1st – H. Schmid, WG, 1:45.90			
10 Apr 1983	Road Race, *Worth*	10 miles	1	50:34
26 Apr	Road, *Oslo*	10km	2	–
	1st – E. Martin, GB			
12 June	*Udine*	800m	1	1:47.64
17 June	Southern Counties C'ships, *Hendon*	800m-heat	1	1:50.39
17 June	Southern Counties C'ships, *Hendon*	1500m-heat	1	3:47.0
18 June	Southern Counties C'ships, *Hendon*	800m-final	DNF	
18 June	Southern Counties C'ships, *Hendon*	1500m-final	1	3:46.45
26 June	*Edinburgh*	1000m	5 (tripped)	
	1st – P. Elliott 2:21.92			2:23.81
28 June	*Oslo*	1500m	1	3:38.81
1 July	*Birmingham*	1500m	1	3:42.17
12 July	*Hengelo*	1500m	1	3:38.94
15 July	*Crystal Palace*	1000m	1	2:17.26
23 July	AAA C'ships, *Crystal Palace*	800m-heat	1	1:46.29
24 July	AAA C'ships, *Crystal Palace*	800m-final	DNF	
11 Aug	*Gateshead*	1000m	1	2:19.08
12 Aug	World C'ships, *Helsinki*	1500m-heat	2	3:39.00
13 Aug	World C'ships, *Helsinki*	1500m-semi	2	3:36.26
14 Aug	World C'ships, *Helsinki*	1500m-final	4	3:42.34
	1st – S. Cram 3:41.59			
23 Aug	*Oslo*	Mile	1	3:50.49
26 Aug	*Brussels*	800m	2	1:45.25
	1st – R. Druppers, Hol, 1:44.90			
29 Aug	*Crystal Palace*	400m-relay	–	48.7
31 Aug	*Koblenz*	1500m	1	3:32.95

4 Sept	*Rieti*	1500m	1	3:30.77*
	*World record			
6 Sept	*Engleheim*	1000m	1	2:20.19
9 Sept	*Crystal Palace*	Mile	2	3:52.71
	1st – S. Cram 3:52.56			
2 Dec	Battersea Park 10km Road Race,	10km	4	–
	London 1st – S. Harris			
7 Jan 1984	Road Race, *Belfast*	Road	1	–
1 Mar	*Melbourne*	1500m	2	3:37.52
	1st – P. O'Donoghue, New Zealand, 3:37.08			
11 Mar	*Sydney*	1500m	2	3:35.36
	1st – M. Hillardt, Aus, 3:34.20			
31 Mar	*Melbourne*	1500m	2	3:36.60
	1st – Hillardt 3:36.26			
23 Apr	Road Race, *Paris*	Mile	1	3:56.12
17 June	*Loughborough*	800m	1	1:47
19 June	*Belfast*	800m	1	1:46.15
28 June	*Oslo*	1500m	1	3:34.50
2 July	*Stockholm*	1500m	1	3:35.65
10 July	*Lausanne*	1500m	1	3:38.43
18 July	*Edinburgh*	1500m	1	3:36.90
19 July	*Larvik, Norway*	800m	2	1:46.41
3 Aug	Olympic Games, *Los Angeles*	800m-heat	2	1:46.66
4 Aug	Olympic Games, *Los Angeles*	800m-heat	2	1:45.72
5 Aug	Olympic Games, *Los Angeles*	800m-semi	4	1:44.81
6 Aug	Olympic Games, *Los Angeles*	800m-final	8	1:52.28
	1st – J. Cruz, Brazil, 1:43.00, 2nd – S. Coe 1:43.64,			
	3rd – E. Jones, US, 1:43.83			
9 Aug	Olympic Games, *Los Angeles*	1500m-heat	1	3:49.23
10 Aug	Olympic Games, *Los Angeles*	1500m-semi	4	3:36.55
11 Aug	Olympic Games, *Los Angeles*	1500m-final	DNF	
	1st – S. Coe 3:32.53, 2nd – S. Cram 3:33.40,			
	3rd – J. Abascal, Spain, 3:34.30			

Sports and activities handbooks now available in Panther Books

Pat Davis
Badminton Complete (illustrated) £1.25 ☐

Bruce Tegner
Karate (illustrated) £1.50 ☐

Bruce Tulloh
The Complete Distance Runner (illustrated) £1.95 ☐

Meda Mander
How to Trace Your Ancestors (illustrated) £1.50 ☐

Tom Hopkins
How to Master the Art of Selling £2.50 ☐

William Prentice
How to Start a Successful Business £2.50 ☐

Susan Glascock
A Woman's Guide to Starting Her Own Business £2.50 ☐

Alfred Tack
Sell Your Way to Success £1.25 ☐

Andrew Pennycook
The Book of Card Games £3.95 ☐

C Lukács and E Tarjan
Mathematical Games £1.50 ☐

Gyles Brandreth
The Complete Puzzler £1.50 ☐

Patrick Duncan (ed.)
The Panther Crossword Compendium (Vols 1 and 2) £1.95 ☐
each
Quizwords 1 £1.50 ☐
Quizwords 2 £1.50 ☐

To order direct from the publisher just tick the titles you want
and fill in the order form.

Health and self-help books now available in Panther Books

W H Bates		
Better Eyesight Without Glasses	£1.95	☐
Ronald Gatty		
The Body Clock Diet	£1.50	☐
Desmonde Dunne		
Yoga Made Easy	£1.95	☐
Laurence E Morehouse & Leonard Gross		
Total Fitness	£1.95	☐
Maximum Performance	£1.50	☐
Constance Mellor		
Guide to Natural Health	£1.25	☐
Natural Remedies for Common Ailments	£1.95	☐
Sonya Richmond		
Yoga and Your Health	£1.25	☐
Phyllis Speight		
Homoeopathy	£1.50	☐
Kenneth Lysons		
How to Cope with Hearing Loss	95p	☐
Dr Richard B Stuart		
Act Thin, Stay Thin	£1.50	☐
Dr Carl C Pfeiffer & Jane Banks		
Total Nutrition	£1.50	☐
Dr Hamilton Hall		
Be Your Own Back Doctor	£1.95	☐
José Silva and Michael Miele		
The Silva Mind Control Method	£2.50	☐
Dr Peter M Miller		
The Change Your Metabolism Diet	£1.95	☐
Slimming Magazine		
30-Day Formula	£3.95	☐

To order direct from the publisher just tick the titles you want
and fill in the order form.

HB881

Guides now available in Panther Books

Brian J Bailey
Lakeland Walks and Legends (illustrated) £1.50 ☐

Mary Cathcart Borer
London Walks and Legends (illustrated) £1.95 ☐

Mary Peplow & Debra Shipley
London for Free £1.95 ☐

Janice Anderson & Edmund Swinglehurst
Scottish Walks and Legends:
   The Lowlands and East Scotland (illustrated) £1.50 ☐
   Western Scotland and The Highlands (illustrated) £1.50 ☐

Showell Styles
Welsh Walks and Legends (illustrated) £1.00 ☐

David Daiches
Edinburgh (illustrated) £1.95 ☐
Glasgow (illustrated) £2.50 ☐

Peter Somerville-Large
Dublin £2.25 ☐

Frank Delaney
James Joyce's Odyssey (illustrated) £2.95 ☐

Paul Johnson
The National Trust Book of British Castles (illustrated) £3.95 ☐

Nigel Nicolson
The National Trust Book of Great Houses (illustrated) £3.95 ☐

Tom Weir
Weir's Way (illustrated) £2.50 ☐

Robert Orrell
Saddle Tramp in the Lake District (illustrated) £1.50 ☐

To order direct from the publisher just tick the titles you want
and fill in the order form.

HB1181

All these books are available at your local bookshop or newsagent, or can be ordered direct from the publisher..

To order direct from the publisher just tick the titles you want and fill in the form below.

Name _____

Address _____

_____

Send to:
Panther Cash Sales
PO Box 11, Falmouth, Cornwall TR10 9EN.

Please enclose remittance to the value of the cover price plus:

UK 45p for the first book, 20p for the second book plus 14p per copy for each additional book ordered to a maximum charge of £1.63.

BFPO and Eire 45p for the first book, 20p for the second book plus 14p per copy for the next 7 books, thereafter 8p per book.

Overseas 75p for the first book and 21p for each additional book.